Language, Form, and Inquiry

Language, Form, and Inquiry

Arthur F. Bentley's Philosophy of Social Science

James F. Ward

The University of Massachusetts Press   Amherst, 1984

Copyright © 1984 by

The University of Massachusetts Press

All rights reserved

Printed in the United States of America

Library of Congress Cataloging in Publication Data

Ward, James F., 1947–

Language, form, and inquiry.

Bibliography: p.

Includes index.

1. Bentley, Arthur Fisher, 1870–1957. 2. Social

sciences—Philosophy. I. Title.

H59.B44W37 1984 300'.1 83-18006

ISBN 0-87023-425-0

Publication of this book was assisted by the American

Council of Learned Societies under a grant from the

Andrew W. Mellon Foundation.

Contents

Acknowledgments

Some of the material in this book has appeared in different form in the *American Journal of Political Science* (1978) and the *Journal of the History of the Behavioral Sciences* (1981). I am grateful to the editors of these journals and to the University of Texas Press and the Clinical Psychology Publishing Company respectively for permission to reprint.

My debts are few but deep. Professor Frank Grace of the University of Michigan, to whom this book is dedicated, has shaped my thinking more decisively than anyone else. Professor Judith N. Shklar of Harvard University helped me refine a number of my thoughts on Bentley. I would like to thank Professor Sidney Ratner of Rutgers University and Mr. Jules Altman for their permission to make use of the Bentley manuscript collections housed in the Lilly Library, Indiana University, as well as for their informative reminiscences of Bentley. Ms. Saundra Taylor, Curator of Manuscripts for the Lilly Library, was invaluable during my research there. Finally, I would like to thank Mr. Richard Martin and Ms. Pam Campbell of the University of Massachusetts Press for their assistance.

Preface

Arthur F. Bentley has an honored, if misunderstood, place in the history of American academic political science, but his true stature as a philosopher of social science has never been properly recognized. In this study I propose to recover Bentley's teaching through a critical examination of his work as a whole and to present his views as accurately as possible. I do not speak for myself or present my own views on most of the issues with which his work is concerned. Moreover, I do not suggest that social science should be reoriented along Bentleyan lines. My belief that his views merit patient study and serious consideration does not entail their advocacy. Rather, I mean to clarify the central issues in Bentley's work and to explore his teaching on its own terms. I do not claim to know better than Bentley what social science should be and I have not attempted to correct his mistakes in the light of some superior teaching. This does not mean that he is beyond criticism or that his enterprise was successful. As I see it, the only proper basis for such assessments must be a correct account of his teaching. This study is not the last word on Bentley or on the basic problems of social science. I am not convinced that all philosophical issues in social science can or must be addressed through the study of Bentley. Recognition of the limits of his enterprise is as necessary to an adequate grasp of it as recognition of his own intentions.

There are several claims I want to make for Bentley's work. I believe that his writing constitutes one of the most profound and penetrating bodies of reflection on the nature and problems of social science available to us. It deserves to be considered as such by students of the history and philosophy of social science. The most important lesson to be learned from it is that the question of the possibility and nature of social science is not self-contained. It cannot be raised, much less explored properly, apart from sustained reflection on the nature of science and on the problem of knowledge. I am in agreement with Bentley in at least this respect. Social science is condemned to parochialism and intellectual incoherence to the extent that it remains closed to what can only be rightly called philosophic inquiry. For Bentley, social science is essentially incoherent if it cannot explain itself. His work may be understood as an inquiry into the conditions of coherence and thus of intelligibility. It was intended to be fundamental in a way that most philosophies of social science, whether produced by social scientists or philosophers, are not.

Bentley's project may be summarized briefly. The systematic study of all human things, among which must be included all things designated as "social," can and must be made scientific, an imperative Bentley never doubted. Unlike many proponents of this view, Bentley was concerned with what gave science its authority. In this concern, I believe, as Bentley himself believed, that his inquiry parted company with that of most major figures in the history of social science. The decisive features in which the authority of science consisted had never been understood, whether by friends or enemies of the idea of a social science, precisely because they were taken as self-evident. A genuine or scientific social science cannot develop as long as social scientists believe that a definitive understanding of science is readily available either in philosophy or in the self-understanding of the natural sciences. Thus, the issues with which the best minds in the social sciences have been concerned necessarily lead, in Bentley's opinion, beyond the conventional boundaries of social science. Few social scientists were willing to follow such a path.

The scope of Bentley's enterprise is the most important reason that so many accounts of his work are deficient. In order to understand him as he understood himself, one must be willing to follow him into disputes in logic, epistemology, philosophy of mathematics, and philosophy of science. In addition, one must be prepared to consider the possibility that fundamental problems in these areas share with basic issues in social science certain common features. For most social scientists, wary of autodidacts and possessed of professional self-consciousness, such a course may seem eccentric. For Bentley it seemed necessary. Bentley's intransigence and a measure of his intellectual integrity lie in his willingness to pursue his chosen problems wherever they seemed to lead.

I should say a few words about the secondary literature on Bentley and the assumptions that have governed the present study. Although he is regarded by many proponents of a scientific social science as a pioneering figure, there are few adequate studies of his work. The most important one is Paul F. Kress's *Social Science and the Idea of Process*.[1] While Kress takes the necessary step of distinguishing Bentley's view of social science from that of most of his self-proclaimed disciples, he interprets Bentley in large part through a sustained and exhaustive comparison of his views with those of sociologists and political scientists. I have not presented most of Bentley's positions in this way. His preferred universe of discourse was that of philosophy of science, logic, mathematics, and epistemology. His views come to light when they are studied in conjunction with the views of philosophers. Kress's focus serves to minimize the importance of Bentley's movement from the problems of social science to the wider horizons in terms of which these problems must be explored. Moreover, Bentley's comprehensive teaching has had a negligible influence on the subsequent development of social science. His concerns have seemed too far from those of most social scientists and his writings that did not appear to address familiar issues in familiar ways have been ignored. As the part of his work with which political scientists are best acquainted, his early book, *The Process of Government*, was his most conventional production. It is hardly accidental that its contents—which challenge the conventions subscribed to by most of its readers—are seldom given their due. The warrant for a study of Bentley must be found in the substance of his teaching and not in its influence.

No study of Bentley known to me makes use of the entire body of his work. I have used all his published and unpublished writings, as well as his published and unpublished correspondence. Bentley insisted that his work was a whole and was intelligible only as a whole. I have studied his teaching with this injunction in mind. In advance of my detailed discussion of his views, I must at least mention the most important theme that becomes visible when his work is studied in its totality. Bentley is often considered a "process" theorist whose aim was to dissolve the boundedness of conventional modes of study in social science. Indeed, Kress's intention is to examine the notion of "process" in social science by means of his study of Bentley. The limits of this approach result from a lack of attention to Bentley's studies of logic and mathematics. I do not believe one is reading Bentley fruitfully or correctly unless one is aware of the issues with which he is concerned in his seldom-read *Linguistic Analysis of Mathematics*. Bentley claims to show in that work that "process" can be made discursively accessible through a development that amounts to a proposal for a radical expansion to all areas of inquiry of the "formalist" program associated with the philosophy of mathematics of David Hilbert. Here I may say only that the maximal development of "form" is presented as the decisive way in which the flux of reality can be captured and rendered intelligible. The complete teaching Bentley sought is an account of the form of science.

Bentley wrote considerably more than he published. In studying his unpublished material I have become convinced that it often sheds light on his published works by implicating them in their originative contexts. Accordingly, I have used unpublished material freely. Bentley was an extraordinarily careful writer. Even the shortest journal article or letter was subjected routinely to numerous revisions. I have learned a great deal from studying his drafts, sketches, outlines, and reading notes. In particular, his notes record his reflections on and engagements with the views of others and reveal the care with which he undertook study in fields other than social science. It is here that one finds, for example, his critical study of Ludwig Wittgenstein, Bertrand Russell, and the revolution of analytic philosophy, carried on when few American social scientists were aware of these philosophers and movements. One of the greatest difficulties in reading Bentley's unpublished or published writings is that his own teaching is often to be found in the interstices of his critical remarks on others. He was quite scrupulous in his attention to the views of other thinkers, in part because he sought to indicate as clearly as possible the points at which he was compelled to challenge their positions.

Another problem in the study of Bentley deserves mention. He is an uncompromising writer who makes almost no concessions to his reader, whom he assumes is willing and able to follow his tortuous paths with few guideposts. His writings are filled with devices intended to replace conventional conceptual distinctions with what Kress calls "concepts of relative stresses and emphases."[2] Among these devices are systems of neologisms such as those developed in *Behavior Knowledge Fact*, his use of a homey cracker-barrel idiom suggestive of his major intellectual influence, John Dewey, and his occasional grammatical experiments in which he disintegrates conventional syntax to convey a sense of "process." In addition, with few exceptions, his style is consistently and sometimes excessively polemical. The most sober debates on the nature of logic and mathematics are punctuated with the outbursts of the muckraking journalist. While Henry S. Kariel draws our attention to his "defiant style, his obstinate stance, his maddening idiom," we must note that Bentley's style was intended to serve his thought by conforming to it as closely as possible.[3]

I begin with an account of the issues Bentley proposed to address. While the introduction offers a brief interpretation of the course of development of social science, it is intended as an indispensable background for the study of Bentley and not as a comprehensive history. I then turn to Bentley's early career and the first stirrings of his interest in social science. Since his most well-known work must be considered to make clear its true place in his enterprise, chapters 3 and 4 are concerned with *The Process of Government*. His journey beyond the boundaries of social science is traced in detail in the next chapter. The heart of his work is reached in the three chapters that follow. Chapter 6 is concerned with his examination of fundamental issues in logic and mathematics and thus with the core of his view of science. In chapter 7 I turn to the new "behavioral science" that follows from his position. Chapter 8 traces his self-discovery in his last years of his relation to the tradition of American pragmatic philosophy. The concluding chapter is a critical assessment of Bentley's teaching.

Several of Bentley's works are cited in the text by abbreviations. In the order of their writing, they are:

PG   *The Process of Government: A Study of Social Pressures* (1908)
KS   "Knowledge and Society" (1910)
MUM   *Makers, Users, and Masters* (1919–20)
RMS   *Relativity in Man and Society* (1926)
LAM   *Linguistic Analysis of Mathematics* (1932)
BKF   *Behavior Knowledge Fact* (1935)
KK   *Knowing and the Known* (1949) (with John Dewey)

I

Introduction:

Philosophy and Social Science

Men "know," but they no longer are so certain that their knowledge will not be re-arranged. A man may believe that his knowledge or some part of it will hold good permanently, but he feels compelled to recognize this as his "belief" in a sense distinct from "knowledge."

"Knowledge and Society"

For Arthur F. Bentley, science properly understood includes within its domain inquiry intended to result in a coherent account of itself. If we remain close to Bentley's view of his own teaching, it must be said that nowhere does he identify his inquiry as "philosophy" of social science. Inquiry into the foundations or principles or nature of science did not for him demarcate a field of "conceptual" issues requiring any distinctly "philosophic" methods or training as distinguished from the field of "empirical" questions with which science is said to be concerned. That there is no self-evident distinction between a nonphilosophic empirical science and a nonscientific philosophic inquiry Bentley took to be shown by the development and practice of science. His study of what we have learned from Thomas S. Kuhn to call "scientific revolutions" showed him that decisive advances in a science were complex mixtures of elements only imperfectly grasped in distinctions between empirical and conceptual questions.[1] What may be called the reflective moment is present, Bentley claimed, in the practice of science at its best. Put otherwise, he attributed the failure to recognize the presence of such reflection, whether by the scientist or the philosopher, to unwitting acceptance of untenable philosophical views.

My use of "philosophy of social science" as a label for Bentley's inquiry is in part for the convenience of readers predisposed to accept distinctions that Bentley rejects, a move I hope will lead them to consider why Bentley did not accept these distinctions. I have, moreover, used "philosophy of social science" and "methodology" interchangeably on occasion. The latter I take to identify reflection on the methods of science and not, as in most present-day contexts, to refer simply to various research techniques. Such reflection, as Leo Strauss noted of Max Weber's methodology, may be philosophic: "Methodology, as reflection on the correct procedure of science, is necessarily reflection on the limitations of science. If science is indeed the highest form of human knowledge, it is reflection on the limitations of human knowledge."[2]

An introductory sketch of the sense in which social science can and must be studied philosophically will prepare us for a preliminary statement of the principal themes of Bentley's philosophy of social science.

The Philosophic Character of Social Science

Social science is a product of, or emerged within the horizon disclosed by, modern philosophy and modern political philosophy. Some such recognition has existed among thinkers often regarded as possessing the best minds in social science or who have devoted careful attention to the character of social science. It will suffice in this connection to mention Karl Mannheim's observation that sociology, as the comprehensive effort to understand human society, is the present-day counterpart to philosophy in the eighteenth century.[3] As the heir to earlier understandings, however, social science does not simply preserve its legacy intact. The "human sciences" in general did not, as Michel Foucault rightly notes, simply inherit a well-defined intellectual domain to be studied.[4] The conclusion I draw from this observation is, so to speak, the opposite of Foucault's, for whom the human sciences exemplify a fundamental break with modern philosophy and political philosophy, to say nothing of premodern understandings. What remains of its origins in the self-understanding of social science consists, first, in a "model of science" which permits the use of science for the study of human things and, second, in a "definition of the social field" which theorizes or grasps the objects of social science in a manner compatible with or in conformity to a model of science.[5]

These considerations may suggest why I do not understand philosophy of social science as inquiry primarily concerned with the methodological unity of natural and social science, which may be described as the conventional account of the principal theme or concern of philosophy of social science.[6] Acceptance of the conventional opinion of the subject matter of philosophy of social science leads us to such familiar issues as the question of whether a single "logic of explanation" can or should be employed in both the natural and the social sciences or whether there are significant differences between the objects of the natural and social sciences that require essentially different notions of science. The constellation of issues ordinarily identified as marking disputes between the "natural" and the "spiritual," "cultural," or "human" sciences is not ignored in the thinking of Arthur Bentley, but is rather made the focus of inquiry that ultimately leads to a radical revision of the intellectual boundaries of this dispute. A more fundamental account of the course of social science is needed if Bentley's teaching is to be grasped adequately.

The assertion that the basic problem of social science is the problem of method connects social science to the primary doctrine of modern philosophy which we may call the methodological premise. Whether in Descartes or Bacon, as well as in their successors, the turn to method is an expression of the conviction of the uncertainty or unreliability of ordinary experience.[7] What is required for Descartes is both an understanding of certitude and a procedure, the use of which issues in certitude. For our purposes only the following needs to be said concerning this task. First, anything whatsoever that is or can be the object of knowledge can be known only by means of a logico-mathematical procedure that exhibits the essential character of things as the homogeneous elements of mathematics. This notion of what it means to know something scientifically, that is to say, truly, is philosophically prior to experimentation or more generally to empiricism. The "ideas" of philosophic empiricism that are transformed, for example, into epistemological units in eighteenth-century Lockean psychology are plainly modeled on the homogeneous substratum accessible to mathematics. Second, the mathematical method by which we know is the creation of or generated by the mind. We may say that the doctrine of method oscillates between the notion that method discloses homogeneity and thus certitude beneath the heterogeneity of things that now appears as "appearance" or superficial ambiguity resulting from the deliverances of ordinary understanding and the notion that homogeneity is invented or generated by and for human aims. Since method itself is not discovered but must be invented, the certitude of method must lie in the mind of the methodologist, taken as a neutral matrix whose contents are immediately accessible.[8]

The most discerning students of the modern doctrine of method recognize the connection between the ontology or doctrine of being indispensable for the methodological premise and the teaching that the aim of philosophy or science is, in Bacon's formula, the relief of man's estate. The "analysis" of anything into homogeneous elements readily becomes the ontological thesis that such elements or parts are fundamental and thus that the properties or characteristics of wholes result from arrangements of parts which can in principle be understood mathematically. This understanding has, in Hans Jonas's words, "technological implications prior to any application in fact," since to know how things are made up of homogeneous elements is also to know how they can be constructed.[9] The question "What is x?" becomes the question of how x functions or is distributed given various conditions. The transformation of the resulting plurality of hypothetical models for the arrangements of things into the actual reconstructions of things according to what Descartes admitted were "dreams" becomes the task of an applied science or philosophy that takes its bearings from human passions or desires.

It may not be quite clear how this aspect of the modern project issues in social science. Modern political philosophy furnishes the substance or content of social science. Put concisely, the founders of modern political philosophy taught that there was no intelligible inner constitution or hierarchy of human purposes or that there was no rational link between human aims and any natural standards in terms of which the ranking or ordering of these aims was intelligible. The place of such a constitution is taken by what eventually is understood as a distribution or uniform substratum of passions, desires, or dispositions. For Machiavelli, the "mass" of ordinary men is both knowable to and the object of reconstruction by the efforts of the exceptional man or prince, in large part because the needs and aims of ordinary men are similar or homogeneous. The prince, in turn, is distinguished from the people by his energies or will to power and his vision or dream of reconstruction. That dream is not anchored in nature or in any standard that transcends the human. It is rather a vision so quantitatively different from the limited vision of ordinary men as to be qualitatively different.[10] A crucial feature of the gulf between the dream of the prince and the needs of the people involves an overt break with ordinary understandings of good and evil. Here it is enough to say that the standpoint from which the prince who follows Machiavelli's teaching can choose good or evil courses of action according to the likelihood of success or failure suggests the thesis basic to virtually all modern social science—that the notions of good and evil exhibited in ordinary experience or understanding are to be theorized as "values" or preferences. Their character is grasped scientifically in terms of their origins in individual dispositions, distributions of "social" characteristics or properties, or the deliverances of history, and not in terms of their connections with anything higher than their sheer facticity.

The major modern political philosophers, allowing for important differences in their teachings, nonetheless shared a remarkably similar understanding of the good or right social order. In saying "social" and not "political" order I intend to draw attention to the gradual erosion, not to say disappearance, of the classical doctrine according to which the best way of life, if it could be actualized, was the product of contrivance or direction. While that direction, in the case of the best regime, was or could be philosophic, it was as ordering continuous with and a perfection of the basic character of ruling and hence of politics. The relief of man's estate, an aim that unites or discloses the common ground occupied by modern philosophy and modern political philosophy, depended upon the possibility and intelligibility of a self-operating human or social order. The principles of such an order are not contrivances of reason or philosophy, nor are they known to the human beings whose conduct, which eventually becomes theorized as "behavior," exhibits and is governed by principles that need not be understood to be exhibited. Social science studies the causal and functional relationships of human beings thus conceived. To the extent, then, that ordinary experience suggests to ordinary human beings something of the character of social order it is mistaken, superficial, or susceptible to replacement by an account that, like the mathematical method of science, penetrates beneath appearances. For political philosophers such as Thomas Hobbes, the methodological premise could be used to prevent what the classical political philosophers had taught was a movement of increasing reflection or clarity from the deliverances of ordinary experience to philosophy or science, a movement Hobbes knew to lead to such dangerous questions as the natural basis, if any, for authority and the natural basis for the right social order.[11]

The right social order is understood as the social order that is necessary given human needs or desires. The ordering impulse, which modern political philosophers at least until Hegel shared with their predecessors, does not vanish but is rather transformed to theorize, in the cases of such figures as Condorcet and others who began to speak in terms of a "social science," a reconstruction of society according to principles inherent in it but nullified by the pressures of tradition or the accidents of history. Conversely, among thinkers often credited with or blamed for the discovery of "history," it becomes possible to assert that the best or right social order is a product of or prefigured in the course of history. When the necessity of this order is understood, the question of its rightness is settled. That question may indeed be transformed or disappear as the necessity of a self-operating social order is emphasized. The gradual erosion of overt concern with this theme in social science is in part the result of the success of the modern understandings that produce social science. Concern with the right social order, when examined in the light shed by modern philosophy and modern political philosophy, appears as an expression of the values of the social scientist. If this thesis is combined with the doctrine that modern natural science has achieved its triumphs by dispensing with qualitative distinctions in nature, the notion that method must be universal requires that such distinctions be dispensed with in the study of human or social things. In the idiom of present-day social science, these concerns become "normative" social or political theory.

The character of the self-operating social order as understood by social science is not fully intelligible apart from its origins in modernity. The principles of such a social order show, when brought to light, the relative unimportance of the "state" and "politics." If society consists of structures and processes that generate order, the "state" appears, if at all, as one of these structures or one set of processes. Crucial to social science is the appearance of "economics" as a science that abstracts a domain of homogeneity from human conduct to articulate universal principles for the explanation of human conduct. While "sociology," at least in the tradition that culminates in Weber, is critical of the "individualism" said to characterize classical economics, it is not wholly incorrect to describe sociology, in Alvin W. Gouldner's words, as a "generalization of a market system."[12] Sociology, then, is primarily concerned with "civil society" or society understood in both the philosophical and political terms of modernity. What cannot be emphasized more strongly is that the idea, if not the reality, of "civil society" was an invention of modern political philosophy.[13]

If sufficient attention is given to social scientists in addition to the order with which they are concerned, we are led to the view that their concerns are related to or constituted by the objects of inquiry. The most serious students of social science cannot avoid the problem of "consciousness" as part of their enterprise. I shall have more to say about this issue in the following chapter and in close connection with Bentley's early views, but a few words here are necessary. The turn to questions of consciousness, while exhibited in the Germanic tradition of social science, is not adequately understood if we ignore its preparation in modern philosophy. When the priority of the thinking subject is linked to the modern doctrine of desires, the result is the appearance of consciousness as a fundamental issue, or the course of modern philosophy from Hume to Kant. The constitutive activities of the mind are increasingly modeled on mathematical or quasi-mathematical structures.

Accordingly, the Germanic tradition of "spiritual" or "cultural" sciences does not, in spite of the claims of many of its proponents and present-day defenders, return to "experience" and thereby overcome the abstractions of empiricism. Indeed, conventional formulations of philosophy of social science that concentrate primarily on the disputes between empiricists and interpretivists obscure the inner agreement that unites these orientations. The originators of the *Geisteswissenschaften* believed they had penetrated to and begun to articulate a science grounded in primordial or prescientific human experience. It is possible to ask whether the nature or sort of experience theorized is any less a reconstitution of experience and thus of human beings into scientific objects than the empiricist teaching. It must be noted that both Wilhelm Dilthey and Weber took for granted that there was and could be only one scientific method and that method as such was most clearly exhibited in natural science.[14] As a methodologist, the interpretive social scientist is not radically dissimilar from the experimentalist of the Cartesian and Newtonian traditions. The questions asked by each scientist are not timeless but rather change according to the drift or movement of history or the changing requirements of science. "Theory," whether in the natural or the social sciences, exhibits, in Jonas's words, "the interminableness of the process by which its tentative hypotheses are revised and absorbed into higher symbolical integrations."[15]

The empiricist and the interpretive visions of social science are in silent agreement on at least the following points. First, the basic problem is that of method. Knowledge of method is prior to knowledge of what is to be studied by method. For the empiricist this means that the everyday or ordinary opinions about social or political things are to be taken as indications of some underlying stratum of processes. For the interpretive social scientist such opinions are intelligible in terms of their locations in conceptual structures that present the distribution of links between material interests and values. Second, the domain of social science is a self-operating social order. Third, regardless of understandings of the role natural science should play in the social scientific enterprise, both traditions agree that modern philosophy has furnished an adequate account of "science."

The Structure of Bentley's Teaching

For Bentley, the beginning of wisdom or of a coherent idea of social science consists in recognition that a tenable account of "science" does not yet exist. In consequence, the notion that philosophy of social science is primarily an applied discipline or a discipline that brings to social science an authoritative account of science as such is an opinion about science. As I have mentioned earlier, Bentley did not doubt that science deserved to be taken as the standard for knowledge. Moreover, he agreed with the methodological premise of modernity and with the general understanding of society I have presented as the teaching of modern political philosophy. What Bentley denied was that these modern understandings had reached a sufficient level of self-consciousness. For this reason Bentley is an intransigent critic of much of social science. He should be studied not because he presents an earlier alternative to these views, as is done by defenders of traditional political philosophy, for example, but because he insists that the revolutions of modernity have not gone far enough.

Bentley was convinced that most philosophers and scientists were insufficiently aware of the categorial premises of their inquiries. The most important categories are those of space, time, causality, and action. The primary source of categorial ignorance lies in a failure on the part of scientists and philosophers to grasp crucial features of the connections between everyday and scientific languages, which in turn arises from a deficient understanding of relations between language and knowledge. As a consequence, science and philosophy all too often retain in their most refined productions remnants of the unconscious metaphysics of the natural or everyday understandings of human beings. Everyday language and the modes of thinking it constitutes encourage us to take some feature of experience as primary and thus as a criterion for knowledge. What present-day philosophers label as "foundationalism"—the belief that there is or can be a rock-bottom basis for knowledge or a basic epistemological condition—is seen by Bentley as a deliverance of the natural understanding. Accordingly, he came to regard his enterprise as a criticism of epistemology as such and not merely any specific epistemological position. Even the most ingenious exercise in epistemology, which may present candidates for foundational status quite remote from everyday thinking, is rooted in the naive belief that there must be something that is primary. In Bentley's terminology, everyday understanding generates "realisms" or opinions about what is "real." A science that remains unaware of these views is likely to smuggle into its thinking any number of ontological commitments. Most of Bentley's critical studies of positions in such disciplines as physics or mathematics or psychology or sociology are concerned with what scientists take as self-evident. The most important problems in a science come to light when we are clear about what is not understood as a problem in that science. I am reminded in virtually all of Bentley's explorations of Hegel's criticism of the certainty that attaches to the familiar:

> Quite generally, the familiar, just because it is familiar, is not cognitively understood. The commonest way in which we deceive ourselves or others about understanding is by assuming something as familiar, and accepting it on that account; with all its pros and cons, such knowing never gets anywhere, and it knows not why. Subject and object, God, Nature, Understanding, sensibility, and so on, are uncritically taken for granted as familiar, established as valid, and made into fixed points for starting and stopping. While these remain unmoved, the knowing activity goes back and forth between them, thus moving only on their surface.[16]

Now Bentley knew he was hardly alone in insisting upon a difference between everyday and scientific understandings. The doctrine of method was developed with just such an intention. What its creators had not understood is that we cannot have any knowledge of reality apart from or prior to language, which is the primary or fundamental condition of knowledge. Bentley's methodology, then, is "linguistic analysis." Since it is difficult to exaggerate the extent to which present-day philosophy, whether in the idioms of "ordinary language" philosophy, or hermeneutics, or semantics, is concerned with language, the recovery of Bentley's views may be accomplished in a more congenial philosophical climate. Bentley sought a comprehensive understanding of language, but recognized that such an account was of necessity a part of what it sought to study. We cannot suppose that there is or can be any "extralinguistic" access to reality. In Bentley's words, language is the "phenomenal form in which science and knowledge present themselves to us" (BKF, 4). Our exploration of the character of science and knowledge is an exploration of a variety of forms of "linguistic behavior" by means of still other forms of this behavior.

The primacy of language must be recognized to make clear the authoritative nature of science. The superiority of modern natural science to any other form of human knowledge has little to do with matters of the determination of "fact." The secret of science lies in its capacity for self-correction. As we shall see, Bentley's understanding of science places him in the tradition of pragmatism to the extent that he regards science as the practice of a community of inquirers engaged in mutual corrective discourse. Unlike pragmatism, however, Bentley understands the progressive unfolding of science and therewith its authoritative character as the emergence of "formalism" from the contradictions of "realism."

The most important difficulties in Bentley's teaching have to do with his "formalism." That formalism is clearly a version of the doctrine of method but is intended to be a decisive advance over all other versions of the doctrine in two general ways. First, Bentley claims that all other versions of the doctrine of method are linked explicitly or implicitly to doctrines concerning the objects of method. Bentley may be understood as having claimed to do more rigorously than anyone before him the modern task of dissolving the connections between ontology and methodology. The second claim is more clearly argued in Bentley's texts than the first. Bentley rejects the notion that there is a general logico-mathematical model or discipline to which science and thereby knowledge must conform. Logic and mathematics, he concludes, face the same problems as empirical science because they are intimately connected with ordinary language and experience. Even the most profound or technical discourse on the foundations of logic or mathematics is dependent upon the ranges of meanings of words and notions found in natural or ordinary language. Bentley's teaching in *Linguistic Analysis of*

Mathematics foreshadows recent arguments (such as those presented by Stanley Rosen) that most proponents of logico-mathematical doctrines do not recognize or consider philosophically significant the connections between analytic discourse and the various contexts of analysis.[17] Unlike Rosen, however, Bentley calls for more formalization. He proposes to formalize the processes by which formal discourse emerges from informal discourse. He seeks sciences that are "systematic" and "consistent" but which do not base themselves on some indubitable or self-evident foundations, whether empirical or mathematical.

Among the major obstacles in the path of formalism in social science is the "individual." Much of Bentley's work consists in a criticism of the notion, present in the most diverse sorts of social science, that the individual or some supposedly fundamental properties of the individual must be taken as primary in social science. His criticisms extend well beyond the context of disputes in philosophy of social science between "methodological individualists" and their critics. First, the status of the individual in social science is related to the more general notion that we can speak intelligibly about "parts" apart from "wholes." Now since we have already seen that the modern doctrine of method seems to teach precisely this possibility, we can also see that Bentley's position is not identical with the modern doctrine although it is presented as an advance over that view. Bentley saw in the "subject" of modern epistemology and in the individual as understood by psychology and social science a systematically and historically connected body of errors. I shall show in the final chapter that this Bentleyan thesis links Bentley with present-day criticisms of the entire epistemological tradition as historically determinate.

Second, consideration of Bentley's criticisms brings us to the question of whether or how a scientific understanding is related to a natural understanding of anything whatsoever. Our belief in individuals is a thesis of the natural understanding. If scientific understanding is both radically different and superior, we must surrender that belief. While science is understood to have effected a break with ordinary understanding, Bentley also insists that it begins with this understanding.

I can present this issue in a preliminary way by directing our attention to a widespread criticism of social science modeled on natural science, which claims that such a social science ignores its dependence upon prescientific experience or understanding. Leo

Strauss's criticism of Weber may be taken as exemplifying this criticism, which may be articulated in a number of philosophical idioms. For Strauss, it is clear that Weber recognized that there is "an articulation of reality that precedes all scientific articulation: that articulation, that wealth of meaning, which we have in mind when speaking of the world of common experience or of the natural understanding of the world."[18] Weber did not furnish an account of that natural articulation, which Strauss takes as fundamental to the proper study of society, because Weber accepted the superiority or the objectivity of the scientific account of the world. While the founders of modern philosophy had understood modern natural science, in Strauss's words, as the "perfection of man's natural understanding of the natural world," their successors taught that this scientific understanding "emerges by way of a radical modification, as distinguished from a perfection, of the natural understanding." Bentley may be understood in this connection to have directed his attention to what is implied by this radical modification of the natural understanding and to have claimed that the scientific understanding must be distinguished decisively from the natural understanding. The modification of the natural understanding required by science is such that it is not correct to view it as a modification. What makes Bentley's thinking unusual is that he agrees with Strauss that there is a "wealth of meaning" in the natural understanding that must be studied by social science. Bentley's sense, then, is nearly the opposite of Weber's, since for him the natural articulation of reality can never be ignored.

What Bentley insisted upon was that the commitment to the development of a genuine social science could not permit understandings of the subject matter of social science that originated in prescientific thinking to remain intact. Since on his view no genuine science was simply or primarily a refinement of ordinary understandings, there could be no compelling reason for social science to derive its themes or subject matter from prescientific concerns and its method from science. At the very least, the notion of "formalism" means for Bentley that a genuine science permits only scientific determinations of its procedures, domains of inquiry, subject matters, and the like. Modernity seems to have meant for Bentley that nothing is or can be taken as "given." The sciences have not learned this lesson with sufficient clarity. Bentley proposes to set science on the right path by showing what is truly implied by the most important modern teachings. His intensification or radicalization of these teachings is an intransigent presentation of a significant alternative. His choice of social science as the primary vehicle for his reflections is significant because it is within the broad and often shadowy realm of social science that inquiry into the connections between the basic modern teachings and their subsequent fate touches the most important human concerns.

2

The Intellectual Matrix of

Bentley's Social Science

Society itself is rather a nexus of actions; and it is a nexus so complex that were the investigator himself of other nature than human, its interpretation would be utterly impossible.
        "The Units of Investigation in Social Science"

"From my point of view," Bentley wrote over fifty years after the appearance of his first work, "I have steadily pursued the same course."[1] This chapter is concerned with the milieu in which Bentley's early thinking was formed and the way in which he began his course of inquiry. The central question is how Bentley arrived at the problem that unifies his work: the search for the foundations of social science. The path to the philosophy of social science led Bentley through a series of intellectual encounters which expanded the horizons of his thinking and which reveal his growing intellectual independence.

My point of departure is the social world of late nineteenth-century midwestern America as it appeared to the young Bentley. Any reconstruction of his impressions is necessarily speculative since examples of his juvenilia are both scarce and fragmentary.[2] What can be determined is that his early interest in social theory was nourished by a reformist idealism that bears the imprint of Progressivism. While his reformism remained intact, his study of economics at Johns Hopkins University and graduate work in Germany led him to subordinate programmatic ideology to systematic social science. The last major intellectual encounter of his early career was his study of pragmatic philosophy. Bentley's understanding of the central problems of social science, derived initially from his self-chosen European masters, and his deepening understanding of pragmatic epistemology energize each other.

Bentley's Early Years

Arthur Fisher Bentley was born in Freeport, Illinois, on October 16, 1870. His father, Charles Bentley, was born in London in 1843 and came to Illinois in 1851. Little is known about the elder Bentley's early career. He became assistant cashier of the First National Bank of Freeport. In 1879 the Bentley family moved to Omaha, Nebraska, where Charles Bentley intended to found his own bank but, finding no opportunities, the family moved to Grand Island, Nebraska, the following year. Early in 1880 Bentley started a bank which prospered during the next two years. He merged his bank with another owned by Samuel N. Walbach to form the First National Bank of Grand Island, with Walbach as president and Bentley as cashier. Bentley became a successful local businessman with a number of real estate holdings and investments and was a leading citizen of Grand Island until his death in 1908.[3]

A self-taught iconoclast, Charles Bentley had an enormous influence on his oldest son, Arthur. Sidney Ratner has described the elder Bentley as a man of "unusual ability and intellectual candor."[4] He was also stern and strong-willed, holding his son to rigorous intellectual standards. Only a few samples of the correspondence between Charles and Arthur Bentley survive. Charles Bentley's letters to his son are almost wholly impersonal and didactic, the letters of a tutor to his student. The correspondence amounts to a series of terse and acerbic treatises on such matters as currency questions, tax policies, land speculation, and the like. Young Arthur's views are, for the most part, brushed aside with merciless logic. Certainly Bentley never had a more severe intellectual master than this probing and sarcastic figure whom he would always regard in some sense as his superior.[5] He sought and received his father's unsparing criticism of his writings, including drafts of *The Process of Government*.

The lessons Bentley learned from his father clearly had a role in shaping his philosophical temperament, so accurately depicted by Ratner: "Bentley . . . was uncompromising in adhering to the most technically exact or precise formulation of his ideas. He believed in challenging his opponents in the most straightforward manner. He did not attempt to conciliate those with whom he differed, and delighted in a no-holds-barred attack on philosophic positions he deemed unsound."[6] In almost all his writings, Bentley's tone is angry and his style is polemical. He does not simply hold other writers to standards of his own devising but insists that they not fall below whatever standards they claim to value themselves, punishing them for their failures with his extravagant sarcasm. A great deal of Bentley's writing consists, on the surface, of microscopic and almost always highly critical examinations of other men's works. His own views lie deep beneath his patient rehearsals of opinions with which he violently disagreed. His chosen standpoint is that of an immensely erudite outsider, determined to vanquish the most distinguished spokesmen for conventional views on their own ground. He usually traces the failures of the orthodox to their acquiescence in received opinions, whether in politics, science, or philosophy. In this practice he resembles his father, whose advocacy of "radical" economic policies to solve the problems of the Depression of the 1890s stemmed less from humanitarian motives or doctrinaire politics than from sheer exasperation with conventions.

Young Arthur's habits were solitary and the demands he made on himself were rigorous. There was an emotional price to be paid. After his education in the public schools of Freeport and Grand Island, he went first to York College and then to the University of Denver. His education was interrupted by the first of several episodes of ill health which were to recur throughout his life, usually in conjunction with periods of emotional turmoil or difficult work. He always described his difficulties in vague language—"neuro-muscular disorganization," "muscular over-strain," and "muscular hypertension"—and sought relief with such eccentric regimes as physical culture, naturopathy, and electrical shock treatments. He worked in his father's bank until he entered Johns Hopkins University in 1890.

Bentley's path to intellectual independence was arduous and while he developed a capacity to sustain his conviction about the merits of his work in extreme isolation from most of his contemporaries, the "ego strength" Paul Kress attributes to him was as much an achievement as any of his intellectual performances.[7] He sought external tranquility to help free him for his chosen tasks. He was eventually able to admit that his recurrent illness was useful, for it gave him time for research and writing.[8]

The most crucial event for Bentley may well have been the death of his father in July 1908. The task of writing *The Process of Government* had taken its toll of Bentley's fragile health.[9] His father's death placed the additional burden upon him of returning to Grand Island from Chicago, where he was employed as a journalist, to serve as executor of the estate. Bentley felt himself ill suited to or unworthy of the role of head of the family now thrust upon him. His "muscular over-strain" soon returned, accompanied by a severe depression which made serious intellectual activity all but impossible. He would refer to this period as a "breakdown" which lasted from 1908 to 1911.[10] Bentley was no more specific about the details of his psychic collapse in 1908 than about the other episodes he suffered. After the earliest occurrence he had been able to retreat for a time to the safety of his father's bank, but no safe haven was available in 1908 to the thirty-eight-year-old son who now had to manage the affairs of the father with whom he had always compared himself so unfavorably. Suffering from chronic weakness, a loss of coordination, and nervous exhaustion, Bentley discharged his duties. He resumed work in 1909 but resigned in 1911, after his mother's death, and moved with his wife to Paoli, Indiana. There he took up the life of a small-town businessman, starting an apple orchard which he owned for many years. Demands on his time and strength were slight and he began to recover slowly. For the rest of his life he would never spend more than a few months away from Paoli.

I believe there are sufficient parallels between Bentley's collapse and the more adequately documented but controversial case of Max Weber's prolonged depression to hazard a speculative comparison which suggests the significance of these events for Bentley's own intellectual career.[11] Students of Weber are familiar with the external circumstances of his breakdown which prevented all scholarly work from 1898 until 1903. Weber had accepted a chair in economics at the University of Heidelberg, replacing the retired Karl Knies. The young Weber, who would later write of his need to be "crushed under the load of work," tried to meet the demands imposed by his academic position, his role as a consultant to government agencies, and his political involvement in reform nationalist circles.[12] His collapse occurred less than a year after assuming his new position. Interpreters of this period in Weber's life have attached great importance as well to the strained relations that existed between his parents and to his own life-long uncertainties about his ability to perform in the role of husband and father. Weber's hard-working and authoritarian father, from whom he became increasingly estranged, and his pious and humanitarian mother, with whom he maintained a close and emotionally charged relationship, are reminiscent of Bentley's acerbic father and his mother, whom Ratner describes as a "conscientious, hardworking, religious person, with a sweet temperament."[13] Weber was evidently deeply divided by the contradictory expectations he believed his parents had of him. His collapse followed a confrontation with his father, whose death several weeks later left Weber with a profound sense of guilt. While it is unclear if Bentley had a similar confrontation, there is a suggestive parallel in the fact that his father, shortly before his death, had criticized *The Process of Government* quite harshly as overlong and excessively polemical. I do not think it necessary to debate the adequacy of an oedipal interpretation of Weber's or Bentley's conditions to recognize the origins of their ailments in a conjunction of professional and personal tensions.

We may draw the lines of comparison still further. Weber's illness divides his work into the massive, competent, but essentially conventional scholarship of his early career and the penetrating methodological reflections that form a major part of his mature work. H. Stuart Hughes suggests that Weber's "four years of intellectual paralysis were only apparently wasted. Actually Weber seems to have been thinking—and thinking hard—a good deal of the time. Indeed, one subsidiary reason why he may have felt unable to read and write was that he was digging into a new sort of problem for which the conventional methods of his youth were proving quite inadequate."[14] We will see that after 1908 Bentley came to believe that the way in which he was beginning to conceive fundamental problems in social science made the inherited categories of social theory radically insufficient for his purposes. *The Process of Government* is the first and last of Bentley's works in which he tries to combine methodological reflections and substantive social theory in a single enterprise. Both Weber and Bentley enjoyed the advantage of a clean break with much of their intellectual legacies.

Throughout the rest of their lives, Weber and Bentley followed similar personal strategies based on their convictions that they enjoyed dubious health. As Hughes puts it, Weber "lived on the careful regime of a semi-invalid," establishing "artificial walls, apparently senseless barriers and taboos against the intrusion of the irrelevant. Unconsciously exploiting his illness for his own intellectual purposes, he used it ruthlessly to strip down to the essentials all the meaningless paraphernalia of existence."[15] In the same way, Bentley moved between the extremes of invalidism and frenetic scholarly activity. His isolation in Paoli allowed him to pursue his own course relatively unaffected by academic fashions. Although he would begin an extensive correspondence in his middle years with a dazzling array of philosophers and scientists, he had arranged his situation so that he always had, if he wished, the last word.

Although Bentley's emotional life is in many respects a sealed book, I believe it furnishes at least some clues that allow us to assemble his impressions of the midwestern society in which he grew up. In Nebraska the young Bentley saw the gradual absorption of what Robert H. Wiebe has called the "island communities"—the small towns, once the core of post-Reconstruction American society—into the new order "derived from the regulative, hierarchical needs of urban-industrial life."[16] Grand Island was an agricultural market and railroad center founded in 1857 by a company of speculators from Davenport, Iowa, who were convinced that the settlement's location in the center of Nebraska held great economic promise, including, in a particularly extravagant vision, the hope that the state or even the national capital might be moved there. The original settlers were largely German immigrants, most of whom remained after the failure in 1858 of the Washington banking house of Chubb Brothers and Barrows, which had backed the development company. The settlement did not begin to grow until the Union Pacific Railroad reached it in 1866. By the early 1880s, when Charles Bentley started his bank, the town was a prosperous commercial center. The German presence remained important; about a quarter of its voting population consisted of German immigrants and their descendants, while the rest of the town consisted of Yankees, and Irish and Danish immigrants.[17] Politics was turbulent, for Grand Island contained political conflicts centered on the opposition of immigrants and nativists. Like so many growing and heterogeneous communities, Grand Island was torn by disputes about the legitimacy of the use of the German language in schools, prohibition, and woman's suffrage. Its German population was divided along religious and class lines as well, with highly assimilative businessmen and craftsmen at odds with less assimilative farmers. In the 1880s some of these differences were expressed in the existence of an English-language newspaper owned by an "Americanizing" German and a German-language newspaper owned by an avowed traditionalist. It is not unreasonable to say that Bentley was exposed very early to group conflict of the sort he would later describe in The Process of Government.

The story of the disintegration of the social order of the "island communities" is a familiar one. For millions of farmers, such as the mortgagees of Charles Bentley's bank, the expansion of American agriculture after the Civil War had been an ambiguous blessing. The number of farms and the amount of acreage under cultivation increased, the result not only of westward migration but of technological improvements, the expansion of the railroads, and the growth of agricultural colleges. The farmer's productivity had increased dramatically but his success had brought entanglement in an economic network controlled by distant concentrations of wealth and power. Commodity prices declined during the 1870s and 1880s, contributing to the general economic contraction that spanned the period from 1873–1898. To both the farmer and the small-town businessman ultimately dependent on him, the hardships imposed by increasing costs for machinery, seed, transportation, storage, and credit, and by declining profits seemed less the result of the laws of the market than of the designs of men and institutions beyond the farmer's control.

The political currents that swept the region shared a common impulse to preserve the world of the island communities. Farmers' alliances, Populists, Progressives, Edward Bellamy's Nationalists, and an enormous variety of Protestant reformers all rested their criticisms on the premises of the self-governing community, composed of individuals whose actions conformed to a conjunction of economic and ethical laws. The virtues of the middle-class property holder were defended in a number of idioms ranging from Bellamy's utopianism and the economic panaceas of Henry George to the eclectic spirituality of Transcendentalism.[18] "Community" was the central term in the vocabulary of social criticism.

A mixture of social radicalism and romantic religious sentiment was Arthur Bentley's initial response to the world. He read Goethe, Hegel, American socialist literature, and popular accounts of Eastern religions and philosophies. He looked, in his words, for a "new reformation of humanism" that would dissolve the frustrations of modern men who had been taught to disparage the "joys of life." He was convinced of the unity of men and the fullness of experience from his earliest reflections. The unity Bentley saw, however, was not that of the constellation of beliefs of his fellow citizens of Grand Island. The small businessman and the farmer, in Barry D. Karl's words:

regulated and managed community affairs in accordance with what they conceived to be American democratic values. They sifted those values through a haze of half-articulated metaphors in which biblical morals, political self-sustenance, and the ownership of property became interchangeable. That system of values certified land and the resources of nature as a gift to all men from the hand of God; sanctified an honest deal shrewdly consummated as an act of political independence; and made political action a holy tribute to the moral cohesion of the community and its commonwealth.[19]

In contrast, Bentley saw social life as a stream of ceaselessly changing forces. His sense of "process," present in his earliest writings, was not a social theory but rather a basic intuition. In a youthful flash of understanding he had seen that the "individual" was mere appearance and not reality. A passage probably written shortly before 1890 expresses his sensibility vividly:

> I, why should I use that personal pronoun? First person, egoistic, unwitting, facts of life, and of thought. These are truly grouped together as me, Arthur Bentley. And they are the real Arthur Bentley. Behind them there is no one at all. Those facts that you group together with a name, the tree and the shrub and the flower, the animal, bird, beast and fish, the stones and the mud of the earth, the winds and the moisture of heaven. All are present now in them & help to give them their meaning. Then why call those facts Arthur Bentley? . . . To those with whom I have talked. To those, also, with whom I have lived: For you, all of you, have your share in that which my pen is now writing.

A favorite couplet from Goethe conveys Bentley's insight: "Nature has neither core nor rind/She's all at once; no need to bind."[20] The continuity of man and nature or of all things made the identity of anything ultimately arbitrary. The "new reformation of humanism" Bentley projected has no content in his juvenilia except for an awkward attack on conventional sexual morality as an example of the kinds of obstacles men put in the path to union with the whole.

The young Bentley found a hybrid political position of "anarchist, socialist and patriot" the best expression for his humanist sentiments. He decided to attend Johns Hopkins because the economist Richard T. Ely, whom he later described as having "startled" the

"American world by using the word 'socialism' in the title of a book," was teaching there.[21] By the time Bentley arrived in Baltimore, Ely had left Johns Hopkins for the University of Wisconsin and his erstwhile student was left without a master. Bentley's capacity for intense and essentially isolated study was revealed in his years at Johns Hopkins. The university did not hire a senior economist to replace Ely. A young instructor, Sidney Sherwood, seems to have had no influence on Bentley, who began to read widely in classical political economy, sociology, and contemporary economics. Bentley had occasional conferences with the economists John Bates Clark and Simon N. Patten, who were visiting professors. Clark may have drawn his student's attention to the theoretical disputes in German and Austrian economics and social science which would soon move to the center of Bentley's interests.

As a student of economics in the early 1890s, Bentley was exposed to a torrent of opposition to Social Darwinism. The fusion of classical political economy and social evolutionism represented in the popular teachings of Herbert Spencer and William Graham Sumner had been repellent to Bentley from his first encounter with it. His study brought to his attention some of the first fruits of the growing professionalization of the social sciences in the United States. Professionalization meant graduate study either in Germany or with teachers who had made the pilgrimage to German seminars. American students of economics encountered a radically different tradition of social theory which had devastating intellectual consequences for Social Darwinism. In the hands of such scholars as Wilhelm Roscher and Karl Knies economics had become a historical discipline. To many Americans, whose views on economics had been formed by rehearsals of Adam Smith, J. B. Say, and David Ricardo, buttressed by divine providence and natural selection, the "historical school" of economics was revolutionary. Joseph Schumpeter summarizes the methodological teaching of the younger generation of economists headed by Gustav von Schmoller, with whom Bentley would study, as the doctrine that "the organon of scientific economics should mainly—at first it was held that it should exclusively—consist in the results of, and in generalizations from, historical monographs."[22] For American students of economics, the approach had the salutary effect of casting doubt upon the universality claimed for the formulas of the classical tradition. Moreover, the parochialism of Social Darwinism became apparent to Americans who studied

German social science. In Donald Fleming's words, "Herbert Spencer fell into perspective as a local writer of the English-speaking tribes and as no Aristotle."[23]

The American disciples of the exponents of *Sozialpolitik* followed their German masters in giving to the state a strong role to play in solving the problems caused by industrialization. Although the founders of the *Verein für Sozialpolitik* did not share a uniform program, they could agree that economic activity should be regarded only as an instrument in the service of spiritual cultivation. Progressive taxation, factory inspection, social insurance, a minimum wage, and the like were not proposed as leveling measures, but rather as parts of the material substructure of liberal humanism.[24] For Richard Ely, a student of Knies, a "new school" of American economists had arisen. In popular works such as *The Labor Movement in America* (1886) and *Social Aspects of Christianity* (1889) he appealed to the Christian conscience of the American businessman, urging him to cooperate with government in solving the problems of the industrial system lest revolutionary socialism penetrate the working class. An industrial system welded together by Christianity as a people's religion would transcend the class struggle. American "socialism" would usher in the Christian Commonwealth of the future.

While his communitarian vision inspired Bentley, Ely's works were innocent of systematic economic theory. Ely had misunderstood the historical school's subordination of classical economics to history as a rejection of systematic theory rather than as a different understanding of the tasks of economic theory. Simon Patten had a firmer grasp of both classical and historical economics. In *The New Basis: The Premises of Political Economy* (1887) and *The Theory of Dynamic Economics* (1892) he argued that the evolution of American society had enabled it to repeal the doctrine of natural scarcity, together with that doctrine's morally undesirable corollaries, and had pointed it toward an economy of abundance.[25] The thesis that America had transcended the laws of Manchester was hardly new. It will suffice to mention the name of Henry C. Carey. But Carey and his forgotten disciples had never reached the larger audience that took classical economics as a subdivision of Protestant theology. The American students of German economics severed laissez faire from social evolution, which was now understood to guarantee a communitarian future.

The young Bentley seems to have taken the ethical criticism of Social Darwinism as self-evident. What absorbed his attention was the methodological criticism of Social Darwinism that had begun to emerge from such leading American social scientists as Patten and Lester Frank Ward. Spencerian sociology and ethics rested on a fatal confusion of biological and psychological modes of explanation.[26] If an evolutionary perspective is taken consistently, we cannot ignore man's capacity to control his natural and social environments. Indeed, the mind has evolved to protect man from the ravages of nature by giving him the capacity for rational and cooperative action. Patten pronounced his judgment in the title of an important article, "The Failure of Biologic Sociology" (1894).[27] Looking ahead to the coming century, Patten argued that the social sciences must rest on psychology, not biology. "Biologic" or Spencerian social science was an untenable combination of sciences or understandings of science that should be rejected by those committed to the scientific study of social phenomena. Psychology and the social sciences would not simply imitate the substantive and methodological features of the natural sciences. As Franklin H. Giddings put it, progress in the social sciences required exploration of the "primary social phenomena," all of which involved psychology. Bentley set out in search of these phenomena as a graduate student.

The Proper Study of Society

Bentley's first major intellectual performance was his undergraduate thesis, "The Condition of the Western Farmer as Illustrated by the Economic History of a Nebraska Township" (1893). It conformed to the scholarly conventions established by the leading Johns Hopkins historians Herbert B. Adams and J. Franklin Jameson, for whom clearly delimited monographs were the model of inquiry. While most students of Bentley dismiss the thesis as conventional, I agree with Richard Hofstadter's claim that Bentley showed in it a talent for shrewd social analysis.[28] The work is a microscopic study of patterns of land purchase, use, and economic yield in a single Nebraska township. Bentley and his father, whom he credited with inspiring the study, collected the data during the summer of 1892. Bentley had in view the larger question of whether the "trouble at the basis of the industrial system" indicated by the growth of militant farmers' groups was "basic or transient."[29] He did not address this question directly and the thesis contains no explicit speculations. The study is methodologically scrupulous. Bentley devised a survey instrument and made numerous drafts of the questions he included in it.

He was aware of the hazards of drawing conclusions from data limited to a single township, but insisted that the virtue of his study lay in its closeness to the data and thus to the farmer and his understanding of the economic world around him. Bentley concluded that the farmer failed to understand his increasing dependence upon such forces as conditions in the international grain market. The machinations of bankers and speculators—favorite villains of the farmers' movement—were much less important as a source of the farmer's difficulties than his own unrealistic expectation that grain prices would always rise. The tacit economic calculus which had been an adequate reflection of economic reality under the simple conditions of the market in the past no longer worked. Bentley, in an early expression of what would become a recurrent view, found neither heroes nor villains. While the farmer had only himself to blame for his plight, debtors and creditors, land speculators and subsistence farmers, and small landholders and international grain merchants had their parts to play in a drama all of which could not be grasped from any single standpoint. Many years later he wrote of his thesis: "Something remote and cold-blooded about it (I am told) . . . it seemed to have a total impartiality to its subject matter."[30] Bentley's detachment was more than the caution of a young scholar concerned with pleasing his professors. Alongside his vision of a world of flux lay the possibility of a comprehensive and dispassionate account of the interplay of social forces. His attitude was not one of moral indifference but rather reflected his growing belief that the path to a genuine social science had to be distinguished from prescriptive social theory. The study of social phenomena required attention to questions fundamentally different from those asked by reformers or partisans.

Although graduate students in the social sciences at Columbia University, which was the only major American university other than Johns Hopkins in which advanced work in these disciplines was well developed, were encouraged to spend a year in Germany, few Johns Hopkins students took a *Wanderjahr*.[31] In the face of Adams's focus on the United States, Bentley's decision to go to Germany reflected his increasing independence. In 1893–94 he studied at the universities of Berlin and Freiburg im Breisgau.

On his way to Germany, Bentley met a wealthy young Yankee, Hutchins Hapgood, with whom he would share a lifelong friendship.

Hapgood, who was taking his *Wanderjahr* after studying with William James and George Santayana at Harvard, is one of the few sources for our knowledge of the young Bentley. He eventually became Bentley's link to the world of avant-garde literature and the arts. Their correspondence is filled with Bentley's eager questions and Hapgood's observations of the literary life of New York, Paris, and London. Hapgood's reports from the fringes of Bohemia not only entertained Bentley but allowed him to express interests he never permitted to become apparent in his own work. For Hapgood, Bentley was a "strangely vivid" young man whose "state of mind was in striking contrast" to his own.[32] Hapgood's German studies were not as serious as Bentley's. The latter was "realistically passionate, with a serious purpose of learning everything known about sociology, and with a determination to add to that knowledge and solve the puzzle of human society." He had a "sense of responsibility which much of the time made him unhappy" and seemed "bitterly critical of himself and his inability to reach the heights." He was sufficiently romantic to have challenged a shipboard acquaintance Kenyon Cox, a young painter and photographer, to a duel. Bentley and Hapgood separated when they reached Europe and met again in Berlin where they took rooms in a house owned by Julius Nehab, a Jewish philosopher. Bentley plunged into his study of philosophy, history, sociology, and economics, while Hapgood eventually went to Strasbourg to study Hegel and aesthetics with Wilhelm Windelband.

A hint of Bentley's development may be found in a letter to Hapgood early in 1894.[33] He wrote a lengthy description of an early morning scene, comparing a crowd of well-dressed men and women leaving a formal ball in Berlin with the paupers they passed in the street without evident concern. Here were representatives of two classes, objectively in conflict, yet oblivious to one another. Each took their conditions as natural, but even their lack of mutual recognition was part of the larger set of relationships of which they were unknowing elements. In another letter Bentley described his experience in the slums of London. "He had been wandering through the slums of London," Hapgood writes, "and had seen such a mass of suffering human beings, he said, so unhappy that they didn't know they were unhappy; an objective impersonal misery that put him into a state almost of insanity."[34] The "mystery of sociology," as Hapgood put it, seemed for Bentley to lie in the contradictions between how men understood their own situations and the objective character of those situations. What Bentley had seen in Nebraska farmers could be found in beggars in Berlin or slum dwellers in London. People were parts of a larger whole, the outlines of which were invisible. None of the systems of sociology with which Bentley was familiar seemed able to account for what he had seen.

At Berlin, Bentley took courses from some of the most important social scientists of the day.[35] During his first semester from October 1893 to March 1894, he studied economic research methods and national economy with Schmoller, finance and economic theory with Adolph Wagner, one of the most active exponents of *Sozialpolitik*, and the history of philosophy with Julius Ebbinghaus, a neo-Hegelian disciple of Windelband. In his second semester, which lasted from April to August 1894, he took more courses from Schmoller and Wagner, although he was disappointed by the lack of rigorous theory in their approaches to economics. He was more impressed by Dilthey's lectures than by the work of the historical economists. During this semester he encountered the social theorist he would later credit with having the greatest influence on his thinking early in his career—Georg Simmel. He took Simmel's seminars in sociology, sociological research, and the philosophy of Kant. Bentley's reading during 1893–94 shows the breadth of his interests and suggests the sort of comprehensive preparation in which he would typically engage while working on intellectual problems. His study of classical economics continued with extensive reading in Say, Ricardo, Adam Ferguson, and Jeremy Bentham. He began to read widely in the works of "scientific" social theorists such as Comte, Spencer, Sumner, and Ernst Haeckel, along with the major works of his professors and those of Roscher, Knies, Ludwig Gumplowicz, Heinrich Rickert, Windelband, and Eduoard von Hartmann. His interest in socialism brought him to Marx, Auguste Blanqui, and Karl Bebel, while his taste in literature ran to the naturalism of Balzac and Zola and the modernism of Ibsen.

Bentley's introduction to the philosophical disputes that marked the emergence of the social sciences in Germany was through the *Methodenstreit*—the "battle of methods" in economics between Carl Menger, one of the architects of marginalism, and Schmoller. It is possible that Bentley may have known something of this issue even before his German study. John Bates Clark, who had arrived at the principle of marginal utility independently of its more prominent exponents William Stanley Jevons, Léon Walras, and Menger, may have directed Bentley's attention to Menger's marginalist statement in his *Gründsatze der Volkswirtschaftslehre* (1871). What can be determined from the lists Bentley kept of his book purchases is that he was familiar with Menger's critique of Schmoller in his *Untersuchungen über die Methode der Sozialwissenschaften und der politischen inbedondere* (1883) and with such important works as Eugen von Böhm-Bawerk's marginalist critique of Marxism, *Kapital und Kapitalzins* (1884, 1889). Menger had criticized the historical economists with having ignored economic theory in favor of historical description, which prompted Schmoller's response that theory and description should not be opposed to each other.[36] Beneath the polemics produced by disciples of Menger and Schmoller it is possible to see more fundamental issues. Neither Schmoller nor Menger was opposing theory to description. Rather, the question was one of the proper character of economic theory. Moreover, the dispute about methods was in large measure a displaced form of a dispute about the place of "values" in the study of economics.[37] The Austrian economists led by Menger challenged the role of *Sozialpolitik* in economics understood as a science and not an ideology. When we reach this level of the *Methodenstreit* it is clear that we cannot limit its scope to economic theory or to economics as a discipline.

The larger context of the *Methodenstreit* is suggested by Hayden V. White's claim that "the intellectual history of nineteenth-century Germany, if indeed not all of Europe, may be conceived as centering about the problem of defining the relation between the human sciences (*Geisteswissenschaften*) and the natural sciences (*Naturwissenschaften*)."[38] The problems with which the leading German academic intellectuals were concerned during the last decades of the nineteenth century had complex roots. I believe Guy Oakes's warning that even the language of German social science debates "is no longer fully intelligible" bears repetition.[39] The ordering of these decades of intellectual activity and of the work of Dilthey, Simmel, and the various neo-Kantian and neo-Hegelian philosophers in such terms as a "revolt against positivism" is convenient and yet inevitably a foreshortening of the disputes. The demarcation of the human or cultural sciences from the natural sciences involved such issues as the nature of science and scientific explanation, the proper methods for the study of social phenomena, the nature of the objects of social science, and the role of values in the construction of social theory. A faithful portrait of the intellectual landscape must include as well an assessment of the importance of German idealist philosophy, the historiography of Leopold von Ranke and his successors, the energizing effect of the constellation of humanist beliefs that made custody of the "higher values" the professional responsibility of academic intellectuals, and the use of "positivism" as a convenient summary epithet for an assortment of philosophical tendencies ranging from mechanistic materialism to the evils resulting from the decline of spiritual cultivation in an age of industrialization. Such a portrait is beyond the scope of my study of Bentley, but of undeniable importance for a full understanding of the ground in which the seeds of German social science were planted.

The tradition with which I am concerned—that of some of Bentley's most important teachers—raised against "positivist" views of the human sciences a teaching considered both more subtle and more scientific by its proponents. The foremost example of a positivist view of the human sciences was taken to be the sixth part of John Stuart Mill's *System of Logic* (1843) on the "logic of the moral sciences." The very term *Geisteswissenschaften*, which German thinkers would use to encompass both history and the social sciences, was the German translator's rendering of Mill's "moral sciences." While Mill doubted that the "moral sciences" could employ without change the methods of geometry and physics, he attributed their backwardness to their failure to imitate the natural sciences. Mill claimed that an associationist psychology was already sufficiently well established to serve as the basis of the moral sciences, since all the properties of social phenomena in principle can be understood in terms of the laws of psychology. Psychological laws, like other laws of nature, are statements of relations that obtain between states of consciousness that are in turn causally linked to natural regularities. For Dilthey, Mill's "dogmatic" empiricism resulted from his lack of "historical erudition." In place of this dogmatism he proposed a study of "authentic experience."[40]

In *Truth and Method*, Hans-Georg Gadamer traces the history and multiple connotations of "experience" in Dilthey's work and that of other German thinkers of the mid-nineteenth century.[41] Among these connotations is the simultaneous sense of immediacy (the *act* of experiencing) and permanence (what remains from or is the residue of experience). The former sense links up with the distinctions drawn in both philosophical idealism and romanticism between the abstractions of analytic understanding and the concreteness of "life" and "activity," while the latter sense establishes an alliance between "experience" and "history." Nor is this all. The notion of "experience" is Dilthey's answer to the epistemological question of what is given. Against the empiricist thesis that experience is analyzable

into units of sensations, he advanced the view that there are fundamental experiential units that cannot be reduced further into psychic elements that are not themselves genuinely objects of experience. In the social sciences, then, the given, the basic units of study,
are units of meaning or significance, since meaning is an undeniable
property of experience. The notion of experience is indeed the foundation for human knowledge as such.[42] Experience is taken as inten-
tional or purposive in character rather than passive as it appeared to
be understood by Mill and empiricism. As such, it is necessarily
what Simmel would call an "element in the life process itself."[43]
Now if we join to efforts to theorize about "experience" the on-going
project of Dilthey and others to develop an epistemology capable of
giving scientific status to "history" as a discipline, we have at least
the beginnings of the distinctions German social scientists would
draw between the objects of the natural sciences and those of the social sciences.

The most important categorial distinction is that social phenomena, unlike natural phenomena, are intelligible as "systems of meanings."[44] From the German viewpoint, empiricist or positivist social
science tries to reduce social relations constituted by and experienced as "meanings" to phenomena from which this property is absent. Social science, with this understanding of its objects, will be
based on an account of "primary experiences" understood as "forms"
or "types." What Dilthey sought, for example, was a "critique of historical reason" that would account for the genesis of "forms" of
thought and a psychology capable of accounting for the formation
process without derailing into the naturalistic mistakes of empiricism. In an unpublished volume of his *Einleitung in die Geisteswissenschaften*, the first part of which appeared in 1883, he proposed a
foundation discipline for all the sciences. His *Grundwissenschaft* is
not intended as a metaphysical system in the Hegelian manner but
rather as a general model of the experiential structure of scientific
inquiry.[45] While Bentley was familiar with the published portion of
the *Einleitung*, there is no evidence that he was familiar with Dilthey's foundation discipline. Bentley's own work in the late 1920s,
however, has a remarkably similar intention.

The search for "primary experiences" required the development of
a new notion of the theoretical task of psychology. Dilthey, in his
Ideen über eine beschreibende und zergliederne Psychologie (1894)
and Simmel, in his *Die Probleme der Geshichtsphilosophie* (1892),
both offered accounts of a primordial experiential unity, prior to de-

terminations of subject and object, as the foundation for the forms of experience. These experiential forms or types were accessible to the social theorist through processes of *Verstehen* or "understanding." We do not need to trace the debates on the nature of *Verstehen* as social science explanation in detail nor consider the many ways in which its advocates understood it in order to see that such a notion entailed philosophic reflection on the process of social theorizing itself.[46] The social theorist, as well as those whose modes of experience he studies, "constitutes" the phenomena with which he is concerned. This recognition is the methodological counterpart of the role played by values in social and political life. As Max Weber would eventually put it, the search for explanations of "meanings" is grounded in our "historical interest" in comprehending "understandable human action." While this means that "intuition" is present in every "domain of knowledge," there may be differences in the "degree to which an approximation to conceptual precision in discursive thought is possible and desirable." In the social sciences theorizing rests upon a "discursive analysis of the objects of 'empathy,' objects which have only been immediately experienced or reproduced in immediate experience."[47]

Social science, then, concerns itself with experiential types rather than with collections of data about the psychic states of individuals. Simmel's sociological research embodies this concern quite clearly in his accounts of varieties of "typical" social experience. Bentley's descriptions of the contrasts between rich and poor in Berlin and the London slums are reminiscent of the investigations Simmel considered central to sociology. Even in Bentley's casual comments one can find the notion that such modes of conduct as "ignoring a pauper" take typical forms or that there are socially constituted ways in which the taking for granted of one's social position is made typical and thus not intelligible solely as a matter of individual idiosyncracy. A sociological theory, for Simmel, had to include a theory of social forms or general structures of typification generated by the conduct of human beings. As Simmel put it, the interpretive methods and formal intentions of social science represented a "declaration of the sovereignty of the category over the material."[48] Simmel's "formal sociology" is not a logically constructed system of classifications but rather an effort to disclose the forms that lend coherence to social phenomena, which are themselves produced by "life's eternal flux." Sociology stands in relation to other sciences of man such as psychology as geometry stands in relation to the natural sciences. Just as geometry determines what the "spatiality" of the objects of natural science is, sociology determines the "forms of sociation," the contents of which may be studied by other disciplines.[49]

For Bentley, the terms in which the problem of developing a genuine social science had to be conceived would always be closer to the German-Austrian tradition of social theory than to any other. It is essential for students of Bentley to realize that he never agreed with "positivist" visions of social science. His exposure to the neo-Kantian currents of German social science immunized him against any version of social science methodology that appeared mechanistic or reductionist. His own interest in economics suggests the course he wished to follow in his inquiry. He had originally intended to study with Menger after the completion of his work in Germany, but the financial reversals his father suffered in the on-going Depression prevented his remaining in Europe. Later he described his intention at this time as an effort "to find how to fit the marginal utility theories of Carl Menger into a fully behavioral sociology."[50] Bentley had been impressed by the theoretical rigor and richness of Menger's marginalism, which he had proposed as the foundation of economic theory. In Menger's view, marginalism was a theory of economic choice based on an idealization of or systematic abstraction from our introspective knowledge of experience. Economic theory sought the "basic forms" of economic phenomena and the principles or laws of their coherence.[51] He arrived at a categorization of human wants and posited mental processes based on desires for additional increments of goods. The principle of marginal utility hovered uneasily between a descriptive psychology and a formal model of rational choice. While Bentley was attracted to its purely formal character, he doubted that Menger was able to account for the origins of the desires and preferences of economic actors. Accordingly, a sociology was needed for this task. It did not seem reasonable to Bentley, however, to accept a division of labor between a formal theory of choice and a descriptive account of the contents of choice. He had learned from Simmel more than any other theorist the need to search for and comprehend the "commonness" of social life.[52] Could the analytic power of marginalism be united with a formal sociology in the manner of Simmel? Bentley would never claim to have answered this question, but I believe it helped to energize his search for a suitable basis for social science.

First Methodological Writings

In June 1894, Bentley was notified that he had received a $500 fellowship in economics at Johns Hopkins and began his graduate work in the fall of that year. While he took courses from Adams, Clark, J. B. Hollander, and Sherwood, in whose conference course he wrote his doctoral dissertation, he continued his wide-ranging studies. His reading concentrated on William Stanley Jevons, Thorstein Veblen, Simmel, and Emile Durkheim, and an evidently growing interest in philosophy is revealed in his reading of Edward Caird, Arthur Schopenhauer, and John Dewey, whose *The Study of Ethics* (1894) appears in Bentley's book lists the following year. By early in 1895 Bentley was lending Simmel's works to Giddings and Clark.[53]

During 1894–1896 Bentley tried to articulate his understanding of the basic questions of social science in five papers, one of which became his dissertation, "The Units of Investigation in the Social Sciences," which was published in 1895. In these manuscripts he made clear the level and scope of his interests. Although the ways in which he formulated his views on social science changed dramatically, his first methodological writings exemplify the sort of inquiry he would undertake in the rest of his work. His debts to American social scientists like Ward, Patten, and Ely is greatly diminished. Although he occasionally claimed that a new social science could be used to solve social problems, reformism and social science begin to separate in his thinking.

"On the Relation of the Individual to Society," written in November 1894, considers the issue of the most suitable level of explanation in social science.[54] While Bentley agrees that there is an "ultimate" level of physical explanation, social science errs when it tries to reduce psychological and social phenomena to this level. Bentley is especially opposed to mechanistic causal explanations in social science. The social scientist is concerned with "teleological human beings" whose actions and thoughts are unintelligible apart from recognition of their purposiveness. More precisely, the best explanatory level is that of "individual volition," which must be understood, however, in terms of the individual's involvement in social relations. The "Austrian theory" or marginalist economics is Bentley's choice as the most advanced account of purposiveness. It is, unfortunately, "logical, but not true." It fails to furnish knowledge of the social, cultural, and historical contexts that constitute all purposive action, including the maximization of expected utilities. Thus,

Clark is unrealistic when he tries to formulate theoretical propositions about "industrial life" apart from a general study of social life.

Bentley then turns to his own proposed synthesis. First, it is necessary to transform the distinction between social and economic "statics" (or purely descriptive theories) and "dynamics" (or historical accounts) from an opposition to a methodological convenience. That is, such a distinction should be drawn only as a matter of research strategy. Bentley proposes to end the *Methodenstreit* by showing that the social scientist does not have to choose between an ahistorical general theory and an atheoretical historical narrative or description. A static or a dynamic orientation becomes the practical choice of the sociological investigator. Second, Bentley proposes to transform marginalism to purge it of what he takes to be its simplistic understanding of and emphasis upon the mental processes and properties of the "individual." What is required, he claims, is an "underlying theory of utility" with which to comprehend the primordial experiential level at which the "individual" and "society" interpenetrate. Bentley's proposal is far from clear. Apparently he did not simply want to extend the domain of the marginalist principle beyond economics. Rather, the marginalist principle as currently formulated was an example of a general explanatory principle whose domain had not yet been adequately recognized.

The impact of Dilthey and Simmel upon Bentley can be seen in "The Individuality As the Basis for Reasoning in the Social Sciences" and "Materials for a Comparison of Organisms and Societies," both of which date from early 1895.[55] The search for "units of investigation" in any science necessarily involves abstraction. Bentley argues that the units used in the natural sciences, contrary to the opinions of many social scientists, are no less the result of abstraction than those of any other discipline. The natural sciences do not have "natural" units of investigation. Instead, since the objects of any science are "complexes" rather than simple entities, all units are theoretically constituted. Bentley agrees with one of Patten's claims in his critique of "biologic sociology" that the scientist's understanding of his own research problem is connected with his choice of an appropriate unit of analysis.

In Bentley's view, the "mind" is the central unit of analysis in social science. It is only by considering the individual's consciousness that the "primary subject-object relation" can be understood. He sketches an account, which appears in his dissertation as well, of the processes by which self-consciousness emerges from a primary "feeling" reminiscent of the primary "experience" theorized by Dilthey. For Bentley, self-consciousness arises through the individual's experiences of others, his own capacities for will and action, and the synthesis of these dialectical moments in organized human life, from which in turn emerges the possibility of rationality and "calculation."

One of the most significant passages in Bentley's early writings marks his discovery of the importance of language. Of all the "social formations" generated by human interests and activity, language is the "most objective." Language alone makes human thought possible. Our thinking is misunderstood if we suppose it to consist in the operations of mental processes. Instead we think in and through "language-forms."[56] That is, while psychology may study mental processes, to the extent that it understands these as observable physical or chemical phenomena somehow located in the bodies of individuals it is prohibited from having anything to tell us about human thought.

Bentley's new social science must be prepared to study a wide range of things not often considered by social scientists. For example, a sociological account of "marriage" must go well beyond legal definitions and the biological imperative of reproduction to provide a comprehensive description of the manifold of "meanings" marriage may have within a given society or part of society, as well as of connections between marriage and other social forms. When the multiplicity of social forms is recognized, it becomes clear that social science must theorize a number of "types of consciousness" rather than assume that persons have a single form of consciousness which simply attends to various social forms. In a move quite similar to that of Simmel, Bentley rejects the notion that there is or could be a general form or characterization of consciousness. To put his view differently, all we in fact experience is our consciousness *of* or consciousness *as* something. Thus there can be no such thing as a general economic theory of value, according to Bentley. A theory of value must be developed for each identifiable economic form. Bentley recognizes that the marginalists—Böhm-Bawerk is mentioned—claim universality for their views, but denies that they have reached or are even aware of the level of generality actually required.

If "economic man" as a utility-maximizer is to be a defensible general concept, Bentley argues that it must be purged of any lingering connections with historically determinate modes of economic behavior. A genuinely scientific concept cannot simply be an abstraction from some set of facts. In this argument we can see the beginning of Bentley's search for purely formal categories for social science. His most frequent criticism of social theories of all sorts throughout his career is that they all too often retain determinate elements or bear the marks of their origins as abstractions from facts. As such they can hardly escape the tacit ontological commitments of the language-forms that nurtured them.

Bentley's comparison of the properties of organisms and societies is an attack on organismic analogies in social science. The "biologic sociologist" cannot demonstrate any experiential counterpart for the organismic mechanisms his analogies require. Natural organisms possess muscles, nerves, digestive systems, and the like, which biology teaches exist in functional relationships. No social equivalents can be found for any of these structures. Organismic teachings are at best suggestive. Moreover, natural organisms, unlike societies, could be understood as intelligible wholes. Bentley had been impressed by Simmel's studies of social conflict and especially with his master's insistence that conflict presupposed a common ground. This presupposition, however, must be distinguished decisively from any normative notion of a "social whole." Organismic sociology traded on the misleading identification of a functioning organism with its components working harmoniously with social concord. Society was intelligible as a "totality" but not as a "social whole." As we will see, Bentley tried in *The Process of Government* to sketch an account of "order" that was free from ethical implications.

The first evidence of Bentley's reading of pragmatic philosophy appears in "Phenomenal Monism As the Basis for the Study of Society," written in 1895.[57] This essay offers an embryonic version of the critique of causal explanation in social science that would run through almost all Bentley's work. Social scientists, according to Bentley, generally believe that explanation must be "genetic" or causal. They fail to realize that this belief is a "postulate" or "principle of sufficient reason" like that of "causality" in physics. Bentley's study of Kant lies in the background of his insistence that causality is a category in terms of which we render the natural and the social worlds intelligible. A social science, however, requires its own postulates. In one of the first expressions of a characteristic argument, Bentley claims that social science cannot rely uncritically on notions furnished by other sciences. It must avoid both the "common sense" and the "mechanistic" understandings of causality. What social science requires is a postulate that can reconcile the "initiative power" of the mind with the undeniable impact of the external world upon it. Mechanistic accounts of human action cannot accomplish this end. Relying on William James's account of the "stream of consciousness" in the *Principles of Psychology*, Bentley questions the adequacy of causal accounts of mental life. With James, Bentley wished to reject as well "spiritual" explanations. Thus he argues that consciousness was neither independent of the physical state of the brain nor identical with some determinate physical state. It is unintelligible to suppose that either the "mental" or the "physical" could have causal status. Bentley's term "monism" seems to have been chosen quite deliberately to suggest the notion that is largely implicit in the essay that "mind" and "matter" are simply different ways in which something reminiscent of Spinoza's "substance" is organized. As for consciousness, Bentley asserts that it simply *is* the "change relation" between the brain and the world, a claim he never clarifies. The conclusion of this essay points directly to Bentley's dissertation. All aspects of the connections between the individual and social forms are accessible to introspection.

The point of departure for Bentley's dissertation is another attack on reductionist modes of explanation.[58] Bentley agrees with Patten's criticism of the "scientific bias" that seeks to "force an explanation of the more complex phenomena in terms of the simplest forces" and transplants "laws and methods found satisfactory in one of these separated spheres of investigation straightway to another." The human mind is the "central point for all study of social phenomena." Bentley hastens to make clear, however, that while this is a self-evident premise, we do not have direct knowledge of the minds of other persons. The raw material of social science is motion or action. Society is a "nexus of *actions;* and it is a nexus so complex that were the investigator himself of other nature than human, its interpretation would be utterly impossible." Although he does not mention Simmel at this point, it is tempting to think that Bentley had in mind his "thought-experiment" that used the mind of a Martian without knowledge of the meanings of human actions to show that this knowledge was necessary in sociology.[59] For Bentley we can only interpret actions "in terms of the content of our own consciousness." He did not wish to maintain a rigid dualism of mind and matter and asserted once more that physical and psychical processes constitute a parallel series without effective causal connections. It is true that there are human actions that can be described in causal terms, but these are without importance for the social scientist since the actions he studies "have their correlates in consciousness." A more concise formulation could hardly be found for some of the views of Bentley's German teachers.

Bentley reiterates his account of the development of consciousness from its primordial state of undifferentiated experience to the initial act by which it distinguishes subject and object. Since subject and object are "abstractions from a primary sense-content" this shows that thought "as a relating and limiting activity involves in its very essence abstraction."[60] The act of knowing constitutes the objectivity of the external world. That objectivity is not synonymous with "materiality" is shown by the fact that we can make the psychic life of others and our own previous psychic life objects of reflection. These "immaterial things are as truly objective to us as the external world can possibly be." Thus it is absurd to characterize psychic life as "immaterial" or "subjective" over against a supposedly "objective" external world.

On this philosophical foundation, Bentley sketches a sociology based on a classification of types of human actions, understood as products of "inward states." His basic types of actions include "impulse," "custom," and "calculation." Impulse is the first "psychic analogue" of primordial human desires, which differentiates itself in the course of experience of the resistance of the external world into the forms "custom" and "calculation." Each of these psychic states has an external correlate that becomes the content of the state itself through the abstraction of thought. Custom, for example, is an "objectified" psychic state that coordinates impulses and is thus the first requisite of society. Beyond custom is the realm of "formations" or institutions. Regardless of its origins, a formation may be understood as part of the "social structure" that "may be objectified by the individual and made the norm or basis of his actions."[61] This thesis has the effect of excluding from social science any effort to explain human action in terms of such factors as instincts or any other forces that supposedly act apart from consciousness. If any proposed explanatory factor cannot be made a basis for action by the individual it is clearly categorially inappropriate for social science. The regulative power of formations results from their status as "representative states" or parts of the "knowledge content of the individual man." Since the social scientist is a human being, he gains access to these contents through the process of interpretation Bentley has already outlined.

The task of social science is not complete, for the objects of investigation—impulses, customs, and calculations—and the various ideational contents—the natural world, other men, and social formations—must be combined through genetic and static analysis. Once again, Bentley notes that the genetic-static distinction is purely a matter of convenience, although his sympathies are clearly with genetic analysis. His own social science, however, will be synthetic. It will be "in the fullest sense explanatory through a synthesis of the social elements which are grounded ultimately in psychology." His dissertation concludes on a note that echoes through every one of his books: the development of social science has just begun.

Bentley's Early Career

After he completed his doctorate, Bentley sought an academic position but nothing could be found for a young economist whose interests lay in European sociology. Adams, who shared none of Bentley's interests, was still quite helpful. He tried, without success, to get Bentley a position at Harvard when he had nothing to offer him at Johns Hopkins. The Depression had dried up resources at public institutions as well. The University of Nebraska had no funds for a new position in its Department of Political and Economic Science, much to Bentley's disappointment.[62] Adams wrote to Bentley in July 1895, "It is absolutely necessary to keep in the academic current if you wish to succeed in your chosen speciality, for which there will be growing room in America."[63] At length Bentley received an appointment as a docent in sociology at the University of Chicago for the academic year 1895–96.

Although the Chicago faculty included such figures as G. H. Mead, Wesley Mitchell, Thorstein Veblen, Franz Boas, John Dewey, and Jaques Loeb, Bentley continued his solitary habits, becoming acquainted only with the sociologist W. I. Thomas. He offered a course on contemporary French and German social theory to a small group of graduate students, but his first experience as a teacher was evidently quite unpleasant. After a few meetings he and his students agreed to dissolve the seminar and he spent the remainder of his appointment engaged in study. There is no evidence that Bentley was an effective teacher or, for that matter, that he had any great interest in teaching.

Apart from Bentley's own inadequacies, the seminar may have failed as a result of the material Bentley proposed to cover. His lecture notes, drafts, and outlines reveal an encyclopedic grasp of contemporary social science. He expected his students to read, among others, Simmel, Durkheim, and Auguste Comte in the original languages and, more important, to have a sufficient grounding in sociology, history, economics, and philosophy to follow the most intricate substantive and methodological debates. To prepare himself for the course he wrote hundreds of pages of commentary on some of the major social theorists to be covered. The largest amount of space was devoted to a massive exegesis of Comte's principal works. A list of lecture and discussion topics gives a sense of what he wished to include: "The Possibility of a Science of Society," "Practical v. Pure Theory," "Social *Science* v. Social Philosophy," "Organic Ideas," "Sociology and Biology," "Progress," "The Social Fact," "Sociology and Psychology," "System of Psychic Forms," "Static and Dynamic," "Subjective and Objective Interpretation," "Function and Cause," "Classification of Societies and Social Phenomena," and "Methods." With each of these topics Bentley correlated a number of readings in an effort to present the forward positions in social theory in exhaustive detail.

A draft of his introductory lecture allows us to see how he understood the history of social theory in 1896. More than a decade before Albion Small advanced a similar argument in *Adam Smith and Modern Sociology* (1907), Bentley traced the origins of sociology to Smith and classical economics. The classical teaching combined economic theory and what Bentley takes to be historical sociology, elements that were gradually separated into the ahistorical pure theory of Smith's intellectual heirs and the atheoretical sociology of the historical school of German economists. In Smith, Bentley found the seeds of what he took to be the central tenet of modern social theory—the order that obtains among people in society is the result of chance or of a manifold of human actions not intended to achieve order.[64] The second major source for contemporary social theory lay in Continental jurisprudence. In an unclear and very sketchy argument, Bentley traces a dialectic of "individualistic" and "organic" doctrines through modern natural rights theories to Rousseau, Hegel, and the historical school of jurisprudence in early nineteenth-century Germany. What Bentley seems to be concerned with here is the emergence of the notion that social forms are products of the unique history of a people or exhibitions of the *Volksgeist*.

Other than his course materials, Bentley apparently wrote only one manuscript while at Chicago, a paper titled "'Causational' and 'Valuational' Sciences of Society."[65] This was one of his earliest efforts to reclassify the social sciences. Most social scientists favored one of three general classificatory schemes. Economists, along with sociologists under the spell of Spencer, preferred a distinction between "static" and "dynamic" sciences, while others found divisions of "realistic" and "abstract" or "practical" and "theoretical" more congenial. Bentley argues that the practice of social science cuts across these divisions. We have already seen that he rejected the static-dynamic distinction except for convenience. The practical-theoretical distinction founders on the fact that even the most avowedly practical social science must employ abstractions. In the same manner, historical economists employ theory while pure marginalists must use historical materials. A new classificatory scheme divides the social sciences into "causational" and "valuational" forms, which Bentley also calls "Science A" and "Science B." Most social scientists drift unwittingly from one form to the other in their practice, as does Durkheim. Bentley is unclear about the extent to which "Science A" is legitimate. Certainly he does not repudiate the criticisms he had already made of causal explanations. Most of his attention is given to "valuational" social science, which requires understanding of psychic states. The social theorist "must have felt and, to some extent, believed with . . . people before he can truly understand them." The methodology of valuational social science is clearly "interpretation" and there is little to distinguish Bentley's idea of valuational social science from similar ideas in Simmel and others.

The most important experience Bentley had at Chicago was his encounter with John Dewey, who had come from the University of Michigan in 1894 to accept the position of chairman of the Department of Philosophy, Psychology, and Education. Bentley audited Dewey's seminars in the logic of ethics and the theory of logic. The seminars were quite large and he had no direct contact with Dewey. The logic seminar made a greater impression on Bentley than the one in ethics. He learned from Dewey that psychology was not a self-evident foundation for social science. Bentley's first significant exposure to pragmatic philosophy led him to doubt the necessity for and the intelligibility of psychological explanations in social science.[66]

For Bentley, the paths taken by Dewey and by his German masters intersected as elements of the revolt against positivism. Dewey's opposition to empiricism and positivism took the form in the 1880s of a defense of philosophic idealism as a teaching capable of furnishing a superior account of human experience. His inquiry was a search for a psychology that would be at once a product and a demonstration of the indissoluble unity of experience. The "ulterior issue" in his focus on experience was his intention to demonstrate the "possibility that actual experience in its concrete content and movement may furnish those ideals, meanings, and values whose lack and uncertainty in experience as actually lived by most persons have supplied the motive force for recourse to some reality beyond experience. . . ."[67] Not surprisingly, Dewey was prepared to defend Hegel against Kant, who was the philosophic touchstone of William James and C. S. Peirce, as *the* philosopher of the here and now or of the totality of experience.[68] Unlike the other major American pragmatists, Dewey's concerns centered on social theory. Psychological knowledge was gained through introspection and the study of the embodiment of mind in collective life. The "abstract" reductionist psychologies like associationism seemed to Dewey a dubious legacy of the Enlightenment, whose philosophers had failed to grasp the interpenetration of individual and collective life:

We see that man is somewhat more than a neatly dovetailed psychical machine who may be taken as an isolated individual, laid on the dissecting table of analysis and duly anatomized. We know that his life is bound up with the life of society, of the nation in the *ethos* and *nomos*; we know that he is closely connected with all the past by the lines of education, tradition, and heredity; we know that man is indeed the microcosm who has gathered into himself the riches of the world, both of space and time, the world physical and the world psychical. We know that our mental life is not a syllogistic *sorites*, but an enthymeme most of whose members are suppressed. . . .[69]

Dewey's thinking parallels that of the major German social theorists with whom Bentley was thoroughly familiar. Unlike the Germans, however, Dewey came to doubt the primacy of the psychological and epistemological "subject" as the locus of experience. In his view, Hegel's notion of "objective thought" shows that there is no "special, apart faculty of thought belonging to and operated by a mind existing separate from the outer world."[70] Against Hegel, he found it untenable to presuppose what he took as "metaphysical" entities such as the Hegelian Absolute. His own reflection on experience had led him to identify one of its structural features as the "problematic situation," a notion for which he could find no Hegelian counterpart. Philosophic and scientific activity are simply special forms of the universal human activity by which indeterminate situations are transformed into determinate situations. The unity of subject and object, which idealism accomplished with metaphysics, could be reached in a more tenable way through the explication of human action. Indeed, Hegel's error lay in his belief that there is or could be a "logic" that can serve as the first principle of philosophy. Any logic, whether traditional or dialectical, is constituted in and by human activity.[71]

What Bentley learned from Dewey was that the various elements of thinking—its categories and modes of judgment—were themselves aspects of human activity rather than faculties, dispositions, or operations of a "mind" ontologically distinguished from an external world.[72] There was no privileged position from which a neutral explanatory instrument could be constructed for social science. The search for some primordial form of experience as the foundation for the study of society was futile. Bentley began to search for a way of describing social phenomena that would dispense with psychological premises. He had been immunized by both the German tradition and Dewey against a reductionist approach. His new science would have to articulate its own interpretive categories, since none could simply be borrowed from other areas of knowledge. Once again, Bentley's thinking had linked up with that of his teachers, who had come to understand their task as the development of an autonomous social science. The pragmatic deposit in Bentley's thinking, however, would lead him eventually to see that the limits of that project were set by presuppositions about the nature of science. Reflection along lines laid out by the pragmatists would take Bentley in what he believed was a more fruitful direction.

After his year at Chicago, Bentley tried once more to find an academic position but without success. His natural home would have been at the University of Chicago, for philosophers and social scientists associated with Dewey at that time began to develop the general view William James called the "Chicago School."[73] Few of Dewey's colleagues and disciples had a first-hand knowledge of currents in European social theory equal to Bentley's. His self-imposed isolation prevented him from contributing these perspectives to the work of the Chicago pragmatists. In 1896 he took a job as a reporter with the *Chicago Times Herald*. Bentley's effort to rethink the basic problems of social science would be done outside the academic world in which he could find no place for himself.

3

The Process of Government and the

Reconstruction of Social Science

A full understanding of the conditions of action is as yet possessed by no one. When such an understanding is achieved . . . when the "conditions" are absorbed into the action, sociology will be an established science, not a struggle to found a science.
                                         The Process of Government

---

The Process of Government (1908) has been the principal medium through which Bentley's views have exerted an influence on American social scientists. With rare exceptions, students of social science have identified Bentley solely with his first major work. The result has been a scholarly literature in which both the early book and Bentley's work as a whole have been poorly served. During the first four decades after it appeared, *The Process of Government* gave rise to two sorts of responses. On the one hand, a series of distinguished scholars—Charles A. Beard, Morris R. Cohen, and Karl N. Llewellyn —praised it as a masterpiece.[1] Their comments do not suggest a close reading of the book nor do they indicate awareness of the fundamental problems in social science with which Bentley was concerned. The book is praised for what was taken to be its uncompromising tough-mindedness about the connections between economic interests and law in American society. On the other hand, Bentley's book helped to inspire a number of case studies of the character and operation of organized interest groups in American politics during the 1920s and 1930s. This literature, which includes monographs by such prominent American political scientists as Peter H. Odegard, E. Pendleton Herring, and E. E. Schattschneider, is equally unconcerned with broad methodological issues.[2]

After World War II, *The Process of Government* was rediscovered by a number of American political scientists who recognized, but misunderstood, Bentley's programmatic intention. Scholars such as Bertram Gross and David B. Truman believed their own studies of interest groups, their "realism" which they opposed to what they took to be the "idealism" of traditional political science, and their commitment to "scientific" inquiry in social science had all been foreshadowed in Bentley's book. Bentley came to light as a neglected pioneer of what was called the "behavioral revolution" in social science, an intransigent critic of the "legalist" and "institutionalist" approaches to the study of politics, and an iconoclast who dissolved the clouds of political philosophy and popular ideology to reveal the raw reality of pressure politics.[3] Gross, a major architect of the Bentley revival, called *The Process of Government* one of the "most important books on government to have been written in any country."[4] Many political scientists began to consider their own research as efforts, in Truman's words, "to elaborate and extend" Bentley's enterprise in a more favorable intellectual climate than Bentley himself was believed to have experienced.[5]

Bentley's book came to occupy a central place in the postwar debates between advocates and opponents of behavioral political science. There was general agreement among supporters and critics of both Bentley and behavioralism that the 1908 work deserved to be taken as a classic formulation of what Heinz Eulau would call the "behavioral persuasion."[6] Read in the terms of the behavioralism controversy, the book seemed to be a call for the use of the methods of the natural sciences in the study of politics and society. None of the disputants seems to have been aware of Bentley's exploration of the possibility of scientific explanations in social science in his earlier works. *The Process of Government* was also understood to have proposed a substantive political theory—the "group theory of politics." Robert T. Golembiewski expressed concisely the view that prevailed among supporters of Bentley:

> Bentley straightforwardly asserted his claim for the greater adequacy of the "group" as a focus for empirical theory. . . . For his core theoretical insights were far ahead of his time and constitute an important part of the century-long theoretical and methodological change which supports the modern study of social organization. . . . The scope of the description Bentley proposed can be suggested generally. It was nothing less than the isolation of the relevant dimensions of reality, and hardly the simplistic classification of "farm groups," "labor groups," and so on.[7]

Opponents of behavioral political science and the group theory disagreed with what they took to be Bentley's teaching, while they acknowledged and deplored its influence. The basic tendency of much of the postwar criticism of Bentley had been anticipated in R. M. MacIver's attack on *The Process of Government*.[8] According to MacIver, Bentley is not only a crudely reductionist social scientist but a scientific purist whose exposure of political myths amounts to an antidemocratic political doctrine. Bentley's book was not an objective or scientific study of politics but rather a political treatise hiding beneath a scientific facade.

There was considerable variety in what I shall call the ideological interpretation of Bentley. For Louis Hartz, Bentley is a typical example of an American social theorist whose premises are shaped by the pervasive liberalism which dominates American political thinking. So much was the Bentleyan group theory a "reflection of the relative conditions of America's liberal life" that it projected "irrational 'Americanism' into the study of America" and elevated "peculiar American phenomena into absolute categories of political analysis."[9] Leo Weinstein's criticism claims that an "implicit democratic assumption" underlies both the methodology and substance of Bentley's work, an interpretation that rests uneasily with MacIver's reading of Bentley as antidemocratic.[10] In Myron Q. Hale's opinion, Bentley's thinking implies a cynical conservatism consistent with the revival of conservative thought after World War II and his political science points toward a "science of control within a closed system."[11] For several critics, Bentley combines Social Darwinist notions of group conflict with a simplistic "social physics" of collective forces to produce a superficial theory of social equilibrium.[12] Bentley appears as a misplaced *philosophe* engaged in a largely unconscious effort to restate a pluralist political doctrine in uncongenial intellectual categories. Finally, Bernard Crick's indictment of Bentley brings together most of the lines of criticism I have identified with his assertion that Bentley's thought "rests upon vast hidden assumptions about what is natural or self-evident." In consequence, his teaching appears "less as a science and more as an uniquely American political doctrine . . . based on faith and on a particular part of a tradition rather than on continuing empirical evidence," which suggests that his thinking is "merely a symptom of or a prelude to a growing intellectual confusion within American liberalism."[13]

The fact that Bentley is praised for having advanced a "scientific" and "realistic" political science and condemned for having produced a derivative political ideology suggests the difficulty of arriving at an adequate interpretation of *The Process of Government*. I am in substantial agreement with Kress that Bentley's critique of causal explanation in social science, which constitutes Part 1 of the 1908 work, establishes a basic distinction between his philosophy of social science and that of behavioralism. In addition, Kress is correct in his recognition of the scope of Bentley's "group theory," which was intended to replace what he believed were inherently untenable causal theories in social science with a comprehensive descriptive theory. Kress fails to connect *The Process of Government* with the rest of Bentley's work adequately because his thesis that Bentley is best understood as a "process" theorist leads him to underestimate the significance of Bentley's search for intellectual categories suitable for the coherent study of the flux of social reality. Put concisely, Part 1 of Bentley's book dissolves both everyday and conventional "scientific" explanations of individual and collective behavior because none of these explanations does justice to the reality of "process," while Part 2 offers a mode of theorizing that Bentley took to be more successful at this task. This mode of theorizing is best understood, I believe, as a "formal" political sociology reminiscent of Simmel.

From Politics to Methodology

The Process of Government participates, as Bentley's writings of the mid-1890s had done, in the on-going debates among social theorists of the first rank about the nature, methods, and philosophical foundations of the social sciences. Bentley employed his encyclopedic knowledge of contemporary Anglo-American and European social science with a greater degree of critical mastery than had been possible for him a decade earlier. For the greatest of his contemporaries such as Weber, Simmel, Durkheim, and Vilfredo Pareto, reflections on the nature of social science were not conducted in a vacuum but rather in a milieu in which the immanent development of social theory and the highly charged political currents of Marxism and its critics interpenetrate. Transformed and muted, the "critique of Marxism" which helped many of the major social theorists of the period take their "first steps toward constructing a more general theory of social reality" is present in Bentley's book as well.[14]

Beneath the surface of his painstaking rehearsals and criticisms of a multitude of social theorists lies the "normative" substratum which Bentley's critics have sensed and to which they have objected. While Bentley's Progressivism undeniably affects his various formulations, it does not thereby render them ideological in the pejorative sense intended by his detractors. Bentley's supporters err in praising him for proposing an objective and value-free social science, while his opponents err in condemning him for failing to provide one. His intention was to begin to develop a social science that would transcend both the "objective" doctrines of positivist social theorists and the "subjective" approaches that had emerged in recent decades as their necessary but equally one-sided correctives. The substantive engagement of *The Process of Government* was to say something of importance about "economic" life. Bentley's dissatisfaction with the state of economics as a discipline required him to concentrate first on "government" and "politics" (PG, 210). The book is esoteric to the extent that its substantive subject matter is not treated directly. The reader is left to draw conclusions, if possible, about the connections between Bentley's criticisms of "social interpretation" and economics.

Bentley did not claim that his theories were completely original. He was convinced that genuine novelty in social theory was likely to insure triviality. On the surface it seemed that each generation rewrote history and even reinterpreted the sciences to suit its own partisanships. If one looked beneath the surface to the "backbone of history," a "solid structure of group relationships" could be seen (PG, 482–83). The task of theorizing about this structure had been recognized, however inadequately, by many students of society. While Bentley thought there was a sense in which his work was built on that of his predecessors, he claimed for himself a decisive role in having brought to light the true scope of this task.

Bentley was a working journalist when he wrote *The Process of Government*. Students of his work who have considered the importance of his experience as a reporter and editorial writer for the *Chicago Times-Herald* and *Record-Herald* agree that it lay in his exposure to politics. After his promotion to editorial writer in 1903, Bentley found the demands of his job quite small. He later characterized his position as a "quiescent spot where I could operate freely outside of the conventional controls."[15] Bentley was able to continue his wide reading in social theory at the nearby Crerar Library, but, in Kress's words, his journalistic work gave him a "sense of tremendous social activity taking place" which was as significant an experience "as any book or teacher Bentley might have known."[16] Bentley

later wrote that "all the politics of the country, so to speak, was drift-
ing across my desk."[17] Sidney Ratner described Bentley's newspaper
work as "the best thing that could have happened to a young intellectual. . . . His nose was rubbed into the harsh facts of life as revealed in the activities, political, social, and economic, going on in
the rushing, strife-torn metropolis of the midwest. . . ."[18]

A "sense of tremendous social activity taking place" had been part
of Bentley's view of society since his youth. His journalistic experience did less to create a radically new orientation than it did to rein-
force a well-established way of thinking. As a journalist he seems to
have been increasingly aware of the differences between the social
reality visible to the reporter and the ways in which that reality was
interpreted. His concern with this issue, which had been present
in his work from its beginning, was energized by his political Progressivism. Bentley came to share the muckraking sensibility in
American journalism. Theodore Dreiser spoke for many intelligent
young men who became journalists during this period when he con-
trasted the editorial office preparing "the most flowery moralistic or
religionistic editorials" on progress and human dignity with the
city-news room where "the mask was off and life was handled in a
rough-and-ready manner, without gloves. . . . Innate honesty on the
part of any one was not probable. Charity was a business with something in it for somebody. Morality was in the main for public con-
sumption only."[19] With few exceptions the social criticism of the
muckrakers was not linked to radical opposition to industrial capitalism. Instead, as Richard Hofstadter notes, "their chief appeal was
not to desperate social needs but to mass sentiments of responsibility, indignation, and guilt. Hardly anyone intended that these sentiments should result in action drastic enough to transform American
society."[20]

The Progressive political formula of faith in good men, strict law
enforcement, and, increasingly after 1900, sound and expert administration made the muckraker's findings the raw data for reform.
The research Bentley undertook in the early 1900s which led to *The
Process of Government* shows the extent to which he shared the
Progressive political mood. As it finally developed, the book was
radically different from its various anticipations in his research. By
comparing the methodological and substantive intentions of his
research with those of the final product, we gain insight into the
transformations in his thinking that would widen the scope of his
inquiry.

Chicago provided Bentley with opportunities to study most of the major social and political tendencies in American society at the turn of the century. The cleavages he had glimpsed in Nebraska that had led him to ask in an early version of "The Western Farmer" whether the "trouble at the basis of the industrial system" was "basic" or "transient" appeared in Chicago on a vast scale.[21] Perhaps the most visible phenomenon was the growth and diversity of the city itself. The population of Chicago was nearing a million and the size of the city had increased severalfold through annexation. Its problems were shared by all large American cities of the period. Inadequate housing, sanitation, transportation, and education were difficulties compounded by a poorly developed city government and a pervasive conflict between the city and a state legislature dominated by rural interests. The tensions between city and countryside were exacerbated by the conflict between immigrants and nativists. Moreover, Chicago had a history of radical labor activity, represented for the popular mind by the Haymarket Riot, the Pullman Strike, and the importance of socialist unions. By the early 1900s the city had become a focal point for the efforts of reformers to replace urban machine politics with "good government," to encourage urban planning, and to raise the cultural level of the city. Alliances developed between the reformist City Club of Chicago and the Commercial Club and reform-minded social scientists at the University of Chicago, including the young and politically ambitious Charles E. Merriam, who had come to the political science department at the university in 1900. Philanthropic promoters of reform financed and encouraged social experimentation. Jane Addams and Hull House were only the most prominent examples. Privately supported schools flourished, including the Chicago Institute of Social Science and the Chicago School of Civics and Philanthropy, which later merged to become the university's School of Social Service Administration. Men like the university's first president, William Rainey Harper, and scholar-activists like Merriam, Wesley C. Mitchell, and Robert E. Park were impressed with the enormous energy of American business and sought, as Barry D. Karl puts it, to "embed in the structure of the university . . . the responsibility for guiding that power in socially responsible directions."[22] What could hardly have remained invisible to Bentley was the common denominator of organization. Immigrants exercised political influence through the United Societies of Chicago and businessmen through the Chicago Association of Commerce. The growth of legislative reference libraries, municipal research bureaus, and the research facilities of charity organizations provided reformist scholars with a national network of communication. The organization of the flow of information so essential to the Progressive view of responsible government had come to resemble yet another interest group.

Bentley undertook three research projects more or less simultaneously from about 1904 through 1907. Two of these projects were quite large: "Municipal Ownership Interest Groups in Chicago: A Study of Referendum Votes, 1901–07" and "The Play of Interests in Legislative Bodies" ran to nearly 400 and slightly over 100 pages of text respectively.[23] Together with a shorter study, "The Play of Interests in a City Council," extremely condensed summaries of these projects appear as an appendix to the final version of The Process of Government (PG, 487–94). Bentley did not believe their findings were proof of the general theory contained in his larger work, but thought of them instead as examples of the sort of research possible under the aegis of that teaching (PG, 487). Bentley says nothing about basic issues in social science in these studies. Their purpose is to document the roles played by organized and unorganized economic interests in the shaping of legislation and policies. As examples of social science research they rank with the best monographic literature of the period and are distinguished by Bentley's skill with quantitative methods. The municipal ownership study employs what is recognizably a multivariate research design with quantitative variables. Its techniques include the use of scaling, hypothesis-testing, and graphic representation of correlations among variables. The legislative and city council studies employ statistical analysis of roll-call votes.[24]

According to Sidney Ratner, Bentley's massive collection of data "spurred him to develop a general theory of social pressures for all phases of government in the United States and the rest of the world."[25] I doubt that Ratner's analysis is completely accurate. Bentley did not believe that collections of data and the use of statistical methods had a fundamental role to play in the development of social science as he understood it. Many years later he stated explicitly a principle that had been implicit in his earlier research: "Mathematical techniques contribute nothing directly to the analysis; and the wider values of the result secured through the techniques are always dependent upon the adequacy of the antecedent classifications and postulatory fixations which the analysis has furnished, though it is of course true that work of this kind may often stimulate a return to the preliminary procedures of analysis."[26]

In fact, Bentley was working on a large manuscript while he was conducting his research on voting patterns in referendum elections in Chicago. His original intention had been to write a book about "practical politics." In a draft manuscript he wrote that while politics had originally meant "statecraft," in America "it means acquiring rulership in a titular democracy. In the not far distant future it will mean the activity of the people, who are now sovereign, but not their own rulers, in exercising their sovereignty as rule." These comments from the preface of his manuscript suggest that his book would have been a contribution to the polemical literature of Progressivism with the findings of his research pressed into service as an exercise in muckraking. Excerpts from Bentley's notes indicate some of the themes he planned to develop:

> Scheme: Abandon private ethical ideas. Trust to will of people. Cultivate knowledge, free play for expression of popular will. These are all that democracy requires—not "high personal virtue."
>
> It is not poor private morals, but popular ignorance of state facts, greed of individuals and popular ignorance of harmfulness of this greed that makes our present government rotten. As to nature of social ethics needed, compare union class ethics (labor).[27]

The final version of *The Process of Government* does not develop these themes. Bentley abandoned the Progressive political vocabulary of popular sovereignty, public morality, and the popular will along with the unifying pedagogical theme of exposing greed and enlightening the public. He did not, and perhaps could not, purge the published version of all evidence of his Progressive convictions, but they are clearly subordinate to the methodological and substantive intentions of the work. His Progressive credentials had already been severely tested by his contempt for "high personal virtue" as a politically significant force. Bentley was almost alone in his reluctant surrender of the temptation to graft an ethical idealism on to the fluid world of group interplay. Wiebe contrasts Bentley with thinkers of the rank of Dewey and Veblen, neither of whom could reconcile their moral doctrines with their own understandings of contemporary American industrial society.[28]

Bentley's suggestion that "union class ethics" offers a model for a democratic "social ethics" vanished. Not only was he overtly unconcerned about the fate of democracy in the final version of his book, but he criticized as well the notion that there was any social force concerned or identifiable with the public or common interest. In his reading notes from a number of socialist writers, including Marx, Jean Jaurès, G. V. Plekhanov, Antonio Labriola, and Karl Kautsky, I believe one can uncover at least some of the reasons for Bentley's new position.[29] Marx and his followers, Bentley believed, had failed to treat the role of "intellectual life" adequately and had reduced it to the restrictive concept of "ideology." For Bentley, Marx was an economic determinist who failed to take into account relations between economic interests and "values." The analytic apparatus of Marxism was simply incapable of furnishing a suitable account of human action. The class struggle encompassed a great deal more than a conflict between owners and workers about the distribution of power and wealth in modern society. Moreover, socialists failed to recognize that the growing political power of organized workers was changing their position to the point where they were able to exploit still lower strata in industrial society. Bentley concluded that socialism was no more able than any other political doctrine to represent the "true interest of society." The very intelligibility of the claim to represent the public interest was questionable.

Behind the transformation of *The Process of Government* from a Progressive tract into a work of social theory lay tendencies inherent in Bentley's earlier work. The central achievement of his writings in the 1890s had been his perspectivism. While its formulation was tentative, we have seen that Bentley's thinking pointed toward the notion that theoretical units of analysis need not be identical with actual social entities. The growth of a "fictional" treatment of the categories of social theory had been stimulated by his appropriation of Simmel's Kantianism on the one hand and his increasing awareness of the idealist component of the pragmatism of James and Dewey on the other. Coupled with this tendency in his thinking had been an increasing skepticism about the position of causal explanation in social science. Bentley came to doubt the causal efficacy of "mind" or its equivalent. By the time he began to write *The Process of Government* he could no longer place "mind" in the center of social theory. Bentley had begun to realize that his thinking was at odds with both academic social theorists and everyday ways of explaining human conduct. The starting point for his reconstruction of social science was the fact that "we are all of us engaged every day in interpreting our social life" (PG, 3–4). Bentley proposed to criticize the modes of social interpretation in general. These interpretive approaches included common-sense views, political doctrines, and academic social theory. Bentley had raised the question of how knowledge of the social world was possible.

Mental Properties and Social Interpretation

In a one-sentence frontispiece Bentley describes *The Process of Government* as "an attempt to fashion a tool." The exploratory character of his theses is evident in his refusal to claim to have produced the comprehensive teaching he sought to develop (PG, 165–66). The first part of the book, "To Prepare the Way," is dominated by two long chapters, "Feelings and Faculties as Causes" and "Ideas and Ideals as Causes." Bentley's critique of social interpretation is divided somewhat unclearly into three themes. The most visible of these is his criticism and rejection of psychological explanation in social theory. Subordinate to this analysis is his attack on causal explanation as such. The connections between these themes are problematic. Bentley opposes both sorts of explanation and seems at times to hold that the principal defect of the former is their status as instances of the latter. The third theme is a criticism of notions of progressive intellectual, moral, social, and political evolution. The coordination of this line of criticism with Bentley's views on psychological and causal explanation is also problematic. The stylistic difficulties of these chapters are an additional hurdle. Bentley's writing is discursive and repetitive, which is perhaps a reflection of the persistence in the final version of themes and sections from the original work on "practical politics." Moreover, his patient rehearsals of the arguments of other social theorists often buries the threads of his own position. What remains for the casual reader is Bentley's cantankerous, debunking, and contentious tone. His stance as a writer is that of an erudite outsider, at once amused and outraged by the defective views he proposes to dissect.

According to Bentley, "the most common way of explaining what goes on in society, including of course the processes of government, is in terms of the feelings and ideas of the men who make up society" (PG, 5). He begins his inquiry by exploring the implications of everyday explanations of social behavior. Bentley does not try to account for the existence of such everyday explanations except by occasional reference to human "purposes." Our ordinary notion of explanation ascribes causal efficacy to various "factors" or "qualities" possessed by human beings. For clarity I shall refer to most of the candidates for causal status Bentley criticizes as "mental properties." Bentley himself recognizes that a "psychological terminology" exists that claims to distinguish such mental states and events as emotions, feelings, instincts, impulses, and the like, but chooses to ignore these distinctions or at least not to employ them because they are notionally vague (PG, 5). The result of our use of the notion of mental properties may be characterized in Wilfrid Sellar's useful phrase as the "manifest image of man."[30] Thus Bentley says that for "most of us all of the time, for all of us most of the time, it is quite sufficient to regard human beings as 'persons' who possess qualities or motives which are phases of their character and who act in accordance with these qualities or this character, under certain conditions of life in which they are placed" (PG, 5). He goes on to say that mental properties taken as causal principles must be criticized before we attempt to "build up an interpretation out of the underlying facts which they dimly hint at, but never actually define." This marks the first appearance in Bentley's thinking of what would become a characteristic move in his philosophy of social science. He does not claim that our conventional vocabulary of mental properties is somehow baseless; instead, he treats it as an inadequate account of a domain of "underlying facts" which are presumably accessible to a more adequate conceptual scheme. Bentley's next step is to make clear his purpose in these early chapters. He will "treat first of the use of the factors in common speech for the everyday purposes of life, attempting impressionistically to reveal their defects; and then to pass to close examination of certain systematic theories built up out of them."

Kress has noted that Bentley's proposed "destruction or redirection of prior thought" is advanced with little "sense of the drama and import of his intentions."[31] Certainly Bentley does not suggest the novelty of his movement from a criticism of everyday social interpretation and its typical language to the theories of social science. His claim that the latter are built upon the former would become a basic tenet of his work. He insisted that a residue of ordinary language and, hence, he claims, of the ontological commitments of ordinary language persists in scientific discourse. Our ordinary categories of social interpretation allow or encourage us to take certain features of our experience as "real" or "true" and thus to use these features as criteria for determining the content and boundaries of possible or admissible accounts of human behavior. We would not accord scientific status to a candidate explanatory theory of human behavior unless it seemed to furnish a model for explanation generally consistent with, but allegedly superior to, our ordinary explanations. Bentley's strategy is to show that what I shall call "mental property explanations" are internally contradictory. He explicitly refuses to "answer a theory with a theory" or to propose his own rival explanation of human behavior over against ordinary explanations (PG, 83). He claims, in other words, to trace a "dialectic" of social interpretation in a manner reminiscent of Hegel.[32] Since Bentley's destination will be a general social theory, it is clear that his theory, like those he criticizes, will be connected with everyday experience and language. Unlike other theories, however, his teaching will have the virtue of self-awareness about its origins.

Bentley's views on language are obviously an important part of his teaching in *The Process of Government*. The majority of social theorists sought what he would later call an "Archimedean point" on which their theories could be based.[33] This search is futile because it ignores the connection between ordinary and scientific language. The social theorist who remains unaware of this connection is placed in the contradictory position of attempting to characterize experience apart from the "language-forms" which are the only medium for its understanding. Bentley's idealist position is obscured in his book by his simplified and nontechnical terminology: "It has long enough been established that there is no 'outer world' except in idea . . . we do not know any outer world except the world that is known to us, or, what is the same thing, *as* it is known to us" (PG, 171). For Bentley, language is the constituent of what Kant calls the "conditions of the possibility of experience in general."[34] We cannot have knowledge about the world apart from the conditions of knowledge. The conventional social theorist, like the ordinary person, falls into this trap because he begins his explanation with some basic unit or interpretive category. The choice of a unit of analysis such as "the individual" or a category such as "progress" smuggles into the explanation built upon it a family of notions about such things as individuals and progress.

There is a resemblance between Bentley's criticism of social theories constructed in this fashion and Kant's criticism of the scientific status of metaphysics. For Kant the natural tendency of reason to attempt to move beyond the limits of possible experience leads to the variety of mutually contradictory metaphysical systems produced by philosophers who claim scientific status for their speculations.[35] For Bentley the multiplicity and ultimate arbitrariness of systematic social theories was the result of a lack of understanding of the impossibility of an extralinguistic foundation for any intellectual activity. Thus, the social theorists whose works he subjects to microscopic analysis all suffer from the same disorder. They have begun their enterprises with what Bentley takes to be arbitrary intuitions. In Bentley's view, the notion of an extralinguistic foundation for social theory is linked to the doctrine that certain empirical beliefs are somehow self-evident or that we can have immediate knowledge the object of which must be taken as having epistemic priority. That this doctrine is unintelligible he believes can be shown by asking its defenders to identify and give an account of any such objects apart from language. Bentley's emphasis on the role of language is more reminiscent of Hegel than of Kant, although I believe the source of his arguments can be found in his critical assimilation of Dewey's pragmatism.[36]

While Bentley's mature theory of language would not emerge for several decades, it is important to make clear the relations between language and the study of society as he understood them in 1908. The study of his views on this issue yields the most significant difference between Bentley's methodology and the leading ideas of his German counterparts. Bentley's earlier interpretive methodology had been based on the thesis that the social scientist's own "human nature" and his participation in the human experiences that are taken to be the raw material of social science allowed him cognitive access to the social actions he proposed to explain. With this thesis Bentley had been in substantial agreement with the forward positions in German and Austrian sociology in the 1890s. Moreover, Max Weber had reached a similar position in his critique of Roscher and Knies at about the same time Bentley was beginning work on *The Process of Government*.[37] In contrast with Weber, Bentley rejected an interpretive methodology. The decisive weakness of any version of interpretive social science was its dependence upon some form of self-knowledge. Because Bentley's position has been confused with the rejection of introspection as a source of knowledge which was central to early behaviorist psychology, a comparison of his view with that of Weber will allow his thesis to become clearer.

Weber's understanding of the connections between the self-knowledge of the social scientist and the latter's inferences about or construction of models of the mental states of social actors was never formulated clearly.[38] He attempted to distinguish his view from the notion that social science was grounded in empathetic participation in or reproduction of the experiences of social actors. Instead, the proper foundation for social science lies in the character of the "immediate experience" we are understood to have of "meaningful" human conduct, which Weber takes to be "axiological."[39] Accordingly, Weber later identifies the "transcendental presupposition of every cultural science" as the thesis that "we are *cultural beings*, endowed with the capacity and the will to take a definite attitude toward the world and to lend it *significance*."[40]

The use of "transcendental" in Weber's formulation suggests the utility of designating as a transcendental methodological premise any thesis that claims to base the central concepts of social science in some allegedly undeniable or irreducible feature of human experience. This move allows us to identify a common ground occupied by both Weber and such social scientists as Albion Small, Rudolph von Jhering, and Franklin H. Giddings, whose works figure prominently in Bentley's criticisms. Moreover, it is possible to see a basic similarity between the positions of some of the most important social scientists at the turn of the century and more recent arguments against positivist notions of scientific explanation in social science offered in the idiom of "conceptual analysis." Here I have in mind claims made by philosophers such as Peter Winch and Charles Taylor that human action must be understood in terms of certain irreducible characteristics such as thinking, willing, purposiveness, and the like. At this point in my explication of Bentley's teaching I will neither summarize nor criticize the positions of these or other contemporary philosophers.[41] Rather, I am suggesting that Bentley's position in *The Process of Government* is his first statement of an understanding of the issues involved in the study of social action that may be an alternative to the views of both positivists and conceptual analysts.

For Bentley what I have called a transcendental premise rests upon the mistaken view that self-knowledge can be immediate: "I know myself, so far as I have any knowledge that is worthwhile, by observation of my actions, and indeed largely not by my own observations, but by what other people observe and report to me directly or indirectly about my actions." Any mental state is, "as it is concretely known to us, supported on a skeleton of language dealing with observed varieties of action in ourselves and in others" (PG,

187). Self-knowledge is necessarily mediated by and constituted through language. Within the context of Bentley's critique of the causal status of mental properties, we should now doubt whether it is intelligible to suppose that we can even identify mental properties unambiguously enough to ascribe causal status to them.

Bentley deploys four principal lines of criticism against "feelings and faculties" taken as causes, in addition to his general criticism of the notion of immediate self-knowledge he believes lies at the heart of the conventional view of how we understand society. The explanation of human behavior in terms of mental properties is not without practical use. It brings a "certain amount of order into what would otherwise be a chaos." Less charitably put, Bentley remarks that he has no wish to "deprive some unhappy being of the anthropomorphism that suits his needs" (PG, 166).

The first argument has to do with the fact that mental properties taken as causes do not produce uniform effects (PG, 5–26). A brief inventory of some of Bentley's examples will make clear his criticism. Most of us would explain the action of a man who knocks down a bully who was threatening a boy on the street by invoking some quality such as "sympathy." Bentley believes this explanation is defective because it fails to make clear why this person does not intervene on behalf of starving human beings who are equally visible to him. Bentley goes on to note that reformers attribute to the evolution of characteristics such as "humanity" a decline in public cruelty to animals, restrictions on child labor, and public criticism of the meat-packing industry. They explain the persistence of the evils they oppose by invoking "wickedness" or "immoral character" as qualities possessed by their enemies while they attribute their victories to the spread of enlightened values. The effects of progressive moral evolution and innate depravity seem curiously selective. The man in whose factory children are exploited is "tender-hearted" toward his own children and the corrupt political boss is scrupulously honest with his friends. The reformer who criticizes Rockefeller's railway rebates tolerates similar practices by his corner grocer. Those who denounce the meat packers as immoral did nothing when brothels were established for strikebreakers during a strike at the stockyards. Bentley's examples are intended to show that if we invoke mental properties as they are popularly understood, their causal operation is subject to numerous qualifications. Now it may fairly be objected to Bentley, I believe, that it is a fundamental misunderstanding of the vocabulary of moral discourse to present such qualities as "sympathy" as actual or possible sources for chains of effective causality. Bentley's argument from the absence of uniform effects suggests that human actions, especially moral actions, may not be intelligible as uniform effects produced by mental properties taken as effective causes, not that mental properties are somehow unreal.

Bentley's second argument seems stronger and depends less upon attributing a causal doctrine to the vagaries of ordinary language. He draws our attention to the complex issue of distinguishing between a social phenomenon we are concerned to explain and its supposed causes that we attribute to mental properties. If a label is desired for Bentley's strategy we may call it his argument from skeptical parsimony. His criticism is developed in connection with theories that take intellectual capacity, whether understood in psychological or physiological terms, as an intelligible cause of social phenomena. He notes that everyday versions of this view seldom, if ever, are specific about physiological properties. He devotes little attention to casual forms of this view and turns to putatively scientific statements of it.

His first point is that the ascription of variations in observable achievement to variations in "brain power" conceals the problem of determining the nature of achievement (PG, 19–21). How do we compare the achievements of Newton or Darwin with those of the Chaldean astrologers who determined the periodicity of eclipses? Do we seriously propose to say that the ancient Greeks and Romans were inferior to contemporary men in intellectual capacity? For almost any modern accomplishment the unprejudiced student, according to Bentley, can find counterparts, both in earlier periods and in the cultures of contemporary "primitives." Bentley does not deny that differences among peoples or societies might exist, nor does his position require him to deny that evolutionary changes might have taken place in the human species. Rather, he rejects that view that such facts allow us to explain observable human behavior in terms of mental properties like intellectual capacity.

Bentley's criticisms are more sharply focused when he turns to the work of Sir Karl Pearson and his followers (PG, 101–7). Pearson's claim to be able to measure such qualities as intelligence and moral capacity suffers from a number of difficulties. In the first place, Pearson fails to recognize that the properties he proposes to measure are not directly observable, unlike the physical characteristics of plants and animals. Thus, Pearson cannot distinguish clearly between mental properties and the judgments that constitute them as suitable objects for a statistical analysis. In his examination of one of Pearson's studies of the inheritance of "mental and moral characteristics," Bentley exposes the methodological defects of Pearson's approach. Pearson had established strong product-moment correlations among siblings for such variables as intellectual ability, moral qualities, including vivacity, assertiveness, popularity, and introspection, and physiological factors such as skull measurements. Although the subjects of the study were schoolchildren, Pearson drew conclusions about adults and even about "man" as a species from findings, ignoring the problems of statistical inference. Moreover, his research relied upon the judgments of schoolteachers to sort the subjects into the categories of the variables considered. In Bentley's judgment this procedure introduces at the outset an uncontrolled source of variation into Pearson's data. Additional uncontrolled variations can be traced to the effects of differences in health, nutrition, and home environments on the children, none of which Pearson had taken into account. Even if he had been more scrupulous about the design of his study, Pearson's research is fundamentally flawed because he believes that discrete physical states underlie and are causally linked with mental properties. The notion that the physical underlies the psychical is necessary, Bentley claims, "so long as we hold the physical and psychical apart by our present terminology" (PG, 106). Pearson is the unwitting captive of ordinary language when he assumes that mental properties are "things" or in any way "thing-like." This belief allows him to describe such properties by the same methods we use to examine an "ear or a thighbone or a skull" and to assume that "lumps of mental or moral qualities can be compared as individual possessions and can be inherited as such." Finally, Pearson's "translation of correlation into causation" which he claims to accomplish by showing strong correlations among his variables "is merely the translation of an untested presupposition into an unproved conclusion."

In a chapter on "Individual Endowment and Race Type" in Part 2 of The Process of Government, Bentley tries to refine his criticisms further (PG, 245–57). Here we can see what I called his argument from skeptical parsimony more clearly. In theories that invoke physical factors as causal forces in individuals and races the confusion of physical and psychical makes the argument "shift at critical moments from one set of terms to the other. . . ." This ambiguity stems from the problem of isolating such terms from the effects or forms of behavior they are supposed to explain. A convincing causal theory containing mental properties, whether these properties are variations in intellectual capacity or not, must be able to identify and describe its chosen variables "in some other way than by mere inference from the facts we propose to explain" (PG, 19). That is, we are presented as social scientists with events or phenomena or objects that are not directly intelligible to us as instances of the operation of causal processes located in minds or bodies. Indeed, social theorists who invoke such processes are often unable to demonstrate the connections required by their theories and turn to comparative and historical data for evidence that the "faculties" that populate their theories actually exist.

Bentley is inclined to regard most of what is typically said about "primitives" or the ancients as expressions of partisanship or of present-day interests. Thus, the characteristics imputed to various races reflect "something of the historical value they have, or have had, for us" and can, with sufficient ingenuity, explain virtually anything" (PG, 253). Bentley does not deny that scientific classifications of race are possible, although he remains skeptical of their soundness. His claim is rather that there is a conceptual gap between any such classification scheme and the forms of behavior it is invoked to explain. We do not observe or experience human behavior that is simply an expression of racial variations but instead we have access only to "social race activities." In other words, Bentley adapts his thesis concerning the impossibility of immediate experience to arrive at the view that our acquaintance with physiological variations is similarly mediated. In this case our partisanship makes the claim that we can devise a causal theory of Pearson's sort absurd. The difficulty of separating our notion of mental properties from our own interests has hardly been recognized in Bentley's judgment.

Bentley's fourth line of argument has to do with the "social forms" in which human behavior appears to the social scientist. Once again, his target is the doctrine of immediacy. The physiologist may study human nutrition, sexuality, disease resistance, or intoxication, but has little to tell us about the eating habits, forms of marriage, public health policies or the politics of temperance we may wish to study (PG, 247–48). For many social scientists a set of propositions about physiological variables is "more real" or more immediate than a set of descriptions of social behavior. A scientific explanation of social behavior is understood as relying upon empirical statements about physiological processes. The "deepest" explanation of this sort is, according to Bentley, the notion that social behavior can be accounted for by appealing to natural selection and the evolution of intellectual capacity (PG, 249–52). An increase in intellectual capacity is alleged to be the result of selection for increasingly complex forms of neurophysiological organization which is in turn reflected or expressed in the increasing complexity of social structures. Bentley offers two criticisms of this explanatory scheme. First, the correlation between neurophysiological and social complexity is dubious, as the case of the social insects makes clear. A complex "social" organization exists quite apart from a highly developed neurophysiological organization. Only "a most desperate prejudice" allows us to maintain this thesis in the face of any careful study of the social organization of animals. Second, there is no reason to assume that other evolutionary developments have not had a role in producing the social behavior we propose to explain. We cannot assume that all characteristics that have been selected for, such as strength or resistance to disease simply covary with neurophysiological complexity. Moreover, the "brain-power variations" posited by this theory "require statement in social forms in order to make it possible to study them." This means that we must be able to distinguish between the social phenomena to be explained and our evolutionary factors we intend to use in the construction of explanations.

In his criticisms of various social theorists Bentley blends these arguments together. A summary of his attack on Albion Small allows us to contrast his understanding of the tasks of social science with that of one of the most influential American sociologists of the period.[42] For Bentley, Small's approach typified the errors he was concerned to bring to light. From a "primary interest" in survival which men share with other living organisms Small derives a classification of desires, which Bentley notes must serve as well for goals, properties of individuals, and labels for clusters of motives: health, wealth, sociability, knowledge, beauty, and rightness.[43] The typology of desires is used to produce a classification of "social forces" taken as the "externalization" of desires. The resulting conceptual apparatus then becomes the basis for an interpretation of history that defines historical periods in terms of specific ensembles of mental properties and social forces, purporting to uncover a pattern of progressive evolution. In Bentley's view, all these moves reveal the fundamental arbitrariness of this approach to theory construction. Small's "social instincts," for example, can be satisfied in ways ranging from "wolfishness" to "brotherhood," while the "aesthetic feeling" can be sat-

isfied in ways ranging from "delight in the hideous" to the "deifi-
cation of beauty." Bentley observes skeptically that Small's list is
less a classification of basic human desires than of social activities
"grouped with a rough empiricism, and attributed for their origin,
in purely gratuitous manner, to desires—as soul-stuff—which are
called into existence to match" (PG, 29).

For Small, the social process can be taken at the level of the individual as the result of the interaction of his six categories of desires,
which now are designated "interests." Since social forces are products of these interests, we can study the interaction of interests at
the collective level as well. A scientific analysis of a social situation
is performed by determining the quantitative variations in the distributions of interests. The relationships between individual interests
and social forces are held to be governed by "general laws." The central methodological problem of social science is to measure the exponents and coefficients in equations such as those that Small suggests in order to represent the desires of individuals and the resulting
"social ends" in Periclean Athens:[44]

$$\text{Desire} = a^x + b^{vi} + c^v + d^{xi} + e^{xiv} + f^{vii}$$

$$\text{Social end} = a^{vii} + b^{iii} + c^{ii} + d^{viii} + e^{xii} + f^{iv}$$

Bentley's hostility to this notion of explanation, which must have
seemed to him a gross parody of scientific theories, is evident in his
scornful description of Small's approach as a "billiard-ball method of
using interests." Small has never "taken the slightest step to isolate
these desires or prove their existence apart from the social phenomena they are intended to explain. His theory taps popular psychology
and the practical terminology of everyday speech for some of the desires. It gets the rest by a cursory inspection of social facts themselves." If Small tried to account for the "transition from extermina-
tion of enemies to the institution of slavery in early times," he
would most likely assert that a "wealth desire" had replaced some
more primitive desire for self-defense. Bentley laments: "But how artificial such a procedure is!" (PG, 36).

Neither in his criticisms of Small nor in his discussions of Spencer
and other social theorists does Bentley reject every aspect of their
work. One of Bentley's characteristic claims is that the best work of
many social theorists often has little to do with their theoretical apparatus or methodological views. Small's most important accomplishment lies in his attention to "interests" taken in their conventional sense rather than in the sense required by his systematic

social theory. For Bentley, Small's intuitive grasp of social phenomena worth studying makes his failure to free himself from everyday
interpretive categories all the more tragic.

Now Bentley has still not provided us with an alternative to the
defective methodological views he has rejected. I think it is possible
to see at least the outlines of his own position by a further consideration of his account of the fundamental errors upon which the defective methodologies rest. First, Bentley proposes a distinction between "causal" and "descriptive" understandings of interests and of
mental properties in general. Any causal explanation requires that
its candidates be treated as "forces in the metaphysical sense" (PG,
31). Bentley provides no full-fledged statement of his proposal to replace causal with descriptive explanations in the 1908 work and we
must defer discussion of his views to later chapters. It should be apparent, however, that Bentley's views even in 1908 are radically misunderstood if they are assimilated to the model of scientific explanation characteristic of behaviorist psychology. Second, Bentley argues
that both ordinary persons and social theorists fail to understand
that scientific inquiry does not and cannot lead to absolutely certain
explanations of phenomena. While Bentley had not yet attempted to
furnish a general account of scientific explanation, his comments
point toward his later formulations. Science must be understood as
"up in the air" since it is "the construction of the scientist's mind"
and matter of "conception, not perception" (PG, 245). Bentley's view
resembles Sir Karl Popper's familiar criticism of the "essentialist
doctrine" that "science aims at ultimate explanation . . . an explanation which (essentially, or by its very nature) cannot be further explained, and which is in no need of any further explanation."[45] Thus,
in place of social theories that require us to treat the "individual" or,
for that matter, "society" as a "thing" with causal powers, a genu-
uinely scientific approach must begin with the notion that the "individual" and "society" should be treated as "points of view" (PG, 83).
Thus, Bentley brought his earlier perspectivism into the methodological debate in a decisive way and was prepared to set it against
the quest for certainty that he believed continued to handicap the
development of social science.

Third, Bentley claims that the dialectic of social interpretation
points toward a radical conclusion. We must consider as problematic
the distinctions between "inner" and "outer" and "subjective" and
"objective" reality. Any proposed description of an "inner" state,
whether a mental property or not, depends upon and is constituted

by a host of "external" factors brought together in the language we must employ in our description. Thus, the traditional "mental" vocabulary does not refer to mental states but instead to a "social something" (PG, 169–70). Any mental property is properly intelligible only as "phases of social situations." Bentley argues that it follows from these considerations that the "individual" is a "highly abstract social idea," a conclusion that must also be true of any properties predicated of the individual as well as of "society." The deeper issue, in Bentley's view, is the intelligibility of the subject/object distinction itself. "If we throw emphasis on either of the two to the exclusion of the other, and deny the complement, we are constructing a world out of stuff that has definition only in terms of the very opposition we attempt to deny." While Bentley was not prepared to explore these issues in 1908, their appearance in *The Process of Government* distinguishes his work from that of most of his American contemporaries in political science and sociology.

Ideas, Ideals, and Progress

Bentley's criticisms of "ideas and ideals as causes" in the second chapter of Part 1 show more clearly than any other part of *The Process of Government* the distance he had put between himself and the political doctrine of Progressivism. The iconoclastic, debunking tone which gave many of his readers the misleading impression that he believed "ideas" should be excluded from social science is nowhere more prominent. As Kress has noted, Bentley is certainly not an amoral or indifferently neutral "objective" social scientist: "Bentley's passion, his anger and scorn, are manifest on several levels: they are directed against the organization of society as well as against the discipline that pretends to study it, and his prose style reflects, in its very crudity and forcefulness, his rejection of the niceties and inhibitions of convention."[46] The "convention" that kindled Bentley's anger was that of attributing social change to changes in ideas. The teachings Bentley attacks claim that ideas are the mainsprings of social progress. The basis of his criticism can be found in the principles he has already developed. Perhaps the most important new theme in this section is his rejection of progressive views of history.

Men invoke the power of ideas in their "everyday talk, moralizing, and exhortation" (PG, 110–17). Ideas, however, are no more uniform in their supposed causal impact than mental properties. Bentley claims that even if a majority of Americans were converted to revolutionary socialism there would be no significant effect on the course of American politics. This rhetorical exaggeration is intended to suggest the causal impotence of ideas. Bentley's argument here is extremely weak. He claims that political systems based on "theoretical socialism" do not necessarily produce recognizably socialistic policies, while such policies may be found in regimes that consider themselves to be based on "individualistic" political doctrines. He does not try to substantiate his claim that we typically attribute to "ideas" a causal role of the sort he rejects.

Bentley's criticisms of social theorists who believe in the causal efficacy of ideas seem to me sounder than his splenetic outbursts against ordinary views. In what is a rare move for Bentley, he defends himself against the charge that he has created a straw man by "falsely attributing to these writers a meaning for the words idea and ideal, and a process of using them, which they do not intend" (PG, 117). His principal targets are the teachings of Lewis H. Morgan, Franklin H. Giddings, and Albert Venn Dicey, although he attempts to buttress his criticisms by offering passages from a number of writers including John Stuart Mill, the American political scientist W. W. Willoughby, Richard T. Ely, Simon Patten, Emile Durkheim, J. K. Bluntschli, and Edwin R. A. Seligman that show their belief in ideas as causes. For Bentley all these beliefs amount to the "same old personifications or, if the term can be pardoned, thing-ification, of the psychic factors. . . ."

According to Bentley, Morgan's influential *Ancient Society* (1877) contains two contradictory notions of social evolution (PG, 123–28). Morgan claimed that social and cultural evolution was the result of technological advancement but also held that "the principal institutions of mankind have been developed from a few primary germs of thought." In Morgan's view the growth of such "ideas" as subsistence, government, language, the family, religion, architecture, and property has been guided by a "natural logic which formed an essential attribute of the brain itself." In his theory of the evolution of the family, Morgan claims that the transition from a "consanguine" form, in which brothers and sisters intermarried in a group, to the "punaluan" form, in which a group of brothers or sisters possessed their wives or husbands in common, was "produced by the gradual exclusion of own brothers and sisters from the marriage relation, the evils of which could not forever escape human observation."[47] Even if Morgan's classification of family types is accurate, his explanation for the transition is defective since he cannot prove that any of these ideas existed. All he has really done is to project "his own opinion of the meaning of the change" into the "minds of the actors" (PG, 126). Thus, when ideas are employed as causal factors in an evolutionary theory, arbitrariness is encouraged.

Bentley's criticism of Giddings makes a somewhat different point. For Giddings, progressive social evolution resulted from the influence of the ideas of exceptional individuals who have the power "to call forth persistent efforts to transform the external order of things into a realization of the ideal."[48] For Bentley it is especially significant that Giddings's intention was to develop a theory of "social causation" in order to solve the practical problem of "social control." Giddings claims that a "growing ethical spirit" promotes "continued stability and progress" and holds that the "rational-ethical consciousness" maintains "social cohesion in a progressive democracy."[49] Now Bentley has no objection to any of these views if they are meant as expressions of a partisan political viewpoint. Giddings, however, presents his views as part of a scientific enterprise. He must be able to demonstrate the existence of his ideal causal factors apart from the effects he purports to explain with them. Failing this, Bentley remarks that he should treat them explicitly as explanatory fictions in the manner in which the chemical atom was treated by antimechanistic physicists (PG, 143).

In his criticism of Dicey, Bentley brings us closer to the roots of his objection to what I will call "causal-progressive" doctrines. Dicey proposes to explain significant changes in English law during the nineteenth century by uncovering shifts in public opinion which produced them. For Dicey "opinion" is more fundamental than "interest" in the shaping of legislation. Thus, he invokes such factors as "humanitarianism" and "reaction" as explanatory categories. Needless to say, Bentley finds these notions, along with such factors as the "habitual conservatism" of Englishmen, woefully inadequate because they are conceptually confused (PG, 146). What Dicey has actually done is to abstract the "essence" of legislation, transform it into a "principle, and then makes the principle explain the legislation" (PG, 149). At length Dicey appeals to "the inner logic of events" which leads men to alter their opinions and finally claims that opinions are governed by the "spirit of the age." Implicit in Bentley's criticism is the skeptical suspicion that events have no "inner logic." Explanations that invoke the "spirit of the age" merely restate in a mystical way the very phenomena we wish to explain.

Any progressive reading of history such as Morgan's or Dicey's is, Bentley suggests, inherently partisan. Theories that make history trace the emergence of "freedom," "self-consciousness," or an increasing capacity to control destiny resemble theories of "race type" since they reflect contemporary interests. Such causal-progressive views share the defects of mental-property explanations by positing an underlying causal agency which is made manifest in or through the course of history. Since some of his critics have described Bentley's teaching as "ahistorical and changeless," the status of "history" in Bentley's thinking must be made clear.[50]

The contexts in which human actions occur, which Bentley somewhat ambiguously labels the "habit background," inherently point toward the past. Bentley does not believe we can ascribe causal efficacy to the "past" any more than the teleologist can rightfully ascribe it to the "future" (PG, 219, 122). That is, an "appeal to tradition" does not constitute an explanation of social phenomena. What goes unrecognized in such accounts is that "if tradition is anything at all, it is an affair of the present. . . . Long, in point of time, as may be the trains of activity which we must follow, we never grasp them except at some present moment."

In his criticism of Bentley's view of history, Bernard Crick argues that the "importance of tradition" is rejected, resulting in a journalistic celebration of the "purely contemporary."[51] Crick fails to realize that Bentley's intention is to explicate the mode of historical experience. For Bentley there can be no possibility of presenting the past as it "really was" and a historical account cannot be a discovery or revival of the past. He was distressed by treatments of history that presupposed that the past can simply be described without consideration of the present in which the historian, after all, lives and writes history. Bentley's position bears some resemblance to Michael Oakeshott's view of history as the historian's construction and thus essentially present. For Bentley, however, as for Oakeshott, this thesis does not mean that the historian can create whatever history he wishes. We must distinguish, in other words, between the causal-progressive views of history that embody a contemporary political or ethical position and historical accounts that are not "objective" in the manner held to be possible and desirable for the natural sciences but are nonetheless in principle devoid of partisanship. Again, a similarity between Bentley's and Oakeshott's positions should be noted. Causal-progressive theories would seem to be instances of what Oakeshott calls a "practical" attitude toward the past which regards past events in terms of their supposed usefulness for us in the present.[52] Bentley doubted the persuasiveness of partisan readings of history precisely because counterexamples could be found for any given progressive interpretation. The progressive theorist must be prepared to distinguish essential from peripheral historical events, a move Bentley always regarded with suspicion. Unlike Oakeshott, Bentley never argued for the study of history for its own sake.

Bentley modestly disclaimed any "aptitude" for history, but he surely possessed a "historical sense" of the sort understood by Hans-Georg Gadamer:

> Having an historical sense is to conquer in a consistent manner the natural naivete which makes us judge the past by the so-called obvious scales of our current life, in the perspectives of our institutions, and from our acquired values and truths. Having an historical sense signifies thinking explicitly about the historical horizon which is co-extensive with the life we live and have lived.[53]

As a student of Dilthey and Simmel, Bentley could hardly have been unaware of debates about the scientific status of history and the nature of historical explanation, but he contributed little or nothing to them. It seemed self-evident to him that "history" is a mode or variety of experience constituted like every other by the mind, a belief he retained even after he had come to doubt the intelligibility of traditional concepts of mind. Certainly there was never any possibility of formulating general historical "laws" in positivist fashion. The notion that historical events are governed by or can be brought under the framework of some deductive-nomological scheme seemed so confused that Bentley never seriously considered it. His nearly boundless skepticism concerning historical progress was qualified only by his conviction that science alone could be understood as progressively developing. Every other form of human knowledge fails Bentley's tests of increasing coherence and consensus (RMS, 190–93).

After *The Process of Government* Bentley's writings scarcely mention "history." He gradually replaced "history" with "temporality." I suggest that he did so for several reasons. First, his notion of the historical field as essentially raw material for the typically arbitrary constructions of historians made him uninterested in history as a discipline. Bentley evidently doubted that there was or could be any distinctively "historical" explanation and accordingly took no interest in historical methods. More important, he began to search for a way of theorizing that would avoid causal idioms altogether. Conventional historical explanations were merely examples of one type of causal explanation and were as such suspect. It is tempting to suppose that Bentley had in mind Kant's notion of time as both the "formal a priori condition of all appearances whatsoever" and the "form of inner sense, that is, of the intuition of ourselves and of our inner state."[54] For Bentley, however, it is untenable to isolate the moments of past, present, and future from the temporal process. He would eventually refer to "durations" and temporal "spreads" that must be understood as constituents or properties of any object of knowledge or act of perception or cognition. Bentley's turn to temporality was something of an escape from history, but it was a move he made without hesitation in his search for social science.

The Psychological Turn in American Social Science

With his rejection of psychological explanations in social science Bentley had entered upon a path that would take him far from mainstream American social science. Simon Patten's prophecy of the 1890s that psychology would lie at the heart of social science was not far from the truth. The major European sociologists, aware, in H. Stuart Hughes's words, that "man as an actor in society . . . was seldom decisively influenced by logical considerations: supra- or infrarational values of one sort or another usually guided his conduct," had turned in their various fashions to the task of linking up this view of human nature with theories about the structure of society.[55] We have already seen how Bentley's masters Dilthey and Simmel had sought a psychology of greater breadth and depth than hitherto available. Weber, often read as a theorist who operated only on the largest historical scale, not only proposed to treat sociological concepts as if they were reducible to statements about individual actions, but engaged in a study of "psycho-physical" aspects of industrial work that was frankly indebted to contemporary experimental psychology.[56] In the United States academic psychology was led by scholars prepared to put the quantitative study of intelligence at the center of their discipline.

A few comments on the role psychology was to play in political science will make clear the distance between Bentley and the discipline that his thinking was to influence. As G. David Garson puts it,

"While Bentley was condemning research on psychological 'soul stuff,' the general trend in political science was in precisely the opposite direction, discovering the importance of the individual as interpreted by social psychology."[57] The work of the leading social psychologist, Charles Horton Cooley, as well as the writings of the Chicago pragmatists, had less influence on political scientists than did Graham Wallas's proposal to quantify advantage, deference, and numerous other "political" variables.[58]

It is essential to distinguish the intentions of the most prominent American political scientists of the period from those of the behaviorist John B. Watson, whose views mistakenly have been held to have influenced Bentley. For Watson the scientific development of psychology required the elimination of all use of or reference to "consciousness."[59] Political scientists ignored, for the most part, Watsonian behaviorism precisely because they wanted access to the sorts of psychological states that Watson had so austerely ruled out of his science. Psychological states were taken as arguably the most important feature of a genuinely explanatory social science. From Bentley's standpoint, of course, this claim was hardly novel. Indeed, he would eventually attack Watsonian behaviorism for admitting a variety of properties and processes that merely replaced "consciousness" with equally untenable explanatory entities.

Charles E. Merriam's 1920 presidential address to the American Political Science Association was an extremely influential programmatic statement of the growing commitment of political scientists to psychological explanation.[60] According to Merriam, the natural sciences had surpassed the social sciences in terms of professionalism, personnel, and research facilities. Among other disciplines, sociology and statistics can assist political science, but "modern psychology" offers "still greater things." It is obvious that "Thorndike and others can tell us more about the *genus homo* than was given to Thomas Hobbes and Adam Smith." The American Political Science Association went on to sponsor a series of well-attended meetings of its new Conference on the Science of Politics during the summers of 1923–1925, at which political scientists responded enthusiastically to such psychologists as Floyd Allport, L. L. Thurstone, and Clark Hull.[61] By 1925 Thurstone was chairing a Round Table on Politics and Psychology at a joint meeting of the American Political Science Association and the American Psychological Association.

From Thurstone, political scientists learned that any scientific problem can be stated in the form of a hypothetical relationship between two variables, which must have a common unit of measurement.[62] Both Thurstone and Allport supported "attitude" as the basic unit of analysis in psychology and recommended it for political science. If a "natural science of political phenomena" is to be developed, Allport held that all statements about political institutions must be reducible to statements about individual attitudes.[63] Political scientists found they could accept Thurstone's definition of "attitude" as "the sum total of a man's inclinations and feelings, prejudice or bias, preconceived notions, ideas, fears, threats, and convictions about a specific topic," as well as his use of scaling techniques to measure attitudes.[64]

In Merriam's hands, the new political science was put to work to create a new politics. With a "genuine knowledge of political and social psychology," he believed it was possible to create new customs, interests, and values that would reflect our increased control of the irrational in human nature. A new politics "woven out of the new elements of modern life and thought" would utilize science to solve social problems.[65] From a Bentleyan standpoint, Merriam's efforts to infuse his Progressivism with a scientific psychology could hardly have appeared as an advance over Giddings or Small. Bentley paid virtually no attention to academic political science after 1908, nor did political scientists seem to read *The Process of Government*.

Bentley explained the dialectic social science followed with its repetitive moves to "subjective" and "objective" explanations:

I will very frankly admit that when an investigator starts out with dead external factors in his interpretation, when he is "objective" to the limit on one side of his work, he will inevitably reach a point, if he is honest with himself, when the "objective" will be recognized by him as not sufficing, when he will be compelled to set up something more "human," something "subjective" to carry his interpretation farther forward. But that is primarily a defect of the hard objectivity with which the start has been made; and whether it is a defect or not . . . it will be no excuse for setting up arbitrary, unreal subjective factors at the upper end of the interpretation. (PG, 135)

In Bentley's view most of his contemporaries were satisfied with a glimpse of the surface of social reality or with the ways in which that reality is understood in everyday life. Again, we must recall that he did not deny the existence of a "real, living, intelligent human social material which is indicated when feelings and ideals are mentioned" (PG, 165). We must find "another manner of statement" that permits a scientific account of the "values and meanings" so inadequately grasped by psychological and causal theories. This new manner of statement would not revive the mistake of positivism by reducing mental properties to some "objective" level of analysis. Rather, the task of a social science is to determine their "proper functioning" in the "system to which they belong." Bentley has brought his reader to the "group interpretation" of politics and society as the adequate manner of statement for the study of ideas and feelings. When we have developed the group interpretation, Bentley believes we will have succeeded in absorbing the "conditions" of social action into "action" itself and thus will have arrived at a social science (PG, 171–72).

4

The Group Interpretation of Politics

Quantity and quality in social science consist in how much and how well we can see, and in how much and how well we can tell what we see. For "how well" understand "how coherently."
        "Remarks on Method in the Study of Society"

Throughout his career Bentley insisted that the "group interpretation" of politics offered in the second part of *The Process of Government* must be connected with his later writings as a preliminary treatment of themes developed more adequately in those works (RMS, iii; LAM, 238; BKF, 219). He doubted that the political scientists who turned to his first book had understood the scope of his enterprise, which they took to have established a theory of "pressure groups."[1] The group interpretation is intended to provide a "full understanding of the conditions of action" which dissolves the distinction between "conditions" and "actions" (PG, 5). I believe it is misleading to characterize the second part of Bentley's book as "more empirical," in Kress's words, than the first part.[2] Bentley's tough-minded, debunking survey of American political institutions is not distinct from but rather a continuation of the philosophic inquiry begun in the first part of his book. This chapter will be concerned with the most important ideas of the group interpretation, the leading examples of its application to the study of politics, and the most serious criticisms of this part of Bentley's teaching. The group interpretation is presented as a teaching that not only accounts for or explains social phenomena but accounts for any explanation of social phenomena. It claims to explain itself as well as its objects. I will examine the intelligibility of this claim through a study of the role of "values" in Bentley's social science. The criticism with which

Bentley's position must contend is that it cannot without contradiction claim to be both an explanation and a product or a "reflection" of its subject matter.

The Basis of the Group Interpretation

Unlike many political scientists who celebrated him as a pioneer, Bentley never claimed that a focus on "groups" was a novelty in social theory. His own position is a more explicit and hence superior formulation of a mode of social interpretation present in "every advance step that is taken in the analysis or understanding of society" (PG, 166, 481). I am reminded of Marx's modest refusal to take credit for either the discovery of classes or of the class struggle.[3] The group interpretation is not simply another social theory set over against defective theories but rather a basic feature of social theory as such which Bentley claims to have raised to a higher level of intelligibility. We cannot help but be Bentleyans in social theory. The best students of politics, ancient and modern, had always recognized the connections between "interests" and politics.

For Bentley it was evident that societies were divided or divisible into various interests. It is this sense that accounts for his lack of concern with any precise definition of "group." David B. Truman, whose *The Governmental Process* (1951) is the finest product of the Bentley revival, was on firm Bentleyan ground when he agreed with John Dewey's remark that "associated activity needs no explanation; things are made that way."[4] We cannot look beneath or behind the notion of "group" in order to account for it. "Group" for Bentley is a categorial term, for it is presented as an indispensable and irreducible part of our understanding of society. Accordingly, Bentley, unlike most of his disciples, was not interested in attempting to draw precise distinctions among such notions as "group," "group activity," and "interest" (PG, 211). There is only one "thing" properly designated by such terms: "so many men bound together in or along the path of a certain activity." A great deal of confusion about Bentley's group interpretation would vanish if both his followers and his critics understood that he intended to exclude as categorially confused any standpoint from which we can *pose* the question of how "interests" cause the formation of "groups." The separation of "interest" and "group" is as untenable as the separation of "purpose" and "action" in the doctrines of social theorists who try to establish causal connections between mental properties and conduct (PG, 63).

If "interest" is understood as a "psychological quality" we cannot, according to Bentley, avoid the hopeless task of developing a causal theory of mental properties that prevents recognition of "interest" as the "valued activity" with which the group interpretation is concerned (PG, 213).

We should not be surprised that Bentley does not claim the authority of "science" for his discovery of groups. We do not learn from any social science that we should study groups. It is for this reason that he appeals to "any experienced reader" to determine the accuracy of his account of the "group process" in American politics (PG, 479). Although such a reader is not a social scientist, he may well be able to judge whether Bentley has chosen wisely the things that deserve scientific study. There is no fundamental contradiction between Bentley's scientific intentions and the prescientific knowledge with which he begins and to which he appeals. Leo Weinstein's criticism that Bentley betrays his scientific program by beginning with a "structured account" of political things is mistaken.[5]

Bentley's decision to begin his science with everyday or natural understanding admittedly makes it difficult to determine, as R. H. Dowling has noted, when he is referring to "group" as a theoretically specified notion and when he takes "group" in its everyday or political senses.[6] Additional difficulties result from the presence in the second part of the book of material written for the original version of *The Process of Government*. Although Bentley may have believed that his muckraking exposure of the roles of interest groups in the shaping of governmental policies could be combined with the methodological treatise he had finally decided to write, the reader is often required to shift from methodological to substantive accounts of groups without warning.

We have already seen that Bentley's primary concern was economics and that his book was intended as a preparation for an account of "economic life." It was clear that political groups are "built upon" certain "underlying groups," which means that the "political process" lies closer to the "surface of society" than the economic process (PG, 209). Bentley's use of the suggestive but problematic metaphor of "surface" and "depth" encourages the widespread but mistaken opinion that the group interpretation is simply a Progressive's or perhaps a sober liberal's version of the Marxist division of society into an economic base and a political superstructure. We have already seen that Bentley found Marxism deficient because it failed to furnish an adequate account of "intellectual life." Marxism, along with all other economic doctrines with which Bentley was acquainted, did not even provide an adequate account of "economic life."

Bentley's comments on the "underlying groups" are modest. He was convinced that so little was known about the "depths" of society that little could be safely said (PG, 460–64). We must stay close to the "surface" of society because we have little possibility to do otherwise. The "underlying conditions" of society include, but are not limited to, such factors as demographic characteristics, technology, and communications. Bentley excludes biological and environmental conditions because we cannot identify their supposed effects on human action independently of the action we want to explain by invoking them. Bentley does not tell us how these various conditions are related to each other or to those levels of society that lie metaphorically closer to us. In *Makers, Users, and Masters* Bentley refers to underlying conditions as the "deeper structure" of society but identifies only the range of skills he takes as necessary for the control of information in the economy of industrial capitalism as part of such a structure (MUM, 224). Clearly Bentley's "deeper structure" is not the material base of orthodox Marxism. Some of his candidates for membership in this structure are assigned to the superstructure by many Marxists. Moreover, he does not claim that any elements of the deeper structure or base of society are related to surface elements as causes are to effects.

My account of the group interpretation will concentrate on three leading ideas: "activity," "government," and "order." Each of these notions has been misunderstood by most students of Bentley. The explication of these ideas restores to the group interpretation the philosophic character inadequately recognized by latter-day group theorists.

Activity. The social scientist must recognize that the "raw materials" of his discipline are "actions" or "activities." The basic phenomenon of social science is "something doing" (PG, 175–77). Now Bentley does not say, as Weinstein incorrectly claims, that the only thing visible to us is "a constant flux, which, as action, carries no indicators of significance or relevance attached to itself."[7] In the first place, Bentley does not identify "raw materials" in any way that might suggest the sense data of traditional empiricism. The "activities" with which social science is concerned are not streams of sense data. In the second place, the social scientist's recognition of "something doing" is already an exhibition of intellectual activity and not a matter of the passive reception of sense data. In general, we may say that for Bentley the human epistemological predicament never begins with an absence of intelligibility of the sort Weinstein attributes to a "meaningless" flux of events. We could not recognize activities as such if this were the case.

For Bentley "there is not a shred of all the activity which does not present itself as an affair of feeling and intelligence. It cannot be stated with these phases left out" (PG, 179). Weinstein evidently ignores Bentley's requirement that we must "get our raw material before us in the form of purposive action, valued in terms of other purposive action." That is, Bentley proposes to begin with the "raw material" as "purposive activity." He thus establishes a categorial boundary for his social science which distinguishes it from simplistic empiricism. The group interpretation is presented as the best way to study the "meanings" that constituted the objects of social science. Students of Bentley who do not give sufficient attention to his agreement with the leading ideas of his German masters do not understand that the group interpretation continues that tradition of theorizing.

Social science cannot study activity properly through the study of individuals. Unlike social theorists who concentrate on "action" such as Talcott Parsons, Bentley was not interested in identifying types of "unit actions" predicable of individuals. In his useful survey, Paul F. Lazarsfeld formulates the central problem of the "empirical study of action" as follows: "A kind of conceptualization is needed that looks at the human being as a goal-pursuing entity whose activities are modified by his socii."[8] For Bentley, this formulation would have been unacceptable since it presupposes both the primacy of the individual and the dualism of "inner" and "outer."

Instead, we must understand "activity" in terms of "relations" among men, which requires a way of speaking about "many men together" which differs decisively from an idiom in which we are simply "adding man to man." Now Bentley does not mean to draw a conceptual distinction between human beings and relations that may exist among them. Indeed, our very knowledge of other persons discloses them "only as participants in such activity." Activities are the "cloth" from which "men in individual patterns are cut." While in an everyday sense groups of men are made up of "thinking and feeling actors," we know "ideas" and "feelings" only through the "medium of action." Failure to understand this condition of our knowledge reduces activity to a "mere abstract relation between given men" (PG, 175–77). That is, Bentley rejects the notion that social science can or should begin with propositions about individuals whose connections are somehow less "real" than their individuality. The distinction between "actor" and "action" is untenable for Bentley. We must see that "the activities are interlaced. That, however, is a bad manner of expression. For the interlacing itself is the activity. We have one great moving process to study, and of this great moving process it is impossible to state any part except as valued in terms of the other parts." Bentley's social science is intended to make this sort of statement possible.

In order to explore "activity" we must first distinguish it from bodily movement (PG, 184–85). We cannot explain social phenomena in terms of bodily movement. Bentley thus excludes explanations of the sort proposed by such later behaviorists as Clark L. Hull, who requires "an ideally adequate theory of even so-called purposive behavior . . . to begin with colorless movement and mere receptor impulses. . . ."[9] The heart of Bentley's argument can be found in his criticism of efforts to explain action in terms of some sort of "interior brain motion." Such an account, in Charles Taylor's terminology, is a "centralist" explanation of behavior that claims to explain behavior by invoking neurophysiological properties and laws.[10] In Bentley's view, a centralist explanation repeats the fundamental "error of the natural scientist who carries his points of view with all their crudities into a field in which they will not apply at all adequately till their crudities have been greatly diminished. . . . Following the error of everyday speech," a centralist explanation takes "brain motion" as a causal force. Bentley notes that we cannot study brain motion directly. The scientist infers the properties of neurophysiological processes from visible bodily motions. In turn, Bentley insists, these visible motions are only intelligible in terms of some social context. To speak strictly, there are no "colorless" movements of the human body since we do not and cannot observe movements as such but rather movements that are identifiable as movements of particular sorts or kinds. Thus, the social scientist has no interest in the motion of a limb as it traverses a certain arc, but is interested in threats, greetings, and the like. By reflecting on the necessary conditions for the identification and understanding of bodily movements we are led, in Bentley's words, to the "logical collapse" of reductionist explanations. A focus on "activity" gives us the standpoint from which the "unity of experience can best be appreciated," a remark that shows more clearly than many of Bentley's extended arguments the extent of his agreement with interpretive social science.

Bentley's notion of "activity" is intended to overcome the dichotomy of subjective and objective modes of social interpretation (PG, 180, 189). As an illustration he offers an analysis of policy making in a corporation. A subjective account would contain statements about the intentions, motives, beliefs, or dispositions of the members of the board of directors, while an objective account would invoke external causal factors or perhaps propositions from economic theory. For Bentley, we begin by taking the policy alternatives under consideration as expressions of the corporation's "contacts with the world around it" which are "reflected" by the directors in various ways. This sort of language seems to reintroduce both psychological explanation and causality, but Bentley asks us to overlook the "disreputable grammatical subject" and to "try to see the corporation activity streaming right through the directors toward realization on one line or another." If we can see in Bentley's fashion, we catch sight of the "social facts" and can describe the corporation's activities "without the misleading structure of hypothetical psychology in which it is ordinarily stated." The policy alternatives must be understood by Bentley's social science as "phases" of corporate activity rather than ideas or thoughts in the minds of the directors. While the policy alternatives are not "visible to the outer world" in any conventional sense of the term "visible," they are not, in Bentley's judgment, subjective.

On the objectivistic side, we err when we understand "activity" in terms of empirical generalizations taken as laws in the fashion of the natural sciences. Bentley's position resembles Weber's rejection of efforts to base history and the social sciences on an objective psychology containing general laws of behavior.[11] Curiously, since Bentley did not know Weber's work in 1908, the two theorists offer similar examples to illustrate their positions. For Weber, an account of the bubonic plague in England qualifies as "history" or belongs to the social sciences "only if its theoretical purpose is not the discovery of laws, e.g., bacteriological laws, but rather the causal explanation of cultural-historical 'facts.'" For Bentley, the activities of men affected by empty granaries, but not the drought responsible for this condition, belong to social science. That is, even if we concede that we have a science that articulates general laws, we do not thereby have reason to base our social science upon it. Unlike Weber, Bentley had no intention of seeking a causal explanation. He would not have agreed with Weber's position that an account of cultural-historical facts is "complete only when we have knowledge of a nexus into which *understandable* human action . . . fits, a nexus which is conceived as a determinant of behavior." Weber's aims are confused from a Bentleyan standpoint because he seeks a causal explanation for what he recognizes as understandable human action. Bentley would have required Weber to choose between searching for "causes" of action and accounting for "meanings." If the aim of a social science is not the discovery of general laws, then it must give up as well any search for a nexus that is conceived as a determinant of behavior.

The proper study of meaningful action requires abandonment of the subject/object dichotomy: "All distinctions between wants and the men who want, and the external acts of these men, and the institutions, or things done by them, and the external world in which these things are supposed to exist, when made concretely and treated as different kinds of 'things,' are very crude" (PG, 195). We err when we treat these "things" as "different parts of a machine" and establish causal relations among them. We cannot separate mental properties and meanings from the external world since "we ourselves, ideas and all, are a functioning part of that very outer world" (PG, 170). If we give ontological priority to either the inner or the outer world, we construct "a world out of the stuff that has definition only in terms of the very opposition we attempt to deny." Thus, when we seek to connect inner and outer by making them "function" together in a "causal system, we are putting two halves together which never possibly on causal lines can make one whole" (PG, 171).

The various distinctions Bentley criticizes may be employed by social science but not in a "concrete" manner. We must keep in mind Bentley's perspectivism. While "group" is a categorial term that designates persons bound together in activity, any classification of groups must be part of a scientific inquiry. In other words, there is no "natural" classification of groups. In Bentley's judgment, Marx, for example, claimed to have arrived at an "all-embracing classification" applicable to all modern societies. The class struggle as a concept is unintelligible apart from the notion that capitalists and workers make up a natural or fundamental classification (PG, 465). At best any such classification is the product of a specific scientific intention, the articulation of which should include recognition of its proper scope. In his reading notes, Bentley suggests that the Marxist class struggle is at best applicable to the conflict of estates in the *ancien régime* and has been extrapolated untenably to industrial societies.[12] Certainly it would be difficult on genuinely Bentleyan grounds to make absolute claims about the constitution of interest groups or to produce a definitive classification of such groups.

In one of his most revealing analogies, Bentley describes the perspectival freedom required by the group interpretation:

If we take all the men of our society, say the citizens of the United States, and look upon them as a spherical mass, we can pass an unlimited number of planes through the center of the sphere, each plane representing some principle of classification, say, race, various economic interests, religion, or language (though in practice we shall have to do mainly with much more specialized groupings than these). Now, if we take any one of these planes and ignore the others, we can group the whole mass of the sphere by means of an outline or diagram upon the circle which the plane makes by its intersection with the sphere, and by partition walls erected on this outline at right angles to the circle. Our principle of classification may include the whole population, or it may have to allow for a section of the population indifferent to it; but in the latter case can equally well be allowed for in the diagram. Similarly, by means of some other plane together with partition walls perpendicular to it, we can group the whole population on a different basis of classification: that is to say, for a different purpose. (PG, 207)

It is only from the perspectivist standpoint that we can grasp the mature social science for which Bentley's book is merely a preparation. He claims that "when the groups are adequately stated, everything is stated. When I say everything I mean everything. The complete description will mean the complete science, in the study of social phenomena, as in any other field" (PG, 208–9). Most interpreters of Bentley have taken this passage as either an extravagant self-advertisement or a proposal to collect large amounts of data and produce elaborate classifications of interest groups. Since Bentley was quite familiar with, but unimpressed by, contemporary efforts along those lines, this can hardly be what he intended. The "complete description" he took as the hallmark of "complete science" is not an exhaustive inventory of facts. We arrive at such a description by adopting a perspectival approach that refuses to take any facts or classes of facts as primary. Second, Bentley's "complete description" is intended to replace causality. Bentley does not claim to have provided such a description. He was not prepared to defend or explicate his notion of "complete description" in 1908. His book is both more and less modest than often supposed. While Bentley never asserts that he has produced his comprehensive social science, he claims to have brought to light the categories upon which it must be based.

Government. Bentley never makes clear how he moves from "activity" to his treatment of the "modern state." Presumably he believed that any sustained study of some other sort of political life than that exhibited in the modern state would be of little interest. That the group interpretation is somehow correlated with the modern state is suggested by his remark that a determinate classification of groups might be possible in societies characterized by such divisions as a "rigorous caste organization" or "very severe slavery." The contemporary student of politics is unlikely to be interested in such cases (PG, 206). Modern societies require the perspectival freedom of the group interpretation. The views of individuals on public issues are best understood in terms of the conflicts among groups to which they belong. Critics who charge Bentley with having produced a spurious general theory of groups from the peculiarities of American society are quite mistaken. If Bentley's vision is limited, then its boundaries are those of "modern" society.

Group activity rests "in a great sea of social life, of which it is but a slight modulation" (PG, 219–21). Bentley refers to the "habit background" which must be considered in the study of groups as a summary term for many, but not all, of the "conditions under which the groups operate." Evidently the habit background must be distinguished from the underlying conditions of society. Among the most important components of the habit background are the "rules of the game," often taken by ordinary men as "moral factors." Bentley insists that the habit background is not to be understood causally. His views are certainly not identical with those of social theorists who treat social conditions as the "causes" of behavior. His habit background resembles the notion of rule-governed social behavior advanced by such philosophers as Peter Winch, who insists that meaningful behavior is by definition rule-governed or involves rule-following, where rules are understood as "the standards governing life in the society."[13] By his use of "background," Bentley means to emphasize that for most men, most of the time, the conventions that may be said to "govern" conduct are not objects of inquiry or even always acknowledged.

We are now ready for Bentley's account of "government" (PG, 259–64). Political phenomena are not identical with "government." They may be taken to have wider application as when we properly describe the activities of a political party as "political" but distinguish the party from "government." In turn, "government" may have wider application when we limit the meaning of "political" to activities of "organized" government and extend the meaning of "government" beyond formal organizations. Bentley establishes a range of meanings for "government." In its most general sense "government" is the "process of the adjustment of a set of interest groups in a particular . . . system without any differentiated activity, or 'organ,' to center attention on just what is happening." This sort of adjustment and hence "government" may be found in societies with no formal governmental structures. In its most narrow meaning, "government" refers to a "differentiated" structure that performs "specified governing functions." Bentley's third or "intermediate" sense of "government" lies beyond the limits of differentiated "governing activities" among those phenomena that are "specialized with reference to government," such as political parties, movements, and the like. That is, "government" in this sense refers to all activities that are relevant to the differentiated structure of his narrowest definition. For example, when the directors of a corporation turn from their "ordinary business" to a discussion of the corporation's role in a political campaign, their activity which a "moment before was industrial or economic, then becomes at once political" and falls under the heading of a study of the process of government. Bentley does not claim that all, but merely some, of the corporation's activities are political. If the operations of nominally nongovernmental organizations come to resemble those of government in his narrowest sense, it may be necessary to develop yet a fourth sense of "government," but Bentley does little in the text with this possibility. For convenience, he proposes to call the "differentiated" or narrow government the "government" and the intermediate range of groups and activities the "process of government."

The activities traditionally classified under the term "state" fall into his third sense of "government." The only advantage of the traditional term is that it allows us to distinguish the "politically organized society" from activities belonging to the "possible fourth sense" of government he has mentioned. That is, we may make a distinction between all activities relevant to "government" and all activities of nongovernmental groups that formally resemble "government." Bentley admits that if his intention had been to "restate theoretical political science" his treatment of the "state" concedes the merits of the traditional concept. Bentley is rarely as conciliatory to those who may use the traditional political vocabulary. He is less respectful of "sovereignty," which he takes as a polemical and not a scientific notion. Nowhere in the modern society or state can we find a locus of sovereignty in the traditional sense. Thus, it is unsuitable for social science since "there is no advantage in trying to sail the clouds in a cartoonist's airship."

For Bentley the "phenomena of government are from start to finish phenomena of force" (PG, 258–59). This claim is qualified in the very next sentence of the text where he repeats an argument from his notes that "force" is a "metaphysical" concept and does not belong in a "positive" social science.[14] One of his early titles for the manuscript had been "The Forces of Government & Their Control," but he came to doubt the worth of "force" as a concept because it carried too many dubious associations with physics. Moreover, use of "force" encouraged the view that "non-force factors of a sympathetic or moral or ideal nature" had no role to play in politics. The criticism that Bentley presents a "social physics" clearly has to contend with Bentley's own appraisal of his strategy. Bentley settled on "pressure" to encompass both force and fraud or to summarize all the actual or possible "techniques" employed in politics. His frequent use of "force" in the face of his disclaimer is an example of the rhetorical exaggeration he admits is present in his book (PG, 434–44). He knows that his treatment of the operation of groups is one sided in some respects but prefers this excess as a counter to the "ordinary point of view" which he insists invests governmental institutions and principles with specious autonomy.

Order. Bentley insists that the "balance" of group pressures simply "*is* the existing state of society" (PG, 219). Since he has been criticized for having given "absolution" to the group struggle, it must be noted that he does not claim that this "balance" is good or even that it furnishes a criterion for judgments of good and evil in politics. In later terms, Bentley's notion of "order" reflects a "functionalist" understanding. For example, he argues that we cannot understand marriage as a social practice except in terms of group interests (PG, 264–70). Human beings do not mate in the statistically random fashion we would observe if their behavior were governed by some combination of biological drives and individual choices. If there are aggregate regularities in marriage behavior, such as persons marrying within their own ethnic groups, there must be a sense in which marriage is a particular "organization of the interests, held in position by effective groups."

Although he provides sketches of functionalist explanations of social practices, Bentley never offers a clear account of functionalism in *The Process of Government*. His comments on "order" must suffice. Society appears as a constantly changing "ordering of the interests" (PG, 267). Regardless of the extent of change, "order is bound to result, because order is now and order has been, where order is needed, though all prophets be confounded." Weinstein is one of the few students of Bentley who had drawn attention to the notion of "order."[15] In his view, Bentley is guilty either of "unwarranted hopefulness" or "question-begging circularity" since we do not know "what particular system or order is assumed" by the group interpretation.

Bentley's understanding of "order" differs decisively from that presupposed in Weinstein's criticism. For Bentley, "order" is not a "normative" term. His functional descriptions make no reference to such conditions as "harmony" or the absence of conflict. Bentley's order resembles the nominally ethically neutral notion of "equilibrium" in economics. There is no room for "disorder" in a Bentleyan social science. Thus, we should not expect to find a "particular system or order" in this teaching. All the activity that constitutes the raw material of social science is ordered. We call some things or conditions disorderly only because we employ a partial or distorted perspective. Bentley writes:

It is of the very definition of activity that it is systematized. Even the simplest motion with which the physicist deals is part of a system of motion. When the geometrician gives position to a point, he admits system. In living beings there is no function that is not systematized. Behavior is a word biologists are now using of the very simplest reactions of the simplest organisms, and except as system it cannot be comprehended at all. All the actions that enter into the behavior of an idiot are correlated, much more all the activities of a mentally competent person. True enough, we can choose many special points of view from which we will say that a certain lot of activity is not systematized, but here we are merely adopting a group's position as our own position from which to view the world, and we are judging along the lines of that group's activity; and the denial of systematization so uttered is a limited denial of a limited form of system, no matter how vehemently or how absolutely phrased. (PG, 285)

In social science, this notion of "order" requires us to recognize, for example, that even the "lowest of despised castes" and the "worst abused" of slaves are not excluded from the systematized activities of groups. There can be no genuine "deviance" and no social element that is not a part of society. Thus, while in an ordinary sense of the term the Russian revolutionaries of 1905 were trying to destroy the Russian "constitution," in the sense of Bentley's social science they were trying to bring about a new systematization of group relations. "Constitution" in Bentley's sense is almost identical with the relations of groups. He agrees with Ferdinand Lasalle's remark that "king, cannon, noblemen, capitalists, all are parts of the constitution—and working-men as well" (PG, 246).

Bentley praises Georg Simmel as a social theorist whose teaching points toward his own science for the "mental power or delicacy" of his analyses (PG, 472–73). Simmel's accomplishment had been to develop an "analysis of the groups which cross one another in a thousand directions in the social mass, and at whose intersections 'personality' and 'individuality' . . . are to be found." He seeks the "typical forms in which group relations occur." Indeed, Bentley goes as far as to say that "almost all the typical social relations—and very many others besides—which have been discussed in this book will be found treated by Simmel, some of them in the most highly suggestive way." Bentley's own "complete description" and his nonevaluative notion of "order" are not far removed from Simmel's efforts to produce a comprehensive account of social forms.

Simmel's formal sociology failed because it still relied upon notions about the nature of the individual. A "psychological content," in Bentley's words, seems to "intrude" into analyses of "social forms and structures." Bentley rejected Simmel's efforts to account for "spiritual structures" such as language, morals, religion, law, and state in terms of the contents of "personal minds." Simmel fails to "allow his own group process full sweep" since he has forgotten "his own demonstration that individuality occurs where the group lines cross" and "uses all sorts of fragments of individuality as material of explanation." Thus, Bentley charges Simmel with having failed to live up to his own methodological teaching which, in his words, was supposed to elevate the "category" over the "material."[16] In Simmel's formula we have as well a concise summary of Bentley's teaching.

The Group Theory and American Politics

Bentley's application of his views to the study of American government and politics contains an implicit challenge to defenders of traditional positions to refute the thesis that any policy or action of government must be linked to an underlying pattern of group activities. His arguments in the chapters of the text concerned with political institutions are often contrived, for they are usually directed against extravagantly naive versions of moralistic understandings of politics. In this section I will consider only the most important of Bentley's observations that strive for some degree of theoretical generality. In order, I will discuss his views of the executive branch, the legislature, law and the judiciary, and democracy.

The executive. In each of his discussions of institutions, Bentley's strategy is to show that the conduct of an institution is ultimately intelligible in terms of the "pressures" brought to bear on it by groups. His treatment of the executive is distinguished by its historical and comparative themes. Not all societies have an executive. Where groups are few and relatively well adjusted, i.e., have fairly stable relations, group oppositions may be mediated without a highly developed executive institution. Even if a king or chief exists, he will not have the types or range of powers nominally available to the modern executive. These powers must be understood as the result of the complex and turbulent universe of groups typically found in modern society. It is interesting that, when a society is not only simple but small, the adjustment of groups may result from processes that approximate the "reasoning" praised by political philosophers. Government by "argument," to the extent that it has ever existed, depends upon factors other than argument. Circumstance, not design, gives men the rare opportunity to conduct their political affairs by means of debate. The ancient city at its best allowed this opportunity, which was furnished by a relatively high level of agreement among its citizens and the ever-present threat of war with other cities. War, either possible or actual, is an important support for the politics of argument. Bentley is tempted to "call this kind of government very highly developed in contrast with our great modern states, but such a way of putting it would easily give a false impression, and, moreover, it is a type of judgment which one should be most cautious in making" (PG, 331–32). Such a government can be described as "very highly developed" because while there is "enough structure to prevent confusion" the structure is unable to "misrepresent large elements in the society or to block the activity." More-over, the stability of such a government is aided by the possibility that disaffected elements can emigrate.

As a preface to his study of the American presidency, Bentley examines despotism. His comments on Russia and on ancient tyrannies express his sanguine, if not precisely favorable, view of despotism. The crisis in Russia is simply a "monster spectacle of the conflict of the interest groups" (PG, 335–37). The czars have failed to mediate the conflicts among large and small landholders, landless peasants, capitalists, and workers. Bentley's hopes for the success of the Duma are guarded and he writes that Russia may "require a new despotism, this time representing some other element than the land-holding class most directly." If this new despotism appears, it will be followed by a "better-balanced governmental structure." Bentley appeals to the role played by revolution in the "history of English liberties" as a point of comparison.

Bentley argues that criticisms of ancient tyrannies such as those of Theagenes of Megara or Nero as instances of "unscrupulous ambition" are "thin and meaningless" when we consider their achievements. According to Bentley, the Greek tyrannies overthrew oligarchies that had ceased to provide "channels" for the expression of group interests, while the Roman emperors appeared when "the provinces were being brutally abused by the richer classes of Rome and the poorer classes were systematically bribed into assent." The "very moment that imperial authority was established, the provinces were more humanely treated." Accordingly, "the ordinary description even of a Nero in terms of morals and personal character is a pitiable caricature. Nero was beloved in the provinces and there was good reason for it" (PG, 338–39).

According to American theory, the executive was supposed to stand above politics, serve as a symbol of national unity, control the excesses of Congress and execute the law. In reality the office has always represented shifting constellations of interests. The history of the presidency has been a "history of the interests which chose it as their best medium of expression when they found other pathways blocked" (PG, 344). Bentley examines Theodore Roosevelt's presidency at some length as a case study to show that Roosevelt's beliefs or ideas have little to do with his activities. Indeed, the president is best understood not as a person but in terms of a "certain number of millions of American citizens tending in certain directions" (PG, 347–49). Roosevelt came to power as the result of the condition of

Congress and the judiciary as vehicles for business interests. Opposing interests, unable to gain access to any other part of the government effectively, temporarily coalesced behind Roosevelt. With a certain amount of access to government secured, the pressures that had taken the form of a moralistic crusade for "good government" diminished. The result was that Roosevelt, like any other president, did not make fundamental changes in the distribution of power and privilege in American society.

The legislature. According to Bentley, the group interpretation provides a simple principle for the study of legislatures. All legislatures originate in and derive their character from the class or group interests present in society. The development of legislatures traces a path from "class" to "group" representation. In no sense is it useful to describe the legislature as the instrument or embodiment of a "social will." His comments are directed against those who suppose that legislatures exhibit a "pure public spirit" which allows their members to deliberate in "Jovian calm" on the public good. Since there "is nothing which is best literally for the whole people," or no public good properly so-called, legislatures can hardly deliberate about it (PG, 370–72).

Now Bentley does not mean to suggest that the legislative process is a struggle without limits. While that process cannot be concerned with an illusory public good, it still goes on within limits established by the habit background. Both the "techniques" of struggle and the "group demands" themselves derive their character from the habit background. These limits can be known only by "empirical observation for the given time and country." The very notion of a "struggle" has "meaning only with reference to its limitations" (PG, 372).

Law and judiciary. Bentley's account of law places him firmly within the camp of "legal realism." Law is not intelligible on its own terms. He would prefer to refrain from speaking of "law" as if it had an independent status at all, for he claims it is best understood as a "forming, a systematization, a struggle, an adaptation, of group interests (PG, 272). There is a form or variant of "law" that corresponds roughly with each sense of "government." The counterpart of government in its broadest sense was formerly called "law" but Bentley believes that current usage has replaced this sense of "law" with "custom." Statutory law and common law correspond to government in its narrowest sense, while proposals for laws, not laws themselves, correspond to the intermediate sense of government.

The scientific study of the "law process" requires us to dispense with traditional modes of legal thinking. "At bottom" the law is only "what the mass of the people actually does and tends to some extent to make other people do by means of governmental agencies." Law is not limited to statutes or even to the decisions of courts or legislatures. A proper account of law must consider the full range of activities by which men in groups affect the behavior of one another. Whether or not any given law is enforced, obeyed, or respected depends upon group relations.

From this standpoint it is obvious that Bentley has little use for "legal theory" (PG, 395–97). He acknowledges that "philosophy of law" is less directly related to the group struggle than other varieties of law, but this makes it even less interesting than if it were otherwise. Constitutional principles and the standards of legal argument are closer to the group process, while the positions taken by disputants reflect groups most directly. Bentley does not claim to be able to establish a point-for-point correspondence between group relations and pressures and legal doctrines. Insofar as possible, social science should try to establish whatever relation is warranted between group pressures and law through a study of the judiciary as an interest group. Jurists as an interest group can then be shown in their relations with the rest of the interest groups.

Democracy. For Bentley the fundamental theory of political science is that the conduct of government should result from reasoning divorced from considerations of interest (PG, 434–44). That is, political science in his judgment is inextricably involved with a substantive teaching about government. It is important to note that Bentley did not consider any of his works as contributions to political science. *The Process of Government* is a work of sociology or a prelude to a work of economics. Against the teaching of political science, he claims that the activities of groups not only "make but also maintain in value the very standards of justice, truth, or what not that reason may claim to use as its guide." Bentley proposes to discuss democracy, representative government, and popular sovereignty in terms of this claim.

In the first place, there was never a period in American history, let alone the history of any other nation, in which "the people" have ruled. Bentley distances himself from conspiratorial readings of American history by observing that legislative bodies are catholic in their plasticity to pressures. There is certainly nothing in Bentley's analysis that limits successful pressure politics to the wealthy. Other elements of society may well have resources they can mobilize for their own advantage. The notion of "popular control" is notoriously imprecise. It is merely one aspect of the process of "control" as such. What is really indicated by such slogans as "popular control" or "rule by the people" is a reaction by large numbers of men against some ruling minority. That is, the notion of popular sovereignty is on the face of it a matter of group politics. To the extent that such control exists, it is "composed of habitual reactions which are adjustments forced by large, united weak interests upon less numerous, but relative to the number of adherents, more intense interests." A government is controlled by the people when the many are able to force the few to take them into account. Now Bentley knows this is hardly what proponents of democracy have in mind. As a self-consciously realistic student of American politics, however, he believes that "representative government" is sustained in the United States by a mixture of formal and informal practices belonging to the "habit background" of American society. He is aware, of course, that Progressives and others have proposed a variety of methods of control such as the initiative, recall, referendum, direct primaries, and proportional representation. While these proposals are made in the name of popular control and advanced as ways of democratizing the American political system, Bentley can find no intelligible connection between them and any so-called public interest. Indeed, from the standpoint of the group interpretation, proponents of these reforms must be understood as constituting identifiable interests. Now Bentley does not mean that reformers are simply advancing these proposals for their own economic gain. The group interpretation does not offer a crypto-Marxist explanation for Progressive reformism. The interests brought to light by the group interpretation are not always "economic" interests as these are conventionally understood. What Bentley insists upon is that while a Progressive may advocate reforms in order to achieve "good government," the standpoint from which he understands what is meant by such a government is always a particular standpoint. He cannot properly be understood to articulate the "public interest" since there is and can be no such general interest.

No matter what sort of classification of governments is employed, Bentley remarks in connection with Aristotle's typology, what is actually observed is the "perverted" or "abnormal" form of government (PG, 298). There would appear to be no standard of goodness for Bentley since he seems to discount the use of a notion of goodness even in order to bring to light the true character of perverted regimes. Bentley recognizes that recent political thinkers claim to trace a pattern of historical development from "despotism" to "democracy," a claim based on numerous "hopelessly inexact" premises. Bentley does not offer his own classification but attempts rather to make clear what must be done in order to classify governments properly.

What Bentley proposes is that political theorists recognize the importance of a multiplicity of groups in all but the simplest societies. This recognition will help the student of politics to avoid schemes that classify governments abstractly. Moreover, the same formal institutions may well have different meanings in different societies according to the nature of the groups that currently play a decisive role in their operation. Thus far, it would seem that Bentley encourages us to ignore or disregard formal governmental institutions. This "realistic" injunction has been taken by some of Bentley's followers as a liberation from the confines of a shadowy but evidently stultifying "legalism" or "formalism."[17] Bentley's own teaching, however, is not one sided. He draws our attention to the opposite error of concentrating on the play of interests as the principle according to which governments should be classified (PG, 301). Thus, we may be tempted to measure the degree of smoothness or friction in the "adjustment" of groups and develop a uniform comparative scale of degrees of adjustment. The next step in what Bentley takes to be such a dubious undertaking is to assume that there are necessary connections between "degrees of perfection of adjustment" and types of government. In principle, many types of governments could meet Aristotle's requirement that a "good" government rules in the public interest (assuming for the sake of argument that we could speak properly of such an interest) (PG, 310–13). That is, such a government need not exhibit a high degree of adjustment among groups. It is rather the case, Bentley claims, that a high degree of adjustment has less to do with the type of government than with the extent to which human activities are simple and uniform. For Bentley this means we cannot rank the varieties of human society on scales of degrees of perfection theorized in terms of adjustment. Such rankings are possible only within sets of societies that have similar degrees of complexity and differentiation and which, in consequence, have similar arrangements of interests and groups. Critics who charge Bentley with an unreflective acceptance of the reconciliatory political formulas of liberal pluralism fail to consider his explicit refusal to define what is politically good in terms of a balancing or adjustment of the claims of interests. Moreover he does not argue that a particular arrangement of groups and institutions is superior to others in securing adjustment. A comparison of governments begins with the notion that we must understand the institutions of government in terms of the interests that are "functioning through them." The next step must be to "avoid letting any system of standards of good whatsoever serve as a test, except so far as those standards are merely the direct and immediate reflection in each particular case of the group process" within the government. While we may certainly ask whether or not Bentley succeeded in understanding each regime as it understands itself apart from any standard of good, we must acknowledge his intention to avoid the sort of ideological parochialism for which he has been criticized.

Bentley applies his teaching to what he takes to be the problem of "despotism." He does not make clear why he takes despotism to be a problem of the "greatest importance" (PG, 305–6). For the sake of convenience, Bentley distinguishes between governments in which a single individual concerns himself with the resolution of every "group antagonism" and those in which "every interest would be able to find a technique for organizing and expressing itself." These are the polar types of "pure despotism" and "pure democracy." Bentley's point is that if either of these "absurd" ideal types of government were realized, the result would be the same. Groups would still operate. Regardless of the claims of the despot, he cannot rule as a single individual. His rule rests upon and is a reflection of the structure of group relations. By the same token, no matter how "democratic" a government seems to be, its power rests upon the structure of group relations. Moreover, "pure democracy" is inconceivable for there will be interests that do not find expression. For both ideal types of regime, the "transformations" of interests create problems. The universe of groups is restless. While the "process of representation" in despotisms may be distinguished from its counterpart in democracies both quantitatively and in terms of organizational "techniques," there is no "deeper 'qualitative' way" in which despotism may be distinguished from democracy (PG, 315).

There is no pattern of progressive social evolution from despotism to democracy. The confidence with which some political thinkers proclaim the emergence of democracy from the darkness of unlimited rule stands exposed for the myth Bentley believes it to be. What students of politics mistakenly believe to be a difference between unlimited and limited governments is actually the result of differences in the structure of group relations. The differences among governments are not essentially differences of principle but rather "differences of technique for the functioning of the interests" that are "adopted because of group needs" and "will continue to be changed in accordance with group needs" (PG, 320). Since governments are, in Bentley's view, everywhere and always representative of the structure of group relations, there is for him no decisive or qualitative difference between democracy and other forms of government. Every government is, therefore, more or less absolute or more or less limited depending upon the vantage point afforded by specific groups and interests.

Values, Interests, and Social Science

Bentley's political teaching, which claims to be compatible with, if not precisely the result of, his new social science, departs from the "ideas" visible as the "surface" of society at which he proposes to begin. This departure consists in Bentley's claim that "values" cannot properly be understood in their own terms. Political opinions, notions of the "public interest," legal philosophies, and the like are all "expressions" or "reflections" of the group process. At the very least this opinion requires us to refuse to take such doctrines at face value. For Leo Weinstein the most important difficulties or contradictions in Bentley's teaching come to light when we recognize that for Bentley the group interpretation itself must be understood in the same way. Other criticisms of the group interpretation—that it furnishes no "operational" criteria for the study of groups, that it does not show social scientists how to study the attitudes of members of groups, that it does not permit prediction and that it does not advance the comparative study of group politics—seem to me misplaced because they apply to Bentley's position notions of scientific explanation with which he disagreed.[18] Because Weinstein takes seriously Bentley's intention to develop a new social science, his criticism is at least based upon a close reading of *The Process of Government* which does not confuse Bentley's aims with those of present-day political scientists.

The teaching that political "values" are reflections of "interests" does not distinguish Bentley's position from any other tough-minded or realistic social science. Bentley claims that his "tool," or the group interpretation, indeed his social science as a whole, is a reflection of the group process:

> When a man writes a book to advance some particular theory about society, he reflects in it a certain phase of the social process, more or less truly. If his book has any bearing, however remote, on political life, it falls within the field before us. Now the reflection of a phase of the social process is the same thing as the reflection of some group interest or set of group interests. His "theory" is such a reflection. It is such an act of "representation." (PG, 428)

Fully aware of the "citizen or partisan orientation" undeniably present in Bentley's book, Weinstein argues that the thesis that any social theory, such as the group interpretation, is a reflection of its subject matter cannot be combined with either reformism or science without contradiction. If every theory is a reflection of interests, "there is no autonomy for reason, not even for the reason which seeks to set this conclusion before us." Bentley seems to face the following dilemma:

> His view of himself and of all other men as group-bound and group-determined in their views does not furnish a basis for discovering the difference between genuine reform and mere random change, or between accurate and inaccurate statements of relevant political problems. More significantly, the group-reflection argument also destroys the possibility of that science of social interpretation which Bentley alternatively presents as his guiding purpose. If description and analysis cannot reasonably seek to be objective, or if the pursuit of objectivity is known in advance to be a futile quest, we are offered an invitation to a Babel where many interests replace many tongues as the insuperable barrier to the erection of a tower of human achievement, whether of scientific description or of practical reform.[19]

In Weinstein's opinion, Bentley's position resembles that of the sociology of knowledge except that Bentley, with greater consistency than Karl Mannheim, does not allow a privileged position for "socially unattached intelligentsia."[20] Nor, it must be added, does Bentley, even in his first book, exhibit a tendency, as Mannheim does, to qualify the application of the "group-reflection argument" to scientific discourse.[21] It is obvious, however, that Bentley also claims that the group interpretation is a better social theory than any other. Moreover, he asserts that the "value and meaning" of a social theory is related to the accuracy with which it reflects the group process. Finally, he believes that even "the most accurate reflection has value only as process through which the underlying interests work somewhat more smoothly," which appears to suggest that social theories should serve the ends of reconciliation (PG, 479). Since Bentley has argued at great length and with great vehemence against such notions as the "public interest," we are forced to wonder how he can appear to speak of the smooth working of interests. That is, we must ask the question, Reconciliation in terms of *what*?

I believe that while Bentley's Progressive political opinions are evident in his identification of social problems, the disclosure of his opinions does not resolve the questions raised by Weinstein. In the first place, Bentley explicitly refuses to define such terms as "reflect," "represent," and "mediate," all of which he uses interchangeably in *The Process of Government* (PG, 177). He thus encourages the misleading impression that he proposes to *reduce* "values" to "interests" in the fashion of social scientists who understand values as "rationalizations" for interests. This is not Bentley's intention, since he argues that the proper study of values and indeed of all social phenomena cannot be conducted through the study of mental processes. This is why he insists on the primacy of "activity," which properly designates "many men together." "Activity," then, is the condition for the social scientist's knowledge of human beings. We do not and indeed cannot properly be said to know a human being apart from the activity in which he is involved (PG, 176). Bentley's rejection of mental states and processes as the causes of behavior is linked with his understanding of activity in his claim that "the individual stated for himself, and invested with an extra-social unity of his own, is a fiction" (PG, 215). We are thus led on Bentleyan grounds to doubt the intelligibility of any doctrine claiming that values or ideas can be anything other than expressions or reflections of the group process since they can have no other possible status.

Now even the self-knowledge of the social scientist on this view is a matter of his inextricable involvement in activity (PG, 187). From this understanding we can perhaps see why Bentley insists that the theories or doctrines of the social scientist are collective products. Scientific discourse, we may say, cannot properly be understood as the product of the isolated mind of the scientist. If individuals have no "extra-social unity," the theories they propose are not and cannot be subjective products. It is possible to formulate Bentley's thesis more precisely than he was able to state it in 1908: ideas are properly understood as expressions or reflections of activity because individuals are properly understood as exhibitions of activity.

Bentley is able to link this thesis, which may be understood as the decisive teaching of the first part of his book, with the group interpretation by identifying or equating "activity," "group," and "interest." We will recall that for him it is categorially absurd to ask whether or how "interests" cause the formation of "groups." This notion may be clarified with a brief glance at his distinction between "discussion" and "organization" groups (PG, 428–33). Bentley recognizes that the group interpretation may be misunderstood as an approach that concentrates on formal or organized interest groups in a conventional sense and thus fails to see that such groups may well originate in the actions of men who share certain beliefs. Since he does not want us to suppose that such "discussion" groups occupy an intermediate stage between the underlying "conditions" of action and the action of more organized groups, he offers the following description of the links between "discussion" and "organization":

> We might picture the process as a flowing stream in which a perpendicular cross-section would represent the discussion phase and a horizontal cross-section the organization phase. Sometimes passing through a narrow channel we have a very deep narrow stream, and the perpendicular cross-section—the discussion—seems to be the whole nature of the happening; again the stream spreads out on a broad level surface, and the organization phase seems so complete that the perpendicular aspect . . . seems negligible. But such a picture is exceedingly crude, however well it may serve to bring out this one aspect of the relationship. We have not a single flowing stream, but a mass of myriads of currents, plastic rather than liquid, and leaving thousand-fold shapes and forms both of discussion and organization differentiated along its course. (PG, 435)

Since we have already seen that Bentley is opposed to causal explanations in social science, it is clear that a metaphorical account such as this is intended in part to suggest the failure of causal explanations. Activity and group, taken as "phases," cannot be linked as cause and effect, just as we cannot link "interest" and group. Thus, "group" and "interest" are equivalent (PG, 211). Now when Bentley asserts that a social theorist is "reflecting" some "group interest or set of group interests," this need not mean that "interest" is restricted to "material" or "economic" considerations. As we have seen, Bentley rejected what he took to be the Marxist understanding of economic determinism. There is undeniably ample evidence that he uses "interest" in its conventional political sense in his book. He also uses "interest" as a categorial term to designate what he takes to be a pervasive and undeniable fact about human beings. His implicit challenge, then, is for us to identify any "thought" that is not a representation of *some* "interest." It is not quite correct to say as Weinstein does that Bentley is "engaged throughout in a dispute with the view that thought rules the world" or with the view that ideas or values lie at the roots of political actions.[22] Rather, Bentley claims to have sketched the outlines of a new social science that accounts for the role of "thought" by exhibiting its status as a phase of activity. Moreover, Bentley can find no justification for exempting that science from the account it furnishes or claims to furnish of connections between activity and thought.

The nerve of Weinstein's criticism of Bentley has to do with the notion of "objectivity." A social science or for that matter a political teaching such as Progressive reformism that cannot on its own terms strive for "objectivity" is doomed, we may say, to either silence or confusion. We have seen that Bentley's notion of "activity" was intended to undercut the dichotomy of subjective and objective modes of social interpretation (PG, 180, 189). In addition, he understands the emergence of social theories based on the former mode of interpretation as intelligible reactions against the deficiencies of theories based solely on the latter mode of interpretation (PG, 135). This sense of "objectivity," of course, differs from Weinstein's. For Weinstein Bentley's teaching is incoherent if it combines the "group-reflection" thesis with the thesis that it is more accurate than other teachings. For Bentley, the accuracy or validity of the group interpretation is identical with the extent to which that theory methodically avoids presuppositions. We will recall that the common denominator of Bentley's criticisms of the work of other social theorists is that they allowed presuppositions about the nature or character of individuals to determine the course of their inquiries. The group interpretation can be both a reflection of its subject matter and more accurate than any other account if it strives to eliminate individuals or properties predicated of individuals as a foundation for its work.

Now it is not the case that any of Bentley's arguments show the impossibility of articulating any notion of the "public interest" or "public good." As Weinstein rightly notes, Bentley not only offers numerous examples of his own view of the public interest but fails to show that we can dismiss as nonexistent any notion of the public interest simply by exhibiting the scope or intensity of political disagreements and conflict.[23] That is, from the admitted existence of numerous and opposed understandings of the public good Bentley has not shown the unintelligibility of the notion of the public good but has at the most shown either that there is no single group that has an adequate knowledge of this good or that participants in the group process do not have an adequate understanding of what is required in order to have such knowledge. He has not even shown that there is any contradiction between the intelligibility of this good and the undeniable fact of "interest," since it is conceivable that the public good could be an object of interest even in Bentley's sense.

We must turn to the unpublished "Makers, Users, and Masters" to conclude these remarks on the role of values in Bentley's teaching. In the introduction to that work he explains the necessity for his theory of reflection: "Whoever we are, whatever we say or do, we express some special phase of the process. We are not supermen. No more are we absolutely individual men. We are representatives, chosen not by popular ballot, but constituted as such by the requirements of thought and expression" (MUM, 3). That is, since thought is possible only in and through what Bentley had identified in the mid-1890s as "language-forms," which are obviously collective or public in character, our discourse is always "representative."

In "Makers, Users, and Masters" Bentley explicitly identifies his position with the interests of the middle class to which he belonged. The theme of that work is that American society is becoming dominated by increasing concentrations of wealth, property, and control of industry and finance. Bentley combines something of the polemical vigor of Veblen with a magisterial command of quantitative material in the fashion of institutionalist economists like John R. Commons to produce a portrait of post–World War I American society at the breaking point. Industrial capitalism had expanded without significant opposition from Reconstruction until the world war. The worldwide economic consequences of that war had demonstrated the fragility of the system. To avoid a catastrophic proletarian revolution, which would probably provoke an even worse reaction by industrial capitalism, Bentley proposes a middle-class "counterrevolution" which would make use of the "ordinary methods of political government in accordance with the old standards and tests" to control and regulate, but not destroy, American business (MUM, 70, 282). This counterrevolution would encourage the growth of co-operatives, small business, a guaranteed minimum income, and the expansion of public-works projects to aid the unemployed workers. A new National Property Rights Party should be created by uniting nonpartisan pressure groups. The American industrial and financial system must be regulated during peace as it was during the war. Its "deeper structure"—the range of skills needed to organize energy and information—can be controlled by a politically organized middle class. Bentley describes his program as revolutionary but possible, since it does not require changes in the "habits and character" of the citizen but rather simply requires him to become enlightened about his position as "maker" and as "user" in the American economy (MUM, 279).

It is impossible to read "Makers, Users, and Masters" as anything other than a proposal for changes Bentley took to be in the public interest. He writes that men are both "adventurers" and sharers in the "common weal." They have aspirations for success and needs for stability. Unrestricted industrial capitalism threatens these aspirations and needs. The changes he proposes would be, he claims, much less drastic than either the subtle changes to which Americans have gradually submitted themselves in the face of corporate power or the changes that must follow either an "autocratic industrial dictatorship or convulsive proletarian revolution" (MUM, 273). Bentley does not believe that his own middle-class interest prevents him from examining these issues with "maximum coldness," as "free as possible from prejudice arising from any special class relationship or from any standard of sympathy or ethics" (MUM, 7). The political teaching of Bentley's massive exercise in muckraking is consistent with his belief that the group process has no terminus or final condition of stability toward which it is tending (PG, 359). For him, however, some conditions of equilibrium are preferable to others.

Nearly twenty years after the appearance of *The Process of Government* Bentley recommends to us that we gain "knowledge of our group attachments and their relativities" or their meanings within the context of the group process as the key to the "virile peace" of which "we all most despair in the hidden parts of our lives, while our values are given us in darkness" (RMS, 199). Bentley's social science does not teach us what we should value but rather assists us in learning our place in society. This knowledge, in turn, Bentley suggests may bring humility. He would later define a humanist as a man "who strips off the arrogance of excessively solipsistic individuality and who seeks for his fellows and himself harmonious living as himself natural within a natural world."[24] The group interpretation and *The Process of Government* as a whole show their limitations in their failure to address the question of what is "natural." For Bentley the path to this knowledge led beyond the confines of social science.

5

Social Science
and the Problem of Knowledge

Science has before it as a matter of direct investigation "minds" which are not only found embodied in an organized, environing world (that world including both the organism that bears the mind, and the organism's own environment) but which are seen to have evolved in that world and which are seen to function in it and nowhere else. On the other hand, having abandoned its first crude guess of inert minds and energetic matter, science finds itself more and more closely facing a world to investigate which it can allege to exist, and which it can give reality to, only as it is known to and tested by those very "minds" which are comprehended in it. It is the problem of a world existing only in mind and yet of mind existing only in the world . . . which is the very essence of the problem of knowledge today.
"Knowledge and Society"

Few scholars have concerned themselves with the period from the death of Bentley's father in 1908 to his resumption of extensive writing in the 1920s. These years were a time for him to rethink the basic issues in social science. He turned to the study of developments in philosophy, logic, the natural sciences, and psychology. The problems of social science could not be stated properly, much less solved, so long as they were not linked up with fundamental issues in other branches of science. Gradually Bentley began to think in terms of a substratum of foundational problems in scientific inquiry which was visible with various degrees of clarity in various sciences. His course was agonizingly slow, for he had to reject the self-confident view of many social scientists that their disciplines could be made scientific by imitating the quantitative methods of the natural sciences. For Bentley the social sciences had hardly begun their journey. The majority of American social scientists were not prepared to address the problem of knowledge, which Bentley found at the core of all areas of science. His retreat to Paoli and the course of reflection he began took him further than ever before from the concerns of his contemporaries in the social sciences.

My first topic in this chapter is Bentley's seldom-read essay "Knowledge and Society" (1910), which is one of the most impressive statements of his agenda. Nearly forty years later he still considered it a suitable statement of a number of his views, an unusual judgment for a thinker who insisted almost obsessively on the inadequacy of his earlier writings. Bentley even considered reissuing *The Process of Government* in a revised version "coordinated" with "Knowledge and Society," but he did not do so.[1] Next I will examine his restatement of his social science in *Relativity in Man and Society* (1926), a transitional work which marks his turn to overtly philosophic themes. Finally, I shall study his work of the late 1920s as evidence of his deepening reflection on the problem of knowledge.

"Knowledge and Society"

"Knowledge and Society" begins with a restatement of Bentley's criticism of the notion of the "individual" (KS, 3–7). He was now prepared to ask the question "In what sense does an 'individual man' have existence for science?" As he did in *The Process of Government*, Bentley draws a distinction between everyday and scientific modes of discourse. In the former, a belief in the reality of individuals may be appropriate but this is not the case in the latter. He does not intend either to absorb the individual into a "higher reality" or to deny the "vital experience of pulsating human life." Rather, he wishes to question the adequacy of "ready-made conceptions" of the individual as the "bearer" of life. We generate a "speculative fog" when we employ our everyday understanding of individuals in domains apart from everyday conduct. In disputes about immortality, for example, conceptual confusion arises when we ask about the sense in which it can be said that "I" survive after death. In a manner reminiscent of, but not directly indebted to, Hume, he claims that we cannot identify an "I" apart from a manifold of "I-doings" and "I-feelings," the survival of which after death is itself problematic. Thus, there can be no experience of self-awareness apart from actions. Bentley does not doubt that there is "something" inadequately represented by conventional notions of the "individual." If such notions fail it will be because the "real life of men" disclosed by science exhaust their capacities.

Both the natural and the social sciences make the individual dubious. The physiologist cannot fix the limits of the individual in space because his "boundary lines" are found to "melt into those of his environment" when "functions" are specified which work through both the individual and his environment. Genetics shows that the individual cannot be isolated in time since the phenomena of genetics are not individual properties. That is, collectivities or populations, rather than individuals, are the bearers of the objects with which genetics as a science is concerned. Bentley claims no originality for his criticisms of the notion of the individual. Instead, he claims to be clarifying a teaching already implied in the theories of various sciences.

There are common experiences that in Bentley's view are not fully intelligible apart from his rejection of the individual. His first example is a person who has acquired some piece of scientific knowledge. Neither the process of learning nor the possession of knowledge can be understood as affairs of a discrete individual. Bentley compares this situation to one of Zeno's paradoxes. The solution to the problem of how knowledge passes from one mind to another resembles the solution to the paradoxes of motion: points are not the "realities in terms of which motion must be explained, but that the motion is the reality and that the points are merely marked off within it" (KS, 7). Thus, social actions such as the transmission of knowledge seem to "lap over the edges" of individuals or to "cut across" them. It is not surprising that Bentley gives qualified praise to objective idealism that takes individuals as instances of the concrete universal or Absolute as efforts to articulate in a defective mystical idiom what should be stated with the clarity of science. Now some might argue that this overlap can be theorized by taking social actions as "relations" among individuals (KS, 8). Bentley insists, however, that the blurred boundaries of the individual are not merely conceptual fictions. "The action 'is' the action of the two or three or thousand as one." Any theoretical "dissection" of the totality of social actions into individuals rather than into "channels of activity" is merely an abstraction from the social process. As long as social scientists insist on the primacy of the individual, the "system" of actions which is the true object of social science will be "forever elusive." For Bentley the notion of methodological individualism is reminiscent of Leibniz's monadology which posited a harmonious universe of radically isolated monads, their order maintained by God. In the absence of God, the identity and stability of the monads become problematic.

In this essay Bentley could not resist the temptation to deploy a novel terminology he acquired from an obscure physiologist, Michael A. Lane, with whom he discussed his views between 1902 and 1910.[2] Bentley was hardly alone in his search for a new vocabulary. Systematic arrays of neologisms littered the pages of many sociological treatises of the period. A. Lawrence Lowell spoke for many social scientists when he complained that political science "lacks the first essential of a modern science—a nomenclature incomprehensible to educated men."[3] As Kress has noted, Bentley's experiments with terminology reflected his intention to purge the vocabulary of social science of its dependence on everyday language and replace it with "concepts of relative stresses and emphases."[4] The most obvious difficulty of such a project is its artificiality. Ordinary terms and concepts must be translated into the new idiom.

Bentley borrows Lane's "Symbiotaxiosis" to designate the "totality of the ordering or arrangement of social life" (KS, 12–13). "Society" then becomes "symbiotaxium" while "symbiotaxiplasm" refers to the combinations of men and "assimilated things" that form society. The human constituents of a symbiotaxium are designated "homoplasm" while the nonhuman constituents or material components of society are "heteroplasm." Bentley defends these coinages by noting that social science has no terms "to designate exactly the mass of material things which have been taken up by socially organized men and incorporated in their common life." It is categorially ambiguous for social science to speak in an idiom indifferent to distinctions between the properties of a thing which have nothing to do with its role in organized human life and properties unintelligible except in terms of this role. Since social science is concerned only with the latter properties, it must be able to identify them clearly.

Bentley then turns to the problem of knowledge. The subjectivity that infects all traditional epistemologies has been rendered obsolete by Darwinism, which recast the problem of knowledge by banishing from science any version of the epistemological subject taken as intelligible apart from an "organized, environing world" (KS, 14). For corroboration of this view, Bentley relies on Dewey's *The Influence of Darwin on Philosophy* (1910). Darwinism and pragmatism agree that the "mind" can only be understood as a part of the world it seeks to explain. Evolutionary theory is required, then, to apply its perspective to science itself. Just as biological evolution has neither beginning nor end, so we must view scientific knowledge in the light shed by an evolutionary perspective. The notions of a "knowledgeless initial status" and a "full-knowledge terminal status" are remnants of obsolete metaphysics. The evolution of knowledge or science is not additive but involves "continual transformation." Bentley had never been comfortable with claims that "science" consisted of the progressive accumulation of facts. Rather, "reconstructability" must be seen as an essential characteristic of knowledge:

> Men "know," but they no longer are so certain that their knowledge will not be rearranged. A man may believe that his knowledge or some part of it will hold good permanently, but he feels compelled to recognize this as his "belief," in a sense distinct from "knowledge." One knows, but one does not know that the knowledge will not reconstruct itself later. To know that the knowing would never need reconstruction would be to transcend the knowledge of actual practical life, or . . . it would be to assert that the limit of the knowing procedure has been attained—the limit toward which all former knowing has been but a gradual approximation. (KS, 20)

Bentley knew that one basic objection to any "process" philosophy has to do with the problem of permanence and change—the question posed in Plato's *Sophist* as "How can being be both at rest and in motion?"[5] Whether we concentrate on the "structural" or the "transformational" aspects of knowledge, we cannot fail to conceive of knowledge apart from some notion of "persistence." Philosophical realists employed the "persistent in knowledge" as a criticism of pragmatism. Against the programmatic "New Realism" of such younger American philosophers as Ralph Barton Perry and William P. Montague, Bentley defended pragmatism as uniquely compatible with evolutionary theory.[6] The problem of the persistent in knowledge brings together the pragmatists and such philosophers as Bergson. Indeed, Bentley prefers to call those philosophers with whom he agrees "evolutionary thinkers" rather than "pragmatists."[7] The problem of knowledge must be approached from a standpoint compatible with evolutionary doctrine. The New Realists, Bentley knew, were sympathetic to the notion that philosophy should model itself on the natural sciences and should employ logic as its method.[8] For Bentley this view could all too easily lead once more to the static epistemologies of the past.

The larger issues Bentley sought to resolve have been stated clearly by Bruce Kuklick in his sketch of the American philosophical climate after William James's death in 1910:

Royce still flourished at Harvard and, exploiting the "subjectivism" and "relativism" attributable to Jamesean pragmatism, proclaimed absolute idealism as the only bulwark of objectivity in philosophy. In this unlikely situation Perry and his friends snatched the banner of objectivism from the idealists. In so doing, the neo-realists widened American philosophic debate. They emphasized doctrinal differences and opened the door to speculative diversity. Suddenly epistemological dispute in the United States became triangular: absolute idealism, Jamesean pragmatism, and neo-realism, each one against the other two. From the realist viewpoint the idealists were correct in believing that truth was absolute and not relative to finite minds, but wrong in insisting that facts existed within a single all-embracing experience. From the same viewpoint the pragmatists were right in their pluralism (the realists also rejected the interdependence of all facts) but wrong in supposing that truth about those facts was relative to and dependent upon the changing experiences of verification. Although disagreeing on the absoluteness of truth, the idealists and the pragmatists joined forces against the realists to deny that existence transcended consciousness.[9]

Bentley's strategy was boldly original. He turns to what seems at first an unrelated topic: the notion of "society" as it "enters into modern logical investigations" (KS, 17). His intention is stated explicitly: "We shall endeavor to bring our facts as to society and facts as to knowledge together into a consistent theory of knowledge as a practical affair of scientific investigation." The philosophic method with which the problem of the persistent in knowledge can be explored cannot be developed within any of the conventional philosophic positions. Bentley proposes to transcend the terms of the triangular debate among pragmatists, idealists, and neorealists by bringing to light connections between the problem of knowledge and the study of society. The philosophers had given insufficient attention to "society" with the significant exception of Dewey, and even he still viewed epistemological issues through lenses colored by the philosophic tradition.

The first step in Bentley's argument aligns him with Dewey's pragmatic teaching that knowledge is the result of inquiry undertaken in problematic situations. Bentley's revision of Dewey's position follows. He begins by asking us to consider the various primordial situations in which "what we know as sensations" first appear. We cannot properly say that we have direct knowledge of sensations, including our own sensations, because we must first have learned what sensations are and how to identify them. Sensations are socially constituted. For Bentley, as for the later Wittgenstein, there can be no purely private experience since to be able to designate something as a sensation is to show our dependence upon language, which cannot be taken as a private creation.[10]

Through his criticism of one of Dewey's paradigm cases for the pragmatic theory of truth, Bentley's own position becomes more clear. Dewey's example consists of a man lost in the woods whose uncertainty gives rise to a practical problem. The "idea" the man forms for saving himself is a plan of action, not a copy of some aspect of external reality. The "truth" of the plan is inseparable from the process of inquiry which may lead to the plan's completion. "Truth" becomes an achievement, not a property of objects that exist apart from some determinate inquiry (κs, 21). For Bentley, Dewey is still guilty of "abstraction." The man does not form his plan of action apart from "groundlore," "weatherlore" and so on, none of which he invented or discovered as an individual. His plan is inherently "social" in character. The "isolated knowledge crisis" is not truly paradigmatic for cognitive situations. The inquiry with which a human being meets a problematic situation is a process that transcends his individual identity. Now Bentley does not mean that "social facts" somehow determine or condition the individual's plan. "It is not a question of the influence of anything 'social' upon anything 'individual.' It is a question merely of the process as one through and through; a question of the whole cloth in which the patterns appear." The man lost in the woods does not simply devise any logically possible plan. Rather, he employs typical or conventional ways of thinking and acting, modes of conduct possible for him only because of his involvement in a shared way of life. The very existence of groundlore and weatherlore means that such experiences as "getting lost" and "finding one's way" are not private but typical experiences. In a more recent idiom, we may say that "being lost" is a rule-governed mode of behavior. Philosophers should rethink epistemological problems with such things in mind. Their speculations would be transformed from discourse about the operation of faculties and the nature of mental properties to discourse about the social forms of knowledge.

Bentley returns to the debate among contemporary philosophers with some reflections on the problem of "truth" which he thinks has been handled poorly by most philosophers. The pragmatist seems to claim that what is satisfying is thereby true, a view that outrages neorealists and idealists alike. Bentley is sympathetic to the pragmatist but proposes to strip the pragmatic view of truth of its subjective taint.

His example is the "grain god" of a primitive tribe who is "real" and whose teaching is "true" in terms of the "life of the group of his worshippers." While we would say from our scientific standpoint that the grain god does not exist, the sense in which our proposition is true is "metaphysical" and is less important philosophically than the function the god performs for the tribe. We do not worship the god because we "have our lives otherwise arranged, our values otherwise symbolized. We have different truths, and yet no truer truth." Now Bentley does not place himself in the position of having to defend the "reality" of the grain god. He distinguishes between the "realistic truths" exemplified by the grain god and the ways in which our own values are symbolized on the one hand and "scientific truths" on the other. The claims made by the primitives for their grain god and our claims for our highest values are both "realistic" in Bentley's sense. Set over against these sets of claims is "science." We misunderstand science if we suppose that it serves the same function as "realistic" claims. For Bentley it is not a scientific question to ask whether or not the grain god exists. "Realistic truths" are antagonistic claims that may pit whole ways of life against one another. The "common matrix" within which the grain god does his work is radically incompatible with our matrix which has no room for grain gods. All of this, however, has nothing to do with scientific truth which "generalizes itself more successfully to cover the past and future, by not merely rejecting the past, but by remaking the past within itself, reinterpreting that past and predicting the future.[11] The realistic truths of the tribe and our own society cannot do this. The power of science consists in its openness to continuous transformation. The process of transformation marks a path from realism to science.

The New Physics and Social Science

It is difficult to determine when Bentley became aware of the theory of relativity and decided to explore its implications for social science. His reading, which had been dominated into the early 1920s by the pragmatists, such philosophers as Bertrand Russell, G. E. Moore, and Alexius Meinong, and sociologists such as Simmel, began to shift toward physics. Notes from works of Ernst Mach, Henri Poincaré, and Wilhelm Ostwald begin to appear, along with a great deal of technical and popular literature on relativistic physics.[12] The fruit of his study was *Relativity in Man and Society*, which he completed in 1924 and published two years later.

Bentley did not claim to base social science on relativistic physics in the manner of cultural and ethical relativists who traded on the evocative potential of "relativity."[13] His point of departure was his agreement with many physicists and philosophers that the new physics, like Newtonian physics and Darwinism before it, required fundamental alterations in human self-understanding (RMS, 7). In the wake of the special theory of relativity (1905) and the general theory of relativity (1916) an enormous literature had emerged. By 1924 more than 3,400 scientific papers on various aspects of relativity had appeared.[14] Efforts to assess the philosophical significance of the new physics could be found in such works as C. D. Broad's *Perception, Physics and Reality* (1914), his later *Scientific Thought* (1923), Samuel Alexander's *Space, Time and Deity* (1920), Sir Arthur Eddington's *Space, Time and Gravitation* (1920), and J. B. Haldane's *The Reign of Relativity* (1921).

A brief survey of some of the reasons why the new physics generated philosophic reflection will enable us to see why Bentley felt social scientists could not ignore it. Recognition of the epistemological features of the new physics is the common theme in studies of relativity theory produced by a distinguished list of philosophers and physicists such as Ernst Cassirer, Hans Reichenbach, Wolfgang Pauli, Hugo Dingler, Philipp Frank, Moritz Schlick, and Hermann Weyl.[15] In Gerald Holton's words, "The theory of relativity was a key development both in physical science itself and also in modern philosophy of science." Einstein's achievement was understood as the result of a philosophical critique of scientific methodology as well as of an effort to explain experimental findings. The domain of the special theory of relativity, according to Einstein, is the "totality of all physical appearance," a concern requiring theorizing which Holton notes "implies its own methodology and its own metaphysics to serve as the philosophical basis of a renewed science." The revolution in physical theory was a philosophical revolution. Relativistic physics had not emerged in the inductive manner advocated by naively empiricist philosophers of science. For Holton, significant parallels between Einstein's 1905 papers and Newton's *Principia* make clear the philosophic character of scientific revolutions. These parallels include:

> the early postulation of general principles which in themselves do not spring directly from experience; the limitation to a few basic hypotheses; the exceptional attention to epistemological rules in the body of a scientific work; the philosophical eclecticism of the author; his ability to dispense with mechanistic models in a science which in each case was dominated at the time by such models; the small number of specific experimental predictions; and the fact that the most gripping effect of the work is its exhibition of a new point of view.[16]

I believe that precisely such an understanding of scientific revolutions is implicit in Bentley's developing views at this time. He had already distanced himself from any notion that scientific theories consisted of collections of data and had from the beginning of his own work emphasized the speculative aspect of scientific thinking. His residual Kantianism led him, in my view, to an understanding of relativity theory similar to that of Cassirer for whom Einstein's new view of nature brought the form of physical theory to its ultimate clarification. The form of physical apperception is determined not by immediate perception but rather by such concepts as space, time, number, and magnitude. The result is the transformation of the natural object into "pure relations of measurement," thus exemplifying the "fundamental cognitive function of physics."[17]

In *Relativity in Man and Society* Bentley calls for a form of explanation in social science that conforms to the spirit of the new physics but is in no sense a simple application of the methods of physics. He claims that *The Process of Government* was a crude anticipation of a relativistic teaching which suffered because the new physics had not yet emerged (RMS, iii, 277). The new physics, Bentley knew, had dispensed with the "absolute" space and time of Newtonian physics. There was no longer any need to suppose that a nonrelational medium such as the traditional "ether" must exist for the propagation of forces. For Bentley, the removal of absolute space and time in physical theory suggested that "absolutes" in less developed sciences were equally dubious (RMS, 24). Now Bentley was fully aware that relativistic physics, contrary to many popular opinions, did not teach that "everything was relative." Recognizing that the velocity of light was merely one of a number of mathematical invariants, he noted that there were no counterparts in social science. Relativistic physics as the most advanced physics exhibited most fully the fact that in truly scientific discourse concepts are defined explicitly and derive their meanings from their roles in systems of concepts (RMS, 10–12, 51–54, 88, 223–24). Physics had broken decisively with everyday or intuitive understandings of physical phenomena. To speak strictly, there is no equivalent in our ordinary understanding of the world for the notion that the presence of matter determines the geometric structure of space-time as taught by the general theory of relativity. "Curved space-time" in this theory is intelligible only within the mathematical, physical, and conceptual contexts of the new physics. Bentley urged social scientists to reach a comparable degree of clarity in their own work. Implicit in his recommendations is the possibility that a scientific account of social phenomena may be as incompatible with ordinary accounts as the propositions of relativity theory are with everyday experiences of the natural world. Social scientists have mistakenly believed that their task consisted of extrapolations from the actions and interpretations which constitute society as experienced by human beings.

Bentley was unprepared to argue the case for a radical discontinuity between ordinary and scientific concepts directly. Instead, he offers his familiar list of criticisms of conventional social science. His book fails to develop its themes with sufficient clarity. Indeed, the book is the most poorly organized of any of his major published works. Nearly a quarter of it seems to have been assembled with little alteration directly from his reading notes. His reflections on the significance of the new physics contend for the reader's attention with his fulminations against a number of defective sociological theories, displays of his customary erudition, and occasional excursions into substantive social theory. Perhaps his most coherent formulation of what I have called the discontinuity thesis concerning everyday and scientific explanations occurs in the context of his discussion of Leopold von Wiese's systematic sociology.

In selecting von Wiese, Bentley expresses his view that the Austrian sociologist was Simmel's intellectual heir and thus the most important figure in his field (RMS, 344–52). Von Wiese believed that sociology should learn the requirements for intellectual autonomy and break with the natural sciences, history, philosophy, ethics, and psychology. Moreover, as a science it must avoid political partisanship.[18] Bentley was familiar with the first part of von Wiese's *Allgemeine Soziologie* (1924), the *Beziehungslehre*. In that work the theorist argued that social relations could be described formally as changes in social distance with no concern for their substance. His procedure was to develop a complex typology of social processes such as association and dissociation, presented in spatial analogies suggestive of Simmel's geometric imagery. Any social relation studied by the sociologist is an arrest in the flow of the social process. Like Bentley, von Wiese criticized any reification of the individual or the collectivity. This orientation was an advance over Simmel because von Wiese's social forms were "not merely logical relations but 'something doing,' something going on, *Handeln*, activity" (RMS, 345).

As Simmel had failed, so von Wiese's system collapsed because it relied upon a substantive psychology. He had not gone beyond the philosophic premises of German sociology since he retained the epistemological subject. His efforts to avoid making unsupportable claims about subjective states or mental properties had the paradoxical effect of smuggling his own tacit views about such states or properties into his theory. Von Wiese took Bentley's criticisms seriously. He began a correspondence with him about the conceptual status of the individual in social science.[19] Howard Becker, von Wiese's American disciple who rewrote much of the *Allgemeine Soziologie* for his colleagues, defended his master by admitting that he and von Wiese "regard the self as the point of initial and fixed focus in any genuine science of interhuman behavior." While he agreed that Bentley's position "avoids the morasses of over-hasty judgments and crude single-factor fallacies," he concluded that it "finally confuses and dismays us by the multiplicity of its facts and branches, by the indistinguishably intricate maze of social occurrences that flashes by."[20] How, von Wiese asked, could Bentley do without the "besouled man" in some form as the "Archimedean point" for his social science?[21]

At issue was the question of what a social science is supposed to explain. For von Wiese and Becker social science takes as its objects phenomena of ordinary social experience. While the theories of social science may employ such abstractions as "role," "status," and the like, these concepts are rooted in notions familiar to us from everyday life. They are used to order the flux of experience into intelligible types. It is because we have a pretheoretical or prescientific understanding of our relations with other persons that we are able to understand "relation" as a formal category in systematic sociology. Bentley, of course, rejected this line of argument. He did not claim that scientific concepts were "objective" in contrast to the "subjective" notions of ordinary thinking. What mattered to him was not so much the fact that the scientist replaces a subjective impression like "warm" with quantitative measurements of temperature but rather that the central problems of a mature science have little or no connection with ordinary experience. Now his position would have been more clear if he had tried to specify what sorts of scientific problems had this character. What can be found in his comments is the view that the propositions of a mature science are not adequately understood as generalizations of claims drawn from ordinary experience.

If what Becker had called the "indistinguishably intricate maze of social occurrences" resisted explanations couched in terms of a limited number of social forms, it was obvious to Bentley that a sufficiently formal approach was the only way in which an adequate theory could be developed. Bentley's distance from the thinking of many social scientists is seldom so obvious. A genuinely scientific theory for him is not a way of simplifying data or organizing data economically. A theory must be prepared to capture the flux of experience on the wing, as it were. It is important to note that Bentley did not argue that a social science explanation should "reproduce" the phenomena with which it is concerned. He does not require social science to convey in its propositions experiences of the sort we might have of the objects of social science.[22] Instead, a formal social science would make possible the complete description of social reality Bentley seeks. The "self" or "besouled man" could no more have priority in such a science than a Newtonian physical system could have priority in relativity theory. Bentley's point was not that social scientists should be barred from speaking of the "self" but that the "self," like a classical physical description, signified a theoretical intention, not a self-evident foundation.

Leading Ideas of Bentley's Social Science

Bentley recognized the role played by epistemology in the new physics and wished to inaugurate a similar movement in social science. His use of notions drawn from relativity theory was intended to be suggestive and did not amount to a reductionist proposal. Although he is quite vague on the issue in *Relativity in Man and Society*, he does not seem to believe there are any general criteria for a suitable scientific epistemology. For that matter, even relativity theory is not presented as having epistemological primacy. Each science must learn to incorporate a reflective or epistemological moment into its practice. It must link up its "own tests of coherence" with appropriate "processes of scientific experiment, prediction and verification" (RMS, 70). There can be no test for "coherence" in a science that is imported from another discipline. Although he suggests that each science is in a sense autonomous, any science must take its bearings from the fact that the "world of knowledge" is "socially constituted" and is thus accessible only in and through language. Language, in turn, consists of the "cross-sectional activities of society" (RMS, 66–70), a Bentleyan expression reminiscent of *Lebensform* in Wittgenstein's *Philosophical Investigations*. For Bentley, epistemology is a mode of "word analysis" concerned with the linguistic and hence the social constitution of knowledge.

Among the most important notions for Bentley's social science is temporality, the importance of which he learned from the new physics. He was convinced that all sciences would have to come to terms with the notion that we live in a four-dimensional space-time continuum in which the motion of anything whatsoever must be understood as a path or "world line." It is, moreover, incorrect to speak of an object "moving" through space-time. Rather, in J. J. C. Smart's words, the object must be understood to lie "tenselessly along the world line."[23] For Bentley the "tenselessness" of relativistic formulations suggests that the conventional understanding of time as a sort of container or matrix within which an asymmetric passage of events takes place is untenable. His principal thesis concerning temporality has to do with the temporal structure of human action. Bentley was convinced that the "time form" appropriate for the understanding of human action was non-Newtonian. That is, reflection on hunan action shows that its temporal structure is not the asymmetric form "past-present-future." For example, the chess master has the "realities of action in periods of time" before him as wholes, not as "mere instants with separate remembered pasts and separate anticipated futures" (RMS, 36). Now Bentley is not arguing that the goals or objects of human action located in the future somehow produce actions in the present. While he takes human action to be purposive, his way of theorizing purposiveness stems from his pluralistic view of temporality that admits any ensemble of the temporal elements past, present, and future. Accordingly, Bentley does not claim that a teleological explanation must account for behavior as a "function of what it serves to bring about," in Charles Taylor's words.[24] A conventional teleological explanation employs an inappropriate classical "time form," the use of which generates the paradox that a future and supposedly as yet nonexistent situation causes present behavior. If we can employ a "tenseless" time form the paradox is dissolved.

Bentley knew that according to the special theory of relativity it is possible that an event that lies in the "future" according to one coordinate system may lie in the "present" or "past" of another coordinate system. There can be no privileged observer or no observer neutral with respect to coordinate systems. This teaching seemed to Bentley thoroughly compatible with his own sense of the plurality of standpoints which should become part of the methodological orientation of social science. One of his somewhat Bergsonian meditations on "duration" presents an impressionistic version of his view of temporality:

Durations remain to us with their pasts and presents, but not with the same definitions of past and present from all points of view, and with no test of rightness as between the varying definitions. We have a substantial time from earlys to lates, knitted up and inseparable. We must take it as such. It is a whole for us—a whole of experience—divided into distance and durations for purposes of study: capable of statement, so far as we know now, not as a whole . . . and finding its unity—if indeed there is a sense of the word unity which will ultimately apply to it—in human experience, which is society. . . . Reverting to rough indications of the reality as existence of past and present one may think of what the psychoanalyst digs out of early life experience from what he calls the unconscious to interpret what he calls the conscious. Amid all his vagaries and sensationalism he does real work. Twenty-five years ago we would have been satisfied with a neurological present to explain to ourselves these results. . . . Today no. We must take it in durations, with no right to attribute an immediate reality to a very short one over a very long one, save as it is useful as a tool or method in our study. (RMS, 39–40)

Psychoanalysis was for Bentley only one example of what he believed was a general movement away from traditional causal explanations in science, a tendency he thought was inherent in the new physics as well. His study of psychoanalysis convinced him that its explanatory style could not be reduced to accounts of effective causality. To the extent that it seemed to transcend temporal asymmetry, a psychoanalytic explanation of neurotic behavior resembled the sorts of explanations offered in physics. Indeed, at several points in his book Bentley refers to his social science as "socioanalysis" because it will study "prospective" and "retrospective" phases of social phenomena as a "system" without reducing one to the other (RMS, 64).

In place of conventional units of analysis in social science, Bentley suggests "events" or cross sections of space-time. Any object of social science can be understood as consisting of "event sections" determined by demarcating portions of the object's world line (RMS, 48–49). Bentley knew that Einstein's use of "event" in the special theory of relativity had been intended to eliminate appeals to some absolute reality that stood behind the flux of physical phenomena.[25] In place of some metaphysical distinction between appearance and reality, Bentley proposed cross sections of space-time specified for determinate inquiry.

The field of study for social science is "man-society," with the hyphen standing as an expression of Bentley's familiar refusal to give priority to either term (RMS, 90–97). "Activity" designates any "event" chosen for study. The notion of "group" from *The Process of Government* is replaced by "cross-sectional activity." A single such activity is intelligible only in terms of an entire system of activities, which means that any one activity is representative of the whole. Conventional units of analysis such as the "individual" are analogous to theoretically specified segments of a relativistic world line.

Convinced that he had produced at least a plausible sketch of the leading ideas of his social science, Bentley offers an example of a "social-fact-complex" and the requirements for its study in his science. If we choose to study the Volstead Act, we must be prepared to examine at least the following:

A vote of Congress. The signature of the President. Many days of debate in Congress. Many weeks of committee hearings. Very, very many man-years of lobbying for and against.

A constitutional amendment. All of its attendant efforts. Its submission to the states.

State and community law and ordinance experiences, local option and prohibition.

A generation or two of writing, speaking, organization, public meetings, addresses, editorials. Temperance societies, political parties, and platform planks.

Brewers', distillers', and retailers' organizations.

Chemists' investigations.

Circles of discussion widening out into principles of government and rights of man.

A changed industrial system, division of labor, machinery.

A changed food complex.

A cross section of the courts, judges, attorneys, marshals.

A welter of private attorneys, legal points, technicalities, relations to other laws and to the constitution.

A new staff of investigators in the treasury department.

A new mass of law breakers, differently law-breaking.

Some new reaches and magnitudes of corruption.

A change in expenditures and in lives, in durations and experiences in men's lives.

We might assume that Bentley's list requires us to furnish a social history of Prohibition, but evidently this is not the case. Kress notes the "fantastic demands" Bentley places upon "adequate description" as the explanatory form of his social science.[26] A cross-sectional study of the elements on this list will not be a historical account since for Bentley historical explanations abstract from the totality of events and usually identify some factors as causes and others as effects. A Bentleyan description, in contrast, will not impose a causal order. It will present all elements and their relationships as a structure with no causal processes unless these are specifically taken as partial explanations.

Categories and Foundation Problems

Bentley eventually felt that his book suffered from an excessively "objectivistic" picture of social facts.[27] He had been unfaithful to his own intention of producing a formal social science. The basic categories of his teaching had been developed casually. He knew that he had not resolved the most important of the issues with which the book had been concerned. After *Relativity in Man and Society* he turned to epistemological themes directly and did not consider the question of the nature of social science as a sufficient formulation of his concerns.

The late 1920s and early 1930s were the most fruitful years of his career. The lines of inquiry anticipated in his earlier works were developed to their greatest extent. Although he was in his late fifties, he was prepared to rethink the whole of his work. He began to search for a common ground underlying scientific inquiry. The *allgemeine Wissenschaftslehre*, which he had admitted to von Wiese was his goal, moved to the center of his thinking. More or less simultaneously Bentley undertook four large and complex projects. Most of his publications in the late 1920s reflected his continuing study of sociology, although psychology began to displace it somewhat. He expanded the range of his philosophical reading and focused on the views of Ludwig Wittgenstein. Alone among American social scientists, Bentley was aware that the new directions in philosophy exemplified by the Russell-Whitehead *Principia Mathematica* and Wittgenstein's *Tractatus Logico-Philosophicus* could not be ignored. In addition, he undertook an intensive study of philosophy of science, concentrating on the "operationism" of the physicist and philosopher of science Percy W. Bridgman. The most important stream of research and thinking during this period was Bentley's investigation of the foundations of mathematics. Here Bentley found what seemed to him evidence of a greater degree of critical reflection than in any other discipline. Chief among his interests in mathematics was David Hilbert's wide-ranging project to produce a completely formalist mathematics. For Bentley a study of the issues raised by Hilbert's program was the best opportunity to explore the nature of scientific inquiry.

After completing *Relativity in Man and Society*, Bentley began a comprehensive survey of American sociological journals to uncover the categorial foundations of contemporary sociological theory and research. His principal focus was the tacit understandings of space, time, the individual, society, and consciousness revealed in the formulation of research problems, the construction and testing of hypotheses, and the analysis of data. He did not offer alternative theories or research designs and was unconcerned with the substance or merits of any piece of research he studied. The fruits of his work were two large unpublished manuscripts in which he identifies and classifies the categorial premises of a number of sociological studies: "'Individual' and 'Social' in Recent American Studies" (1926–27) and "The Data of Sociology Examined with Respect to Time and

Space" (1927).[28] Sociological researchers almost without exception took over notions of space and time from everyday experience or Newtonian physics. For Bentley there was little advance in their work over philosophers like Locke, who had begun the unwarranted extension of notions from Newtonian science to the study of man and society.[29] The empiricist tradition had sought ultimate units of intelligibility such as "ideas" or "sense data" in the manner of Newtonian physics. While an ontology of particles might be appropriate for classical physics, there was no good reason to suppose that equivalent units must be found in any other realm of knowledge.

In his published writings Bentley made clear his continued dissatisfaction with contemporary views. In "A Sociological Critique of Behavioralism," which appeared in the *Archiv für systematische Philosophie und Soziologie* in 1928, his target is Watson's influential position.[30] In "L'individuel et le social: les termes et les faits," which was published in *Revue International de Sociologie* in 1929, he presented an especially clear summary of his criticisms of psychological explanations in social science.[31] While it broke no new ground, this article is distinguished by the systematic comparison Bentley makes between his position and that of Durkheim, a strategy he followed to acquaint French sociologists with his views. The same year he published another summary of his position as "New Ways and Old to Talk About Men" in the British journal the *Sociological Review*.[32]

Sometime in 1927 Bentley read Wittgenstein's *Tractatus*. His familiarity with the historical background of the emergence of the logical views of Russell and Whitehead, as well as his study of philosophy of science, allowed him to consider the *Tractatus* in terms of a larger philosophical context than was recognized by most English or American readers. He thus avoided the parochialism of readings of Wittgenstein that took the *Tractatus* philosophy, in David Lamb's words, as "an unprecedented phenomenon, exploding into the Anglo-Saxon tradition with revolutionary ideas unparalleled in the history of Western thought."[33] While the style of the *Tractatus* might be novel, Wittgenstein's view of philosophy as a "critique of language" located him within a tradition extending to Kant.[34] Bentley, in spite of his awareness of the Kantian context of Wittgenstein's thinking, thought that Russell had been correct in linking the *Tractatus* philosophy with his own logical atomism and accepted the testimony of the Vienna Circle philosophers that Wittgenstein belonged in part to their camp. Since Bentley found little novelty in the views of Russell or the logical positivists, however, he seems to have read the *Tractatus* as an especially stimulating rehearsal of erroneous doctrines.

Nevertheless, there was a great deal in the *Tractatus* with which Bentley could be sympathetic. As Janik and Toulmin have recently argued, Wittgenstein may be understood as having proposed to determine the logical limits of the sayable or to "map" the limits of language from the "inside."[35] While Bentley was indifferent to the ethical dimension of Wittgenstein's teaching emphasized by Janik and Toulmin, he certainly agreed with the notion that the "limits of my language mean the limits of my world," and doubtless found much to admire in Wittgenstein's rejection of the view that there is any a priori order of things. Bentley in his own way had insisted for decades that it was impossible, in Wittgenstein's words, to go beyond the limits of the sayable and "view those limits from the other side as well."[36]

What Bentley could not accept was Wittgenstein's insistence that there is a sufficient degree of structural similarity between language and reality to permit a characterization of sentences as "pictures" or models of objects.[37] The "picture theory" of the *Tractatus* was simply a reformulation of the empiricist doctrine of sense data. The "atomic facts" modeled by *Tractatus* propositions were as dubious as empiricist sense data. Bentley would not have been surprised to read in Wittgenstein's *Notebooks* that "simple objects" must exist as a "logical necessity."[38] As Bentley later put it, the "historical tendency" of philosophies concerned with definitions is to seek some ultimate "elements." While Russell was the most famous contemporary example of this tendency, the "push is that of Wittgenstein."[39]

The most important difference between Bentley and the early Wittgenstein has to do with the limits of the sayable. Bentley held that Wittgenstein's failure to develop an adequate account of language had led him to limit unduly the scope of what could be said. The famous doctrine of the "mystical"—the things, including the existence of objects, the "metaphysical subject," and good and evil that are beyond the limits of language—seemed to Bentley a needless admission of impotence. An adequate view of language, according to Bentley, shows that nothing is "beyond expression." The relation between knower and known, which Wittgenstein ultimately reduces to intuition or silence, must be taken instead as a "social language phenomenon."[40] From the standpoint Bentley took in *Linguistic Analysis of Mathematics* Wittgenstein's empiricist legacy is linked to the problematic notion that a mode of statement can be created whose elements and internal relations are stable. Wittgenstein's use of such devices as the propositional function and logical quantification could not remedy the defects in his position which result from his belief that he must establish connections between a "subject" who thinks, constructs pictures, and the like, and a "world" consisting of "states of affairs" that are configurations of "simple" objects.[41] Regardless of its logical methods, the *Tractatus* philosophy is firmly traditional, a fact revealed by Wittgenstein's talk of the "metaphysical subject." He had failed to see that the conditions that allowed "the world" to be "my world" were to be found in the cross-sectional activity made intelligible to us only through language. It is not too much to say that from Bentley's position there was no reason why Wittgenstein could not have written the *Philosophical Investigations* rather than the *Tractatus* in 1918 if his masters had been Dilthey and Simmel and not Gottlob Frege and Russell.

The third of Bentley's projects—his study of philosophy of science—brought him to Bridgman's "operationism" during the late 1920s. He began an extensive correspondence with Bridgman after reading his *Dimensional Analysis* (1924) and his influential *The Logic of Modern Physics* (1927). During the 1930s they exchanged a number of manuscripts and commented extensively on each other's work. Bridgman admired *Linguistic Analysis of Mathematics* although he found some of Bentley's purely mathematical discussions excessively difficult. He even modestly described his own *The Nature of Physical Theory* (1936) as "puerile and naive" when compared with *Behavior Knowledge Fact.*[42]

Bridgman believed his operationism was simply an extension of Einstein's own methods as employed in the development of relativity theory. For Bridgman there were no meanings for "space" and "time" in relativity theory apart from propositions about measuring rods and clocks. A scientific concept is definable in terms of a statement about "operations" which we are able either to perform or to conceive. Operationism proposes both a rule for the formation of scientific concepts and a criterion for their meaning. In Bridgman's words, "If a specific question has meaning, it must be possible to find operations by which an answer may be given to it. It will be found that in many cases the operations cannot exist, and the question therefore has no meaning."[43]

In Bentley's view, the merit of Bridgman's thesis lay in its unification of the "empirical" and "rational" elements in scientific thinking implied by the connection between "operation" and "concept." In his own idiom, "concepts" and "operations" are "stresses in the one common situation of man-experiencing-fact." Operationism does not depend upon the passive reception of sense data nor does it ignore the continuity of scientific thinking with scientific practice. Bentley seems to read Bridgman as if he had translated Dewey's instrumentalist epistemology into the language of measurement. Unlike many social scientists and psychologists who later discovered Bridgman, Bentley had no interest in providing "operational" definitions for scientific concepts. Instead, he saw in operationism the possibility of overcoming the subject-object dichotomy. He ultimately rejected Bridgman's teaching because it failed to bridge this gap.

In a lengthy unpublished study, "The Postulates of Operational Physics," Bentley argued that Bridgman relied on "mental operations" in the construction of scientific theories and took as unproblematic a dubious view of the "direct experience" to which we are supposed to refer to determine the results of employing operational definitions.[44] As he became more familiar with Bridgman, Bentley found that he, like most philosophers of science, was an empiricist at heart. He had failed to reflect adequately on the role of language. This shortcoming left Bridgman unable to explain what it meant for a scientist to "have a concept" because he took for granted that he could rely on our everyday notion of what having a concept meant. That understanding, when clarified, was that thoughts of a specific sort were localized in a traditional epistemological subject. Bridgman, then, believed that scientific "concepts" were a sort of mental object, a thoroughly traditional and untenable position.

Bentley's study of operationism was the last of his efforts to understand scientific inquiry by relying on the thinking of natural scientists. Natural scientists still believed they had access to some extralinguistic or extratheoretical reality. To require a scientific concept to be defined in terms of measurements is to presuppose the ontological thesis that the objects of a science correspond to our efforts to measure them. More generally, natural scientists paid little attention to the form of scientific statements and theories. Bentley turned to mathematics as the science concerned more than any other with "form." As we shall see in the following chapter, here too he found controversy.

6

The Logic of Scientific Inquiry

It is true that [the] identity of problems centering around the presentations "one" and "some" and "all" in mathematics and in sociology is not often emphasized, perhaps indeed is not generally recognized. It is concealed from view beneath a very prevalent attitude and distinction under which mathematics is regarded as "abstract" in the extreme, while social presentations, by contrast, are regarded in their characteristic of immediate experience and behavior as the most vitally "concrete" of all. If one accepts such a distinction of abstract and concrete as basically sound or true, and if, along with this, he regards the abstractness as implying a certain "unreality," while on the contrary the personal and social experiences seem to him to have the truest and fullest "reality," then he of course sees the problems of the two fields as of entirely different nature. But the distinction abstract-concrete is far from possessing theoretical rigor, whether in psychology and logic, or in practical and scientific life; it is far from being a firm basis of classification within knowledge; and, beyond this, the implications of "reality" and "unreality" are even less secure in their meaning. Given any such uncertainty in these basic forms of discrimination, then the comparison and correlation of the problems of "one" and "some" and "all" in these two regions, mathematical and sociological, becomes at once of the greatest importance; and the way is open for an inquiry as to whether any light may be thrown by the situation in one of the regions upon that of the other.

"Sociology and Mathematics"

Linguistic Analysis of Mathematics contains Bentley's mature teaching on the nature of scientific inquiry and is the principle text for the study of what I have called his "formalism." It establishes beyond reasonable doubt his credentials as a serious philosopher and by itself it furnishes ample warrant to consider Bentley as a major philosopher of social science. That this work has not been studied extensively by Bentley scholars is, I believe, an indication of the degree to which his position has been misunderstood. Although its role in Bentley's work as a whole is as a methodological prelude to *Behavior Knowledge Fact*, his study of issues in the foundations of mathematics and their implications for scientific inquiry seems to me both more profound and more indicative of the scope of his project than his later products. The teaching of *Linguistic Analysis of Mathematics* distinguishes Bentley's philosophy of social science from both the work of his contemporaries and that of present-day scholars. Regardless of the merits or defects of that teaching, it represents a fundamental alternative to the ways in which philosophers of social science have understood their tasks.

Social Science and Mathematics

Bentley, unlike many contemporary social scientists, never took quantification to be a significant methodological issue in social science. Accordingly, he never entered debates about the merits of quantification and took little notice of the development of statistical techniques for social science research. He criticized the "mensurators" who, by restricting methodological issues to questions about quantification, had unduly limited inquiry in social science.[1] While measurement and statistical analysis were indispensable in social science, Bentley never believed that quantification was the foundation of any science. There remained in his thinking a permanent residue of the interpretive tradition in sociology which made him doubt that an adequate explanation of social phenomena could result solely from uncovering measurable relations among data. While he had distanced himself from the subjectivism of interpretive sociology, he always stood close to the spirit if not the letter of Weber's view in *Wirtschaft und Gesselschaft*: "If adequacy in respect to meaning is lacking, then no matter how high the degree of uniformity and how precisely its probability can be numerically," a correct causal interpretation of an action "is still an incomprehensible statistical probability, whether dealing with overt or subjective processes."[2] Bentley's agreement with this premise of interpretive sociology helps to account for his refusal to join the rising chorus of voices in social science calling for a thoroughgoing operationism. The thesis that all social science concepts could or indeed should be "defined" in terms of "operations" or types of measurement seemed fundamentally confused to Bentley.

The identification of "science" with "quantification" was, from

Bentley's standpoint, a reflection of the metaphysical doctrine that the objects of science or the properties of the objects of science are determinate entities, the most important characteristic of which is enumerability. In a larger sense, the very rationality of science is then understood to consist in counting, which in Ernst Nagel's lucid formulation is "the delimitation and fixation of our ideas of things."[3] The mathematical physicist or, for that matter, social scientist follows the Cartesian teaching, as summarized by Stanley Rosen, that "the essential structure of the world consists of abstract, symbolical mathematical objects. The study of order and measure is at once the study of mathematics and of physics, but it is also the study of thinking or *ratio*."[4] Very few social scientists possessed a clear understanding of the ontological commitments necessarily implied by the notion that the essence of science is quantification or measurement. One important consequence of this ignorance is the naive notion that the objects of social science are somehow "given" to the social scientist as "facts" to be assembled with the aid of statistical methods into organized collections of facts. In Bentley's words, "sociology is much more than a manipulation of data assumed as factually well established and adequately provided for its use. Mathematics is much more than a compendium of technical devices."[5]

From Bentley's standpoint, the failure of social scientists to grasp the character of mathematics could be seen in their practice of using quantitative methods to study the same sorts of things they had previously studied without such methods. Sociologists and political scientists employed statistical techniques to study phenomena known to them through prescientific means. Social scientists had not considered the possibility that the use of mathematics might require radical revisions in their disciplines. The proper use of mathematics, for Bentleyan inquiry, requires acceptance of the fundamental discontinuity between everyday and scientific accounts of things. The advanced sciences, which were the most mathematical sciences, had begun to dispense with determinate "things" or properties of "things." The objects of physics had little or nothing in common with everyday objects. Physics was not simply a discipline which employed mathematics but rather a discipline unintelligible apart from mathematics. A truly mathematical sociology, political science, or psychology would have little in common with social sciences in which the role of mathematics, in Paul F. Lazarsfeld's words, is "to translate ideas into empirical questions and to look for regular relations between the variates so created."[6]

When Bentley turned to mathematics itself he discovered a number of fundamental philosophical conflicts. For him this meant both that the foundation discipline for the advanced sciences was problematic and that reflective inquiry was more developed in mathematics than in any other discipline. For Bentley, as for Heidegger, "the real 'movement' of the sciences takes place when their basic concepts undergo a more or less radical revision which is transparent to itself. The level which a science has reached is determined by how far it is *capable* of a crisis in its basic concepts."[7] In Bentley's view, the issues in the foundations of mathematics all had to do with "consistency" and reveal that the "investigator is involved thereby, directly or indirectly, clearly or confusedly, in the broadest problems of the appraisal of knowledge in its many forms and in its entanglement in the practical living of mankind" (LAM, 1). The ferment among philosophers of mathematics had implications for our understanding of knowledge at least as important as those flowing from relativistic physics. Social scientists could no more ignore developments in mathematics than they could in physics. The study of human things had been fundamentally transformed by Newtonian and relativistic physics, and was likely to be similarly affected by the philosophy of mathematics. Convinced that knowledge was unitary, Bentley never doubted that even the most abstruse issues in the natural sciences and mathematics were linked, when understood correctly, with both social science and larger human concerns.

Some remarks are in order concerning the foundations of mathematics since many social scientists may be unfamiliar with this branch of philosophical study. "Foundational studies" or "foundations of mathematics" identifies both a number of technical issues within mathematics and philosophical views of the nature of mathematics that result from and, in turn, clarify the problems that give rise to these reflections. I shall be concerned with general topics in the philosophy of mathematics since Bentley concentrated on these areas and, moreover, did not claim to have made significant contributions to mathematics in his own right (LAM, vii).

Modern foundational inquiry begins with the "crisis" in mathematics that resulted from the emergence of non-Euclidean geometries.[8] Arithmetic and geometry, as the mathematical sciences of number and space, were grounded in what most philosophers took to be necessarily valid intuitions concerning the nature of the physical world. For ancient and modern philosophers, mathematics was the best example of or even the standard for a priori knowledge. The systematic character of mathematical theories, the abstract nature of mathematical objects, and the existence of rigorous methods of proof were properties that made mathematics both a science of "ideal" objects and the basis for a stable account of nature. With the discovery of non-Euclidean geometries a gulf was opened between the rational structure of classical geometry and what had been taken as our necessary intuition of the structure of physical space. Ernst Cassirer has described the implications of this discovery with extraordinary force:

> It was obvious that no simple mathematical question had been raised here; the whole problem of the truth of mathematics, even of the meaning of truth itself, was placed in an entirely new light. The fate not only of mathematics but of logic as well now seemed to depend upon the direction in which the solution was sought and where it would be found. . . . If geometry owes its certainty to pure reason, how strange that this reason can arrive at entirely and wholly incongruous systems, while claiming equal truth for each! Does this not call in question the infallibility of reason itself? Does not reason in its very essence become contrary and ambiguous? To recognize a plurality of geometries seemed to mean renouncing the unity of reason, which is its intrinsic and distinguishing feature. Still less than in earlier times could mathematical thinking in the nineteenth century hope to evade the problem thus posed by recourse to an infallible and absolutely evident "intuition." For through recent advances in mathematics intuition had not only been steadily driven back but a real "crisis in intuition" had come about.[9]

Mathematicians began to treat the various branches of mathematics such as geometry, algebra, and arithmetic as the study of what Morris Kline calls "arbitrary structures."[10] What Felix Klein called a "wholly intellectual mathematics that has been purged of all intuitions" began to emerge, "a theory of pure forms with which are associated not quantities or their symbols, numbers, but intellectual concepts, products of thought, to which actual objects or their relations *may*, but *need not*, correspond."[11] The internal development of mathematics links up with the course taken by logic in the nineteenth century in the pioneering work of George Boole whose *The Mathematical Analysis of Logic* (1847) showed that such arithmetical operations as addition and multiplication are possible with logical notions like classes. Logic as a theory of relations had obvious parallels with mathematics as a theory of pure forms. The central questions in logic and mathematics seemed to have to do with formal operations and structures. While geometry had been stripped of its status as an a priori description of the physical world, its axiomatic formulation was still paradigmatic for mathematics. Other branches of mathematics could be axiomatized as well. Such programs as the deduction of number theory, central to the work of mathematicians like Richard Dedekind, Georg Cantor, and G. Peano required the integration of logic and mathematics. In John Passmore's words, the task of presenting mathematical theories "in such a way that their logical structure would be immediately apparent and gaps in that structure would be readily discerned" gave logicians their most important issues.[12]

The stage was set for the emergence of "logicism" as the first of three identifiable schools of thought concerning the foundations of mathematics by developments in the arithmetization of mathematics. Arithmetic, rather than geometry, was understood by many mathematicians as the appropriate foundation for mathematics.[13] For Cantor, Gottlob Frege, and Bertrand Russell, the epistemological premise of number theory was that mathematics describes ideal objects or classes of ideal objects. Thus, in Cantor's set theory, sets become ideal objects. For Dedekind and Leopold Kronecker, number theory is based on "ordering" as the constitutive activity of pure thought. Thus, for the former orientation, number theory will be based on cardinal numbers, while for the latter it will be grounded on ordinal numbers. As Cassirer notes, such opposing positions transcend the purely mathematical issues involved, since "what was at stake was no longer the concept of the object of mathematics but the universal condition of how knowledge is actually related to 'objects' and what conditions it must fulfill in order to acquire 'objective meaning.'"[14]

Logicism contends that mathematics is an extension of or is reducible to logic. Frege was the principal architect of the logicist teaching, while its most influential statements were Russell's *Principles of Mathematics* (1903) and *Principia Mathematica*. Russell sought to reduce number theory to set theory and set theory to logic, where logic is taken to be the theory of propositional functions.[15] The logicist program requires the axiomatization of all branches of mathematics in order to show their ultimate derivation from logic.

The second major foundational approach is "intuitionism," represented by the Dutch mathematician L. E. J. Brouwer, with whom

Bentley corresponded. For Brouwer, mathematical theorems are synthetic a priori truths. These truths are based on our intuition of the structure of time which gives rise to the sequence of ordinal numbers and thus to the primary constructive operations that generate all mathematical ideas.[16] The logicists are mistaken in holding that mathematics presupposes logic, for logical principles are themselves established intuitively. Accordingly, Brouwer refused to give the canons of traditional logic a privileged position.

One of Brouwer's most interesting arguments, given Bentley's predilections, was that the principles of logic and mathematics could be understood in terms of their historical origins. In a speculative reconstruction of these origins, which Max Black has usefully called a theory of the "sociological basis of mathematics," Brouwer supposes that early man found himself in a world of structures such as the family and the tribe.[17] "Science" emerged as the observation and eventually the creation of ordered activity, issuing in mathematics as the idealization of the primary temporal intuition of ordering. As Brouwer puts it, "The reliability of logical principles, in practice, rests upon the fact that a large part of the universe of experience exhibits far more order and harmony in its finite organization than mankind itself."[18]

The third major orientation in the foundations literature was formalism. Formalism, prior to its articulation as a school, was the implicit position of mathematicians concerned with ridding mathematics of metaphysical claims. As William and Martha Kneale put it, "mathematicians who call themselves formalists have tried to maintain that in pure mathematics there is no need to go beyond symbols and their rules of combination, that is to say, beyond material over which we ourselves have complete control."[19] The principal formalist was David Hilbert, who produced a successful axiomatization of Euclidean geometry in his influential *Grundlagen der Geometrie* (1899) and presented a famous list of twenty-three unsolved mathematical problems in 1900 which comprised the so-called "Hilbert program."[20] Hilbert proposed to eliminate the paradoxes that had disconcerted mathematicians by axiomatizing logic, arithmetic, set theory, and analysis. It was possible in principle to show that all branches of mathematics and hence mathematics as a whole could be "consistent" and thus free from contradiction. The epistemological issues in mathematics defined a distinct domain Hilbert called "proof theory" or "metamathematics." In order to show that one branch of mathematics was consistent it was necessary to show that the branch upon which it rested was also consistent. The task of metamathematics was to develop methods that would allow us to decide in a finite number of steps such matters as whether or not a given theorem was provable, and thus to locate it in a consistent larger structure.

For Hilbert, axiomatization had implications far beyond mathematics:

Everything that can be the object of mathematical thinking, as soon as the erection of a theory is ripe, falls into the axiomatic method and thereby directly into mathematics. By pressing to ever deeper layers of axioms . . . we can obtain deeper insights into scientific thinking and learn the unity of our knowledge.

Especially by virtue of the axiomatic method mathematics appears called upon to play a leading role in all knowledge.

[The axiomatic method] now and for all time is the instrument suited to the human mind and indispensable for every exact inquiry, whatever its field may be. . . . To proceed axiomatically in this sense is simply to think with knowledge of what one is about.[21]

While logicism probably won more adherents among philosophers than either of the other foundational schools, neither logicism, intuitionism, or formalism ever enjoyed unchallenged supremacy. Andrej Mostowski speaks for many philosophers of mathematics when he writes: "The philosophical aims of the three schools have thus not been achieved, and it seems to us that we are no nearer to a complete understanding of mathematics than the founders of these schools."[22] The followers of the schools thought they had at least entered onto the path toward such an understanding. In spite of their disagreements, most philosophers of mathematics in the 1930s would have agreed with the spirit of Hilbert's confident assertion in 1928 that "to the mathematical understanding there are no bounds. . . . our reason does not possess any secret art but proceeds by quite definite and statable rules which are the guarantee of the absolute objectivity of its judgment."[23] Bentley was less concerned with the "rules" than with the conditions of their statement, which he was convinced were not adequately grasped by mathematicians. Put concisely, mathematics could not provide an adequate account of itself, a deficiency that must at the very least severely qualify its claim to achieve absolute objectivity.

The Linguistic Structure of Mathematics

Bentley prepared himself for the venture into mathematics with considerable care. In addition to his voluminous reading, he studied with the Vienna Circle philosopher Friedrich Waismann in 1929.[24] He also began a correspondence with the physicist and philosopher of science Hermann Weyl, whose interest in broad epistemological issues resembled his own.[25] Bentley's initial thinking led him swiftly to the conclusion, offered in an unpublished manuscript in 1929, that "organized expression" is the basic problem shared by social science and mathematics. The question of the "form" of knowledge lay at the roots of the most fertile and profound debates in a number of disciplines. The stage was set, Bentley believed, for a convergence of hitherto unrelated fields toward the common denominator of form.[26] The foundations of mathematics disputes allowed Bentley to explore the problems of the discipline he took to exemplify form above all others. He had originally planned to call his book *Symbol and Meaning in Mathematics* but decided to call attention to the methodological novelty of his "linguistic analysis."[27]

In the first part of *Linguistic Analysis of Mathematics*, Bentley's intention is to establish a "firm construction" for the "embedding language" of mathematics. Even mathematical symbols, usually taken as "abstract," cannot be isolated from the "surrounding forms of expressions and assertions through which the symbols are developed, communicated and interpreted" (LAM, vii). As a philosopher of mathematics, Bentley aligns himself with Hilbert and presents his own teaching as a continuation of and improvement upon that of Hilbert. I believe that the originality of Bentley's views is obscured if his connection with Hilbert is given excessive emphasis. Hilbert did not consider the linguistic context of mathematics as a domain worthy of investigation. Bentley proposes to place the clarification of this context "under the control of mathematical consistency itself," a procedure he contrasts with the logicist appeal to the external and problematic standards of logic. The philosopher of mathematics should begin with "accepted consistencies" in algebra, geometry, and analysis, and should try to extend consistency "across all of mathematics, taken as in one system" (LAM, 1). The logicists, in Bentley's opinion, do not see that every branch of mathematics already has some understanding of "consistency" which is not simply taken over from formal logic. Moreover, there is nothing mystical or unacceptably vague in such notions, unlike the "intuition" of Brouwer and his school. The search for consistency in mathematics must begin in the midst of mathematical discourse itself. Philosophers of mathematics cannot seek an external standpoint from which consistency can be legislated.

Bentley's principal target is the logicist position as presented in *Principia Mathematica*. He remarked later to Dewey that he had decided in the late 1920s that if *Principia* were correct, his own views were seriously threatened.[28] What Bentley had in mind was both the logicist veneration of formal logic and, more important, the ontology of logical atomism. Logicism failed to realize that its faith in logic amounts to reliance upon a "distillate of everyday language" and thus upon the implicit ontology of that language. There was for Bentley no advance over the vagaries of everyday understanding with Russell's belief that the expressions contained in "atomic" sentences must refer to logically independent data of immediate experience. Russell's effort to theorize a "logical atom" as something that cannot be further analyzed was nothing more than a rehearsal of familiar empiricist theses. Bentley could never understand precisely why philosophers who prided themselves on their advanced views continued to accept a teaching as thoroughly discredited as he took empiricism to be. The doctrines of *Principia Mathematica* seemed to Bentley to rest on the absurd notion that the logician or mathematician can somehow step outside the language he employs to appeal to the standards of logic.

Hilbert's merit is that he presents the "objects" of mathematics such as the natural numbers, operations such as addition and subtraction, and the "primary logical elements" of mathematics such as "and," "all," and "some" as symbols, where the very "locus of consistency is in the symbols themselves, and not in some other region of fact for which the symbols are merely representative" (LAM, 3). Now Bentley does not go so far as to agree with the opinion of some formalists that the "ideal statements" of mathematics are merely meaningless combinations of signs or arbitrary "marks on paper." Indeed, one of Bentley's central claims is that there can be no such thing as an uninterpreted formula as asserted by advocates of axiomatization.[29] Any assembly of symbols is "interpreted" simply by being constructed by a mathematician.

In order to make Bentley's program clear, I shall begin with Hilbert's dependence upon intuition in metamathematics. The finitary method, according to Hilbert, relies upon "direct reflection on content that proceeds without axiomatic assumptions but by means of thought-experiments on objects imagined in full consciousness," an admission that led Weyl to describe Hilbert as a formalist in mathematics, but an intuitionist in metamathematics.[30] For Bentley, this approach suffers from two fatal difficulties. First, Hilbert takes as unproblematic the condition of "being 'before him'" when he investigates a mathematical object. In less Bentleyan language, Hilbert has offered no account of what is meant by entertaining a notion or carrying out a thought-experiment on a mathematical object. In Bentley's opinion, there is no good reason to assume that, simply because we believe we know what is meant in ordinary language by the "appearance" of an object to us, we can simply extend this everyday meaning to mathematical thinking. The "appearance" of a mathematical object before the mind cannot be modeled on the "appearance" of a physical object. Second, Hilbert "posits a certain conventional psychological status—an 'inner' power or faculty or condition" called "intuition." A consistently formalist approach cannot resort to these conventional mental states or powers. Thus, formalism cannot employ a notion such as "intuition" until or unless it has produced an account of intuition acceptable to the formalist orientation. It must be understood that Bentley is not advocating the formalization of a natural language. Rather, he seeks to formalize the processes by which the operations of metamathematical intuition are carried out.

Since philosophers of mathematics have not clarified intuition, they do not understand what they are doing: "What it is that they themselves mean, and more particularly what it is that they mean for the purposes of mathematical construction, has never been directly established by an adequately complete study of the situations they describe, and it cannot be inferred from their conventional employment, nor by appealing to some inner power of appraisal: it must be established by studying them in the very systems of presentation which they contain or offer" (LAM, 5). Among various possible senses of "intuition" Bentley is most concerned with the nonconceptual knowledge claimed by the mathematician who conducts a thought-experiment.[31] In a discipline concerned with the elimination of arbitrariness, Bentley believed it was absurd to resort to ordinary views concerning the direct apprehension of objects. Intuition for Bentley, as it is for Hegel, is essentially a "silent" or radically subjective process about which the mathematical philosopher or logician can say nothing.[32] It is hardly possible to achieve consistency in a discipline in which the private intuitions of system builders are at odds.

His reflections upon the problematic character of intuition led Bentley to question the whole notion of mathematical "foundations." The very expression suggests that mathematics has or needs some sort of extramathematical supports. If the philosopher of mathematics has not uncovered and eliminated the implicit metaphysics of these supports, mathematics will inevitably have shaky foundations. What Bentley requires is, to use non-Bentleyan language, the complete philosophical speech about mathematics. That speech, moreover, cannot import any extraneous notions into mathematics. Mathematics, then, must become self-conscious. If we insist upon "foundational" imagery, we must realize that foundations are to be sought in mathematics or nowhere at all. The formalist quest for consistency must proceed outward from technical mathematical discourse to the discursive context of mathematics. Accordingly, the mathematician turns in vain to conventional logic. Bentley knew that it is possible to discuss consistency and axiomatization apart from some determinate branch of mathematics, but this possibility simply shows that we can abstract from the practice of mathematics, which he never denies. We can no more arrive at a consistent mathematics by the application of principles drawn from some foundation discipline than we can arrive at a consistent natural science through the application of rules of "scientific method" which are nothing more than abstractions from the practice of science.

Bentley was aware of the parallel, drawn more recently by W. V. Quine, between the foundationalist reduction of mathematics to set theory and the reduction of empirical knowledge to sense perception or experience.[33] The problems involved in doing the latter could also be found in doing the former. The deeper issue for Bentley has to do with the intelligibility of conventional views for which it is self-evident that mathematics is a matter of pure reason. We have seen how Bentley criticized conventional epistemological divisions in the social and natural sciences. He saw no reason why mathematics or logic should be exempt from these criticisms. The implicit challenge in *Linguistic Analysis of Mathematics* is for philosophers of mathematics who have objected to particular versions of the traditional opinion that mathematics is a form of a priori knowledge to press on to reject this thesis altogether.

We are now ready to look at Bentley's arguments more closely. The linguistic tools used in foundational studies are less precise than the mathematical symbols employed and bring into these stud-ies numerous presuppositions. Complete consistency in Hilbert's sense of freedom from contradiction cannot be reached without the development of "fully clarified postulation" in the embedding lan-guage of mathematical discourse. By "postulation" Bentley means the "most general form of linquistic control which we may estab-lish" in some area of inquiry (LAM, 21–22). Bentleyan postulation is more comprehensive than procedures by which so-called primitive or uninterpreted terms are introduced into a logical system. He sug-gests a family resemblance between his notion of "postulation" and Hilbert's "formal axioms," as well as parallels with the logician Henry Sheffer's usage in his unpublished "General Theory of Nota-tional Relativity." Sheffer, however, "makes his postulates rest in a 'language function' or 'base' which at once becomes a field for fur-ther analysis and further postulation" (LAM, 21). Finally, Bentleyan "postulation" designates both a formal structure and the processes by which the structure is produced.

There are two general sorts of postulations: "realistic" and "se-mantic." Although Bentley had used the term "realism" for many years, he defines it carefully only in *Linguistic Analysis of Mathe-matics.* "Realism" designates the "status of any linguistic situation prior to any direct use of postulation" such that when a system or any part of a system is "taken naively and immediately as '*man-ifest,*' '*intuitive,*' '*true,*' or '*necessary,*' then that system is to be called a Realism" (LAM, 16–17). He makes clear that "realism" is not identical with "materialism" or indeed with any traditional meta-physics. Whenever we take the status of an entity, class of entities, or properties of entities as intuitively clear, Bentley is inclined to la-bel this view "realistic." He distinguishes further between "explicit" realistic postulations where this status is admitted and "implicit" views where a realistic notion "lurks unsuspected in the postulatory materials." A "semantic" postulation, in contrast, has no realistic elements. Inquiry in terms of semantic postulation seeks consis-tency and the identification of all alternative postulations in the same domain. The only "reality" or "existence" admissible in a se-mantic postulation is "that of the separately inspected elements within the system with respect to one another."

The fundamental premise of realism is that some or all of the parts of a system are isomorphic to some extralinguistic "reality." Bentley labels with a lower-case "x" any member of a system defined wholly in systemic or mutually reflective terms and with an upper case "X" any member of a system defined in explicit, implicit, partial, or complete independence of the system to which it belongs. The "realistic postulate" then refers to a system S_r constructed so that all orderings of its members depend upon orderings of the form "x-to-X" or upon the isomorphic assertion. The "semantic postulate" refers to a system S_s constructed so that any X appears in it only as a contextually defined element. The ordering of members of S_s is independent of any external ordering.

Now Bentley is aware that his formulations lack the precision of efforts by conventional logicians. The student of logic may find Bentley's various notations and expressions peculiar since logical notation was widely standardized by the early 1930s. Bentley's defense is that the "appearance of exactness" is "specious for the very reason" that the "underlying postulations" of conventional logic are unclear (LAM, 22–23). The use of standard symbols or notation could not give precision to a discipline riven by confusion. Bentley's own formulations are preferable to those "which make pretenses to precision where precision is not available." It cannot be doubted, I believe, that Bentley's refusal to employ conventional symbols and notation makes his presentation needlessly obscure. In fairness to him, however, it must be noted that his starting point is different from that of conventional logicians. Bentley does not believe that he possesses a metaphysically neutral instrument with which to study a variety of problems. He rejects out of hand the notion that we can "formalize" or "axiomatize" a scientific theory or a scientific discipline by turning to mathematical logic. Bentley warns the reader that he proposes to begin by employing ordinary language, a move he recognizes as paradoxical and which lends what he calls an "impressionistic" character to his arguments. What must be established first is a "small region of precision" as an "island" in the "sea of linguistic confusion" (LAM, ix). That the precision of logicians is illusory he takes to be shown by the very existence of rival schools of logicians. We know much less about inquiry than most philosophers suppose, for no one has developed a "form of accepted expression adequate for the general development of knowledge" and given it a "technical language of the type we call scientific." His two forms of postulation are intended as indicators of "certain phenomena or situations, as yet not fully analyzed, with which all of us are in a general way acquainted, but with which no one of us is precisely acquainted." Thus, even Bentley's own conceptual divisions are exhibitions of the postulational method he proposes.

In Bentley's thinking, the use of "semantic postulation" is linked with the goal of understanding inquiry in a "systematic" manner. Conventional philosophers or logicians, regardless of their systematic intentions, had never grasped the notion of "system" adequately. A correct account of "system" requires the complete and consistent development of whatever we are concerned to understand. That is, the property of being "systematic" is an emergent property. Even if we do not have before us the complete and consistent development of a subject matter, we may still understand "system" as "any organization of meanings, implications, or references" with which we are concerned. Within logic and mathematics, Bentley realizes, "system" has a different meaning, designating a formal structure consisting of symbols, formation rules, logical axioms, and the like. Since Bentley does not understand consistency and completeness in the same way as philosophers for whom logic is paradigmatic, his use of "system" is unlike the conventional usage (LAM, 73–75).

The conventional notion of "system" is thoroughly tainted with subjectivity, a criticism made clear in Bentley's correspondence with Weyl (LAM, 164–70).[34] Like Bentley, Weyl had insisted that mathematical and physical systems be treated as wholes, but he had made a rigid Kantian distinction between phenomenal and theoretical knowledge. For Bentley, Weyl's claim was that we could describe something as a "system" if we could construct it. This claim ignores the difficulties posed by two unrecognized premises upon which it is based. First, Weyl takes for granted our immediate knowledge *that* things exist. Second, he believes we know that certain *sorts* of things exist. For Weyl, "persons" and "things" are known directly. Bentley rejects this "Aristotelian" view and finds a form of it at the roots of mathematical intuition. In a letter to Weyl, he says that he has "never had such existences exhibited" to him in any immediate sense. A system cannot simply be the subjective product of an especially inventive logician. Since there was no adequate account of intuition, any system claiming to be based on intuition could hardly be considered complete or consistent. That is, for Bentley mathematicians cannot develop systems in isolation from accounts of the processes by which systems are formed. These processes, in turn, cannot be understood to consist in the application of standard logical methods. Bentley proposes a more fundamental level of reflection in mathematical or logical discourse than he believes is exhibited in the work of philosophers of mathematics.

Bentley's Semantic Analysis

Bentley's view of language lies at the core of his semantic approach. For most of us language is an instrument used by "minds" to communicate with other "minds" about "things" (LAM, 32). As a realistic postulation, our everyday view of language requires us to assume some sort of correspondence between "mind" and "external" reality. Thus, ordinary language is metaphysically realist. Rather than enter directly into the epistemological debate about connections between language and reality, Bentley chooses to characterize language in terms of a manifold of various degrees of consistency. Language is the totality of "connected expressions . . . consisting of a nexus of smaller systems; some consistent and some inconsistent; some sharply outlined and some almost everywhere . . . vague; some rabidly dogmatic and some freely open to reformatory organization." Bentley's notion of grades of consistency is intended to cut across both conventional classifications such as "parts of speech" and functional views that take language as "expressive" of ideas, thoughts, and the like. Language contains such terms as "Experience," "Knowledge" and "Fact" which "when realistically set up within it, claim to control it. By the same token, however, Experience and Knowledge and Fact, as established and developed in language, are analytically within its scope." During the late 1920s Bentley had theorized the field of scientific inquiry as consisting of four elements—experience, knowledge, fact, and language—a division that forms the basis for his new classification of the sciences. Conventional understandings of language, according to Bentley, claim that language "represents" facts, "constitutes" knowledge, or gives us "access" to experience. Such opinions do not permit us to bring these four elements together in a systematic way. When we employ semantic postulation we do not assign any priority to one of these elements. However, since semantic postulation is a linguistic activity, our systematic theorizing of the organization of these elements cannot avoid reflection on language.

According to Bentley, many of the most advanced thinkers recognize the importance of the "linguistic problem." Language is a fundamental issue for Poincaré's philosophy of science, the philosophies of mathematics of Felix Klein and Karl Menger, and the social science of Simmel. Bentley's study of language, while occasioned by his interest in the philosophy of mathematics, is intended to address larger epistemological issues. He does not offer a "theory" of language set over against defective views. Rather, he begins with a tentative division of language into four levels of organization: "inchoate implication," "words-common," "terms," and "symbols." The "linguistic field" consists of a domain of inchoate implications which includes as successively smaller and internally more consistent sets the domains of words-common, terms, and symbols. "Mathematics" is the smallest and most consistent subset of the domain of symbols. We find, however, that the symbols that compose mathematical language bring with them "implications of meaning" from less consistent linguistic domains (LAM, 34–36). Bentley proposes to trace the emergence of consistent forms of language from the least consistent linguistic domains, since for him it is unintelligible to suppose that we can begin anywhere else.

The conduct of Bentley's linguistic inquiry requires several rules or procedures. None of these procedures is intended to characterize or identify a mental process. Bentley sought to avoid any hint of "psychologism" in his semantic method. Instead, his procedures are designated as "sociological" in what he calls the "methodological and critical sense" of the term. For Bentley this means that the procedures have to do only with the form or structure and not the substance of inquiry. A sociological account is both a formal account and an account of form.

Bentley's six rules may be stated in less eccentric fashion than their presentation in the text (LAM, 38–41). First, any linguistic analysis is based on some "preliminary provisional dissection and organization of linguistic materials." We can never begin without taking something for granted. As an example Bentley offers Hilbert's reliance upon the axiomatization of arithmetic as the basis for his axiomatization of geometry. What is crucial is that the investigator understand precisely what he is taking for granted. Second, the "final court of appeal for maximum certainty" is the agreement of "experts." Bentley denies that there is any taint of subjectivity in this rule by claiming that his notion of agreement has nothing to do with any "individualistic psychology." The mathematician is not an "individual" who employs various methods of reasoning in isolation, but is rather a member of a larger community of mathematicians. Moreover, the language of mathematics cannot be a private language. The mathematician cannot do mathematics apart from the public language of mathematics. Thus, Bentley claims to be studying the "whole procedure of mathematicians-at-work-with-mathematics-in-language," where the string of hyphens is intended to suggest the "process" with which he is concerned.

The remaining rules may be stated briefly. The third is that all "meanings, references, implications and connectivities" must be intelligible in systemic terms. Fourth, there can be no privileged position within a system. The structure of a Bentleyan system is not the hypothetico-deductive "tree" or "pyramid" of the conventional logician who begins with primitive terms and axioms, but is instead a circle that can be entered at any point. Fifth, any supposed correspondence between systemically defined terms and "external reality" must be transformed into an intrasystemic or contextual correspondence. Finally, no realistic interpretations of "word-clusters," which are sections of the linguistic field identified for analysis, or "connectivities," which are the structures of word-clusters, are admissible. Such interpretations Bentley dismisses as "Aristotelian."

Bentley's criticisms of "Aristotelian" logic resemble familiar pragmatist opposition to the supposed formality and sterility of traditional logic, which is understood as linked to a discredited metaphysics of substance. He was also sympathetic to Fritz Mauthner's linguistic conventionalism which treated logic as a form of behavior or as a branch of social psychology.[35] In this spirit, Bentley claims that he does not use logic in any "formal sense" in the development of his own position. While he realizes that some readers might well consider semantic postulation a "logical" doctrine, he does not want to identify his position with any conventional logical viewpoint. Bentley describes formal logic as merely one "technique" for scientific thinking and refuses to consider it to be normative for scientific thinking. He notes that pragmatic logic implies a rejection of the logicist foundational view of logic. Indeed, the logicists are simply traditional logicians who employ more refined methods. Bentley agrees with Jan Łukasiewicz's reading of the history of logic which distinguishes Aristotle's own logic from its more dogmatic and inflexible Stoic descendants, especially the logic of Chrysippus (LAM, 301–2). The "apotheosis of Chrysippian logic" is to be found in *Principia Mathematica*. While Bentley recognizes that alternative logics such as those of C. I. Lewis, E. L. Post, Łukasiewicz, Alfred Tarski, and Alonzo Church can be formulated, he believes that none of these logics is free from tacit ontological views. If the system of *Principia* could be purged of logical atomism and given complete consistency, it would be preferable to alternative logics because of its greater comprehensiveness (LAM, 308).

The bulk of the first part of Bentley's book is concerned with the study of word-clusters and connectivities in mathematics. His intention is to uncover ways in which the use of mathematical notions in foundational studies is affected by the indeterminate fringe of meanings attached to these concepts stemming from their use in ordinary language. Until these connections are uncovered, confusion will be endemic in the philosophy of mathematics.

Bentley's survey of the foundations literature suggests to him the presence in the mathematical field of eight word-clusters, several of which have numerous subdivisions. He does not claim to have devised a totally exhaustive and mutually exclusive classification scheme but rather to have reproduced the situation in philosophy of mathematics since mathematicians themselves are uncertain about the meanings of "number," "set," "object," "intuition," and "element," for example. Each word-cluster designates a "situation in language" which is necessarily a "situation in knowledge" and thus has implications reaching beyond its purely mathematical importance. For example, the word-cluster "Symbol" includes a number of notions from algebra, geometry, and analysis, but for Bentley the "situations in knowledge" are, respectively, of "things discretely taken," "things taken as capable of subdivision," and "situations of change, transition, motion." Moreover, there are many knowledge situations for which no types of mathematical consistency have been theorized, such as those designated by terms like "soul, mind, behavior" and "the virtues, the instincts, the feelings, the purposes" (LAM, 45). Such terms identify unexplored territory. For Bentley all branches of mathematics began as efforts to theorize knowledge situations. The unexplored territories suggested by Bentley's lists will not be mathematized in the sense that an existing branch of mathematics will be applied or extended to them. Rather, each of these areas stands in need of the development of consistency.

The word-clusters include character, symbol, number, extension, cardinal, class, intuition, and "the Hilbert object." In Bentley's view most mathematicians treat these word-clusters in a realistic fashion, but a semantic treatment is obviously superior. Two additional classifications are needed to complete a complex classificational scheme in terms of which the foundational issues may be studied. Nine "connectivities" or forms of mathematical organization are identified, including five semantic connectivities and four realistic connectivities. For example, "analytic consistency" illustrates a semantic connectivity while Hilbert's notion of freedom from contradiction is a realistic connectivity. At a more fundamental level, Bentley identifies fourteen "common-reference descriptions" which are carried into mathematical thinking from ordinary language. These descriptions permeate mathematical discourse about word-clusters and connectivities. Indeed, such descriptions can be found throughout the sciences and amount to a kind of table of categories. The descriptions or categories are paired concepts: Objective/Subjective; Inner/Outer; Mind/Matter; Particular/General; Part/Whole; Finite/Infinite; Thing/Operation; Abstract/Concrete; Discrete/Continuous; Structure/Function; Existence/Transition; Individual/Collective; Temporal Instantaneity/Duration; Spatial Instantaneity/Extension.

For Bentley there is nothing inherent in these pairs to require their use. Instead, he has simply identified notions he believes are used by mathematicians who give no attention to the ways in which they determine both the questions and the answers of foundational inquiry. The semantic approach may use these notions if they are purged of realistic premises.

A general characterization of Bentley's semantic apparatus is in order now that we have followed some of his initial steps. In the first place, Bentley attempts to trace the course of mathematical concepts through microscopic analysis of the writings of philosophers and mathematicians. He concentrates on the contexts in which concepts are introduced, their shifting meanings in the course of a mathematician's career, and the various ways in which mathematicians try to explain what they are doing. If we can determine, for example, the precise contexts in which Hilbert aṅd Brouwer refer to "discreteness" we gain some insight into the origins of the differences in their teachings. Through such inquiry we come to understand mathematics as a form of linguistic behavior and not as an a priori science of ideal objects. Although technically difficult and often presented in laboriously baroque language, Bentley's patient examinations resemble what Gilbert Ryle has described as the "tea-tasting method" of the later Wittgenstein: "Tea-tasters do not lump their samples into two or three comprehensive types. Rather they savour each sample and try to place it next door to its closest neighbors, and this not in respect of just one discriminable quality, but along the lengths of various lines of qualities. So Wittgenstein would exhibit the characteristic manner of working of a particular expression, by matching it against examples of expressions progressively diverging from it in various respects and directions.[36]

Now it could be objected that, whatever such analysis might tell us about the genesis of a mode of thinking within mathematics or about the origins of a term or notion, it tells us little or nothing about the issues with which foundational theorists were in fact concerned. We cannot know whether or why a formalist philosophy of mathematics is superior to a logicist philosophy of mathematics except by logical analysis. Bentley firmly opposes this view. For him the study of the "history" or perhaps the "sociology" of mathematics cannot be separated from the practice of mathematics. He did not think he was simply writing the intellectual history of the foundations debates. Rather, his work requires a rethinking of foundational issues that cuts across the school distinctions among logicists, intuitionists, and formalists, since few of these theorists understand mathematics as a "great historical-social development, susceptible of empirical presentation and investigation in its own right" (LAM, 72). The failure of mathematicians to grasp their own discipline in this way lies at the core of the foundational disputes.

Only recently have some philosophers of mathematics begun to consider the possibility of viewing mathematics as an empirical discipline, the history of which is indispensable to an adequate understanding of its basic philosophical issues. Imre Lakatos, for instance, recommends "historico-critical case studies" to explore the "informal" theoretical contexts of mathematical issues.[37] Bentley's studies of the work of Hilbert, Brouwer, Kronecker, and Poincaré have precisely such a task as their central theme. Indeed, it seems to me that Lakatos's work does not address as directly as Bentley's does such crucial questions as the nature of mathematical intuition and the connections between ordinary and mathematical language. According to Bentley, the mathematician's everyday and thus unclarified understanding of "experiential discreteness," for example, conditions his understanding of "mathematical discreteness" (LAM, 66). Unless the ways in which the former is typically transformed into the latter are brought to light, the notion of mathematical discreteness is not completely clear. For Bentley, if mathematics is to learn the most important of lessons from its own development, it cannot permit a continuum of meaning to connect everyday and properly mathematical notions. That is, while the first step in Bentley's philosophy of mathematics is to uncover the links between everyday and mathematical notions, the next step is to achieve full consistency in mathematics by employing semantic postulation, which is the methodological correlate of Bentley's familiar discontinuity thesis. Put concisely, Bentley prohibits any appeal to extramathematical considerations if our intention is to develop a complete and consistent mathematics.

Now the goal of completeness and consistency in mathematics was the heart of Hilbert's program and it has been suggested that Bentley's agreement with this goal makes his own position vulnerable, as Hilbert's was, to Kurt Gödel's demonstration that in any consistent system in which elementary recursive arithmetic can be generated, there will be undecidable propositions of number theory.[38] While Bentley agrees with the intention of the Hilbert program, his own understanding of consistency and completeness does not seem to me to be vulnerable to Gödel's theorem. Bentley criticizes Hilbert for having appealed to extramathematical premises (LAM, 105−16). He had failed to apply mathematical consistency to the categorial pairs such as part/whole and finite/infinite, which play important roles in his system, nor, as we have already seen, was he prepared to explain how thought-experiments on ideal objects were possible. Hilbert could see neither the temporal nor the spatial character of mathematical thinking. Bentley argues that Hilbert failed to understand that since mathematical thinking is a form of linguistic behavior, it must be "durationally social." The result is that his system is a study in "maximal instantaneity." Put in less Bentleyan terms, Hilbert understands the certainty of mathematics in the traditional sense of timeless and a priori truths. A Bentleyan system, unlike a Hilbertian system, is consistent and complete if it employs no realistic premises and does not depend upon notions imported from everyday language. While Bentley never took up the challenge posed to Hilbert by Gödel, he found Gödel as much a "realist" as most mathematical logicians because he appeared to believe in ideal objects.[39] Although it may be the case that Gödel showed the impossibility of formalizing mathematics in a single formal system, Bentley's notion of formalism is sufficiently unlike conventional logico-mathematical understandings of formalism that Gödel's results are not applicable. Equally irrelevant for Bentley's teaching is the extension of the significance of Gödel's theorem reflected in claims that it shows the limits of knowledge or has far-reaching epistemological importance. I believe Bentley would have been sympathetic to Barry Hindess's treatment of this question.[40]

Hindess argues that, properly speaking, the domain of interpretation for mathematics is "theoretical" and that epistemological extensions of Gödel's theorem, which often take the form of claims about the "limits" of knowledge, must invoke extramathematical interpretive criteria that make the original extension baseless. The implications of Bentley's position are, if anything, even more far-reaching than Hindess's criticism of extensions of Gödel's theorem. While one may argue that Gödel's demonstration applies only to a limited class of logico-mathematical systems, Bentley's position suggests that even these systems are misunderstood if they are taken in their conventional sense as atemporal structures having no connections with everyday discourse. As Bentley repeatedly claims, a notion like "consistency" is unintelligible apart from its own history in the work of mathematicians. Indeed, it is only because the mathematician is a part of the historical discourse of mathematics that he is able to understand "consistency" in the first place. Thus, both the problems with which Gödel was concerned and his solutions are, from a Bentleyan standpoint, constituted within and in terms of a variegated but historically identifiable tradition of discourse.

Among contemporary philosophers of mathematics, Hilary Putnam has developed several arguments that parallel leadings ideas in Bentley's work.[41] Like Bentley, Putnam has expressed serious doubts about the search for "foundations of mathematics" and has linked up his skepticism to reservations about the "foundational" view of empirical knowledge. For Putnam the most important aspect of mathematical propositions is "the very wide variety of equivalent formulations that they possess."[42] Most philosophers of mathematics take a specific sort of formulation as primary. For the majority of philosophers of mathematics, their discipline describes a universe of objects understood as sets. Putnam's claim is that an "equivalent picture" of mathematical facts can be constructed employing modal logic, a move that changes our picture so that mathematics does not describe a domain of eternal objects but "simply tells us what follows from what" by using notions of mathematical possibility and necessity. While this view certainly suggests Bentley's rejection of ontological language in mathematics, the parallel is even more specific. Bentley argues, for example, that from his semantic point of view there is no need for philosophers of mathematics to debate the priority of natural numbers or to decide whether number theory should be based on cardinals or ordinals (LAM, 132–44). In general, mathematics can dispense with such questions as what number "really is." For any specific theory of number it is possible to propose an alternative view. Thus, in a number theory characterized by "semantic consistency" we view "number" as having a variety of what Putnam calls "equivalent formulations" or what Bentley calls "mathematical operations." For Bentley it is the use of "number" in a particular branch of mathematics that is primary rather than its supposed general meaning. That use, in turn, is not the free invention or arbitrary creation of the mathematician but is rather embedded in a history of mathematical thinking. Again, we find a similar notion in Putnam, who writes that "the construction of a highly articulated body of mathematical knowledge with a long tradition of successful problem solving is a truly remarkable *social* achievement."[43] Unlike Bentley, however, Putnam does not claim that the "social" character of mathematics is inseparable from its technical character.

The second major point of similarity between Bentley and Putnam lies in their opposition to the traditional distinction between "empirical" and "mathematical" discourse.[44] Bentley's studies of the work of mathematicians convinced him that significant new mathematical notions were typically introduced in what may be called an "experimental" vein. For Putnam, similar reflection leads to the thesis that mathematics employs, but all too often fails to recognize, "quasi-empirical" strategies rather than proofs in the strict sense. Thus, the practice of mathematics challenges the conventional a priorism of the philosophy of mathematics. That a priorism is in part the legacy of the untenable view that an a priori mathematical theory of physical space is possible. Foundational thinking itself must be rejected, in Putnam's view. What Bentley believed he had shown was that the search for completeness and consistency in mathematics and the search for foundations must part company. A complete and consistent Bentleyan system cannot have an a priori foundation.

Semantic Analysis and the Sciences

Bentley's criticisms of the foundations of mathematics literature are grounded in his methodology of semantic analysis, which is presented and employed to produce a philosophy of science in a remarkable section of *Linguistic Analysis of Mathematics* (LAM, 229–79). The self-contained essay "Semantic Analysis" presents Bentley's philosophical position with greater clarity than any other single text.

In Bentley's opinion, his semantic analysis, which developed from his study of underlying issues in mathematics and sociology, has shown its utility in the examination of foundational disputes in logic and mathematics (LAM, 231). Its clarification of these disputes suggests its general applicability. Bentley begins his presentation of the semantic approach by distinguishing between "scientific" and "metaphysical" discourse (LAM, 232–35). The traditional view he wishes to reject presents science and metaphysics as if they were concerned, respectively, with "objective" and "subjective" subject matters. For Bentley, the cut should be made between domains in which "primary propositions" serve, explicitly or implicitly, as criteria for knowledge and those in which no such propositions can be found. The former domains belong to metaphysics, while the latter belong to science. Accordingly, there are likely to be both general viewpoints and specific theories in the sciences that are metaphysical in his sense, while it is conceivable that positions typically taken as metaphysical might be scientific in his sense. Subsumed under his distinction is also the cut, criticized as well by Karl Popper, between science as "empirical" and metaphysics as "non-empirical."[45] Bentley's distinction is intended to account for what seemed to him a crucial characteristic of science—that it could undergo a complete transformation without collapse. Metaphysical systems either "rule or ruin" for Bentley since they require us to accept some "realistic" account of the world or of essential features of the world. In contrast, rival scientific views do not engage in the global conflict Bentley sees between metaphysical systems.

While there is a great deal in Bentley's teaching that resembles on the surface the views of Thomas S. Kuhn and other historians and philosophers of science which emphasize the discontinuous development of science through successive confrontations of rival world views, this aspect of Bentley's position is not all of his understanding. It is incorrect to see in the transition from classical to contemporary physics a conflict similar to those that exist between rival metaphysical doctrines. Science, unlike metaphysics, possesses a methodology, the essential character of which is the possibility of self-correction. While Bentley was prepared to grant "revolutionary" status to relativity theory, he also believed that Einstein's work was both intelligibly connected with and in a number of ways strongly dependent upon a variety of physical and mathematical notions already well established. The Bentleyan view is that in science, as in politics, a revolution never marks a complete break with the old regime. The continuity of science is furnished by self-correction. Bentley's thesis is that semantic analysis in his sense lies at the heart of this self-correction. Since scientists themselves may practice, but not understand, semantic analysis, its characteristics must be stated explicitly.

The underlying problems Bentley finds in mathematics and sociology have to do with "parts" and "wholes." In neither discipline can be found systematic efforts to solve these problems in what Bentley takes to be the genuinely "scientific" way—"solution 'from within' the field of the investigation itself"—since metaphysical presuppositions permeate both sociology and mathematics (LAM, 238). In more general terms, scientists of all sorts take for granted a "naively-given extra-scientific background" consisting of "(a) real human beings with presumed definitely real mentalities; (b) an actual, or in some sense real and actual, world of matter and events; (c) a general, vaguely-characterized realm of knowledge (science) related to or relating with (a) and (b), and embodied or formulated in language or language structures of varying degrees of exactness" (LAM, 239). Most scientists or philosophers of science accept all or some of this background casually. Thus, the social scientist may make extremely crude and simplistic assumptions about the physical world, while the physicist is likely to possess an equally crude understanding of psychological or social phenomena. To the extent that a feature of the "conventional background" is taken as obvious or self-evident, it is for Bentley necessarily misunderstood and, more important, its constitutive role in or for a particular science is rendered opaque.

Bentley's semantic analysis proposes to theorize a "field of investigation" consisting of fact, experience, knowledge, and language. Most scientists or philosophers have taken one of these terms as a firm basis for science. Bentley gives each term a "semantic" interpretation without realistic claims. Thus, "knowledge" represents the totality of currently accepted "science" with no suggestion that it must be taken as a property of the "minds" of scientists or that it is identical with "empirical facts." "Language" indicates the "formalized embodiment" of knowledge and is to be taken as "activities" or "behaviors" without assumptions connecting it to the operations of individual minds. The conjunction of knowledge and language, then, will indicate the "ranges" or domains of science. "Experience" designates all references to the ways in which knowledge and language appear to be concretized in psychological or mental states. "Fact" represents the "content" of science. The conjunction of experience and fact, then, will indicate the ranges of (a) and (b) as specified in Bentley's presentation of the "conventional background" of scientific thinking. Since the domains designated by the terms "fact," "experience," "knowledge," and "language" are unintelligible if taken in isolation from each other, the field they constitute is an "intricate never vanishing connectivity."

"Language" has the unique status of being the necessary condition for our identification of any object in any of the four domains of the field of investigation. Moreover, Bentley claims that in each domain we find multiple levels of linguistic organization and degrees of consistency of the sort he has identified in the foundations of mathematics literature. When the multidimensional character of language is not recognized, we are likely to settle on one of the domains as the foundation for our understanding of the field of investigation as a whole. The result is a "world interpretation" such as the foundational doctrine of "fact" offered by materialism, intuitionist appeals to the authority of "experience," idealist appeals to "knowledge" and contemporary "logistic realism" that gives "language" the foundational position (LAM, 254–55). It is not surprising that Bentley distinguishes study of a domain based on a world interpretation from genuinely scientific or "semantic" study of a domain. Semantic analysis requires both that any study of a domain must be concerned with relations among domains and that any formulation of these relations may be taken as an "alternative formulation" of foundation problems (LAM, 256). That is, semantic analysis is intended to show that equivalent formulations can be produced for the foundation problems of all sciences. Finally, in what Bentley calls a "linguistic adaptation of the mathematical use of limits," semantic analysis will make clear the limits of complete and consistent formulations in any one domain insofar as these limits are dependent upon the rest of the field of investigation. For example, how might the limits of what we can presently theorize about "experience" affect what can be theorized about "fact"?

Bentley's next move is to identify various categorial pairs such as subjective/objective and mind/matter as word-clusters that serve in semantic analysis as "indices," which give access to the "structure" of the field of investigation as a whole (LAM, 258–59). Two sets of word-clusters are distinguished which may be summarized by subjective/objective and individual/particular. The result of Bentley's analysis is a presentation of the four domains of the field of investigation as a coordinate space generated by an objectifying/subjectifying dimension as the horizontal axis and a particularizing/generalizing dimension as the vertical axis. The x-axis is a continuum ranging from experience to language or from subjectifying to objectifying viewpoints. The y-axis is a continuum ranging from fact to knowledge or from particularizing to generalizing viewpoints. The result is a space divided into four quadrants designated "subjectively particularized," "objectively particularized," "subjectively generalized," and "objectively generalized." This scheme permits Bentley to locate and classify both the various world interpretations he rejects and the various sciences. Since the two axes mark off continua rather than dichotomies, Bentley can identify and locate viewpoints along the axes as successions of transformations from one domain to another.

While Bentley is not interested in classifications of the sciences as an important philosophical issue, he claims that the scheme he has presented leads to a better understanding of relations among the sciences than can be found elsewhere (LAM, 265–66). In the first place, the nineteenth-century doctrine of the hierarchy of the sciences is obviously untenable. Against Comte and Spencer, Bentley argues that the sciences cannot be arranged with physics as the foundation discipline and the other sciences as its subdivisions or special cases. Any version of the hierarchy of the sciences doctrine theorizes the inclusion of one science in another by means of "quasi-localization," which Bentley believes invariably conceals ontological premises (LAM, 266–67). If we assume, for example, that "mental processes" are a subset of "neurophysiological processes," which in turn are a subset of "biochemical processes," the door is opened to reductionist explanatory strategies of the sort to which Bentley had always been opposed.

In contrast, Bentley distinguishes the sciences of "description," physics and socialization, from the sciences of "technique," mathematics and psychology. Physics is concerned with the domain of fact, but Bentley appeals to contemporary physics to make clear that no materialistic teachings are permissible. Socialization is concerned with "organization and coherence" and is thus the science located in the domain of knowledge. Mathematics and "linguistic interpretation" constitute the science of semantic analysis. Psychology is the least clearly demarcated science, since Bentley has in mind a discipline concerned with all connections between experience and fact on the "subjectifying" side of the field of investigation. The sciences occupy the termini of the x and y-axes and are concerned with transformations between the poles of fact-experience (psychological analysis), knowledge-experience (social analysis), fact-language (physical analysis), and knowledge-language (semantic analysis). The figure is adapted from one of Bentley's diagrams to include the most important features of his system.

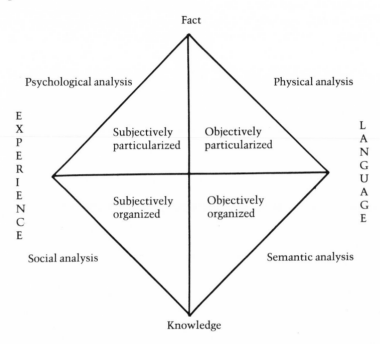

The four principal modes of scientific analysis are not intended to replace but rather to make possible a better understanding of the conventionally identified sciences. For example, while biology is ordinarily located in the domain covered by physical analysis, Bentley claims that many of its important theoretical and research issues are understood better if they are located in the domain of social analysis, since these issues have to do with parts/wholes or "organizational" questions (LAM, 269). Semantic analysis of the foundations of mathematics, in contrast, purges this discipline of the "implied reality" of its objects and makes possible full formalization (LAM, 270–71). The social sciences, when mapped onto Bentley's scheme, must incorporate complete spatio-temporal frameworks into their inquiry (LAM, 271–72). Physics, which already operates in Bentley's approved manner to a great extent, is encouraged to become even more semantically oriented. Indeed, Bentley invokes Werner Heisenberg's uncertainty principle in quantum mechanics as an analogous notion in one branch of physics to his own semantic approach to "all knowledge" (LAM, 273). Psychology must divest itself of all realistic premises and formulate such notions as cognition, sensation, and the like as "limits" (LAM, 274–76).

The Bentleyan system as I have presented it so far, however, is not complete. Bentley generates this system from only two categorial oppositions. We should recall that he has already presented a number of other such oppositions in his discussions of the foundations of mathematics. He describes the fourfold division of the field of investigation as "crude." It is the "merest sketch" in two dimensions of what is actually a "many-dimensioned field of study" (LAM, 264). Thus, the door is opened to an n-dimensional presentation generated by additional categorial pairs.

Bentley's semantic analysis may be clarified by comparing it with recent "semantic" approaches to the study of the structure of scientific theories as summarized by Frederick Suppe.[46] According to this view, advanced by Suppe, Patrick Suppes, Bas van Frassen, and others, scientific theories are intended to provide a generalized description of some class of phenomena that permits the scientist to answer a variety of questions about the phenomena by abstracting a set of parameters from them which it takes as influencing them. Thus, the theory characterizes "idealized replicas" of the phenomena. In the physical sciences these replicas are the "physical systems" with which we are concerned. A specific configuration of a physical system is a "state" of the system and the behavior of a system is its change in state over time. This behavior can be represented as a "trajectory" traced by the system as it intersects the coordinates of successive states. The parameters of a scientific theory, then, establish coordinates that define a "phase space," the configurations of which represent the behavior of the system. Configurations are imposed on the phase space by the laws of the scientific theory. Thus, deterministic laws specify as physically possible certain subsets of a phase space, while statistical laws specify probability measures over the phase space. The elementary statements of a scientific theory are organized according to the particular logic required by the topological structure of the phase space of the theory. That is, we need not assume that there is a single logic according to which a scientific theory must be organized. In Hilary Putnam's useful formulation, we "read the logic off" from the infinite dimensional vector space or "Hilbert space," in the case of quantum mechanics.[47] Accordingly, this procedure may be generalized to other scientific theories.

To return to Bentley, his full-scale program which would call for generating a scheme from all relevant categorial pairs may be described as a proposal to map scientific disciplines in a way analogous to the mapping of specific scientific theories within a given science as proposed by advocates of semantic analysis as I have just sketched it. For Bentley, a particular science may be mapped onto a set of subspaces of the Hilbert space. This would mean, on Bentley's view of science, that the totality of the objects, theories, methodologies, and "foundations" of a science must be mapped as well. The "complete description" Bentley presents as the task of science consists in precisely this mapping operation.

For Bentley it is necessary to show that "realism" in any science is untenable. His semantic teaching depends, he believes, upon the intelligibility of his claim that we cannot assert a "one-to-one correspondence" between a proposition and some aspect of reality unproblematically (LAM, 75–77, 277–79). I shall conclude with an account of Bentley's position as the logical basis of his semantic approach.

If we assert a one-to-one correspondence between a term S and a fact T, symbolized here by S:T, Bentley claims that a paradox results. First, it is not the case that we can characterize T apart from some word or term, since we cannot even speak coherently about extralinguistic knowledge. Our correspondence, then, is not between S and T but rather between S and a term P which designates or represents T. The distinction between S and T "vanishes with the transformation" of T into P. Our proposed S:T cannot be established. Now in order to produce S:T or, for that matter, S:P, we must be able to identify S, T, and P unambiguously. That is, for logical discourse to be possible S must be identical with itself such that S = S, P = P, or T = T. This is, of course, the principle or law of identity. We should note that for Bentley it is impossible to assert T = T, for this would amount to making an ontological claim about the identity of a thing, whereas we can only speak properly of terms.

Extending Bentley's analysis, if we are to identify S or P, we must be able to identify the properties that allow us to distinguish S or P from everything that is non-S or non-P.[48] There is no reason why the difficulties inherent in the notion of isomorphism cannot reappear, since to identify S as S, we must be able both to identify a set of properties V and to connect V with S. While Bentley appears to agree with this argument, his own direction is somewhat different. In order to identify S we must know the larger system R to which S belongs. Thus, we cannot establish S:P without consideration of the place of S within R. If we do not identify S within R, we cannot distinguish S from non-S. Now since S:T dissolves into S:P, then P as well as S belongs to some larger system. If S and P both belong to R, we require a way of distinguishing them from each other. If S and P belong to different systems R and Q, we must find yet a third system U to which both R and Q belong, pose the same questions concerning the differentiation of R and Q, and so on. It is essential for us to understand that Bentley cannot turn to intuition to determine these identities and relations. He cannot say, with Arthur Pap, for example, that we cannot teach logic to someone who "simply does not see that 'q' follows from 'p and q,' or that 'p' and 'not-p' cannot both be true."[49] The terms of logical discourse are unstable. They may be stabilized only through a semantic analysis that makes explicit the structure of the space to which they are applied. In the final chapter of this study it will be necessary to ask if Bentley's formalism is itself rational.

7

Bentley's Behavioral Science

The discovery of fact, the development of theory, and the consideration of method, are phases of one procedure. . . .
  "Sociology and Mathematics"

Behavior Knowledge Fact is the most comprehensive statement of Bentley's behavioral science. It employs the philosophic teaching of *Linguistic Analysis of Mathematics* to criticize the categorial premises of contemporary psychological theories and presents Bentley's alternatives more clearly than his earlier criticisms of psychology permitted. In Part 1 of the book he offers "an appraisal of psychology as itself a form of knowledge" through a study of the premises of a number of contemporary psychologists.[1] Part 2 presents "semantic postulation" as a method that permits the study of "men and things in systems" in the fashion of the advanced sciences. Part 3 develops behavioral science as the science of general forms or types of behavior.

Unlike most of Bentley's books, *Behavior Knowledge Fact* was well received by scholars, including such sociologists as George A. Lundberg and Edward S. Robinson, and the psychologist J. F. Brown.[2] The book addressed a range of topics more familiar to sociologists and psychologists than the themes of *Linguistic Analysis of Mathematics*. It belonged to a growing genre of writings concerned with the possibility of a scientific approach to the study of social phenomena. The book appeared at a time when the impact of European emigrés was beginning to be felt in American psychology, social science, and philosophy. Such psychologists as Kurt Koffka, Kurt Lewin, and Wolfgang Köhler figure prominently in Bentley's discussion, reflecting the growing importance of Gestaltist psychology and other tendencies opposed to functionalism and behaviorism.[3] Proponents of "scientific" sociology like Lundberg had begun to turn to contemporary philosophy of science and thus were prepared for Bentley. The "unity of science" movement initiated by the logical positivists Otto Neurath (with whom Bentley would correspond during the 1940s) and Rudolf Carnap seemed a straw in the wind, while in a popular vein Alfred Korzybski's "general semantics" both reflected and helped to foster an interest in connections between linguistic precision, science, and progressive social theory.[4] The issues with which Bentley had been concerned for decades were now part of the mainstream of academic social science.

This chapter will concentrate on Bentley's criticism of the categorial bases of psychology, which provides additional insight into his view of language; on his rejection of behaviorism; on his restatement of the semantic method; on the roles of observation and theory in his teaching; and on his behavioral science as a whole. Since Bentley's criticism of the primacy of the "individual" in social science explanations is developed to its greatest extent in *Behavior Knowledge Fact*, the final section of the chapter includes a comparison of his position with P. F. Strawson's arguments on behalf of "individuals."

Linguistic Analysis of Psychology

I will dispense with complete summaries of Bentley's rehearsals and criticisms of the views of most of the psychologists whose work he studied in order to make clear the larger issues at stake in the first part of his book.[5] The effects of the absence of serious critical inquiry in psychology can be seen in the insistence of most psychologists that their discipline studies "individuals." Bentley was aware that many social scientists continued to understand psychology as the foundation of social science. Behavioral science will not be a foundation discipline but rather the dialectical *Aufhebung* of psychology and conventional social science.

Bentley limits his study to psychological systems that aspire to the status of science. At first sight, scientific psychologies appear to divide into teachings that understand "science" as "report, reproduction, reflection, or display of 'fact,'" and teachings that stress the interpretive "construction" of "complex systems of 'meanings'" (BKF, 3–5). This division, however, is premature since proponents of both notions of "science" have not considered the role of "language" in science. Both notions rest upon a priori claims about the subject matter of psychology. As usual, Bentley's criticisms do not present a rival account of this subject matter set over against defective positions. His reasons for rejecting out of hand the views of a number of psychologists furnishes a convenient summary of what he was opposed to in the study of behavior:

> They all accept as "known" in advance of inquiry, and as the point of support for their procedures, some "certain" or "definitely expressed" or "sufficiently well understood *fact*." Their "points of support" lie, then, in a sense, *outside* their own ranges of workmanship. No single formulation of this characteristic will do justice to all the cases. In some it is clearly expressed, or with equal clearness, implied. In others it shows itself in the manner in which problems are formulated. In still others, it takes rather the form of constraint, of stumbling, in the shadow of some "philosophical" cloud. This statement is not to be understood as meaning that the rejected systems are *wholly* under the influence of some conventional or dogmatic or other unappraised attitude toward factuality; nor that the accepted systems are *wholly* free from such attitudes. (BKF, 17–18)

What decided the issue for Bentley was evidence of a psychologist's or philosopher's intention to rely as little as possible on assumptions about "facts" or "truths" on which a psychology could be built. His only admitted hesitation was over Koffka's Gestaltism as presented in his *Principles of Gestalt Psychology* (1935). While Bentley was sympathetic to Gestaltist experimentation, he found Koffka's distinctions between the "behavioral environment" and a cognitive "locus" untenable, for they led inevitably to a choice between two equally unacceptable alternatives: "positivism" and "mentalism." Bentley, like Koffka, was an opponent of positivism, but he could not see how Koffka could avoid reviving a traditional dualism of inner and outer.

In his familiar fashion, Bentley produces a classification scheme for the positions he proposes to criticize. In place of conventional schools of psychology, he theorizes a number of underlying "traits" based on "varieties of presentation of spatial and temporal frameworks of observation and construction" (BKF, 18–20). The choices psychologists make concerning fundamental variables, concepts, modes of explanation, and the like define abstract psychological "spaces" and "times" in the same way that mathematical functions define abstract mathematical spaces. His discussions of "space" in *Behavior Knowledge Fact* take their bearings from his reflections in "Sociology and Mathematics," which appeared in the *Sociological Review* in 1931.[6] Bentley distinguishes five spatial types. "Vulgar" space is the space form taken for granted in everyday life. It is similar to but not identical with the three-dimensional space of Newtonian or classical physics, since the latter is defined by an explicit logico-mathematical conceptual framework. This framework is a "mathematical" space that is given a physical interpretation, thus defining, precisely in the sense intended by proponents of "semantic" notions of scientific theory, a "physical" space. Societies, Bentley argues, may be understood as creating and using "limited sets of space and time forms" which we may identify, such as notions that define membership in a society, social distance, and the like. The social scientist organizes social objects in a space that is not identical with that created by a society when he conducts research and develops social theories. The result is a "sociological" space analogous to the "physical" space defined by the natural scientist. It is categorially absurd to claim that these various "spaces" can or should be arranged in a deductive hierarchy. That is, Bentley is skeptical of the intelligibility of arguing that any spatial type is primary. In particular, he wishes to draw attention to the assimilation of Newtonian physical space into the "prevalent vulgar space" which is then taken for granted by social scientists and psychologists as the self-evidently appropriate or even necessary spatial form for their theories.

Scientific psychologies exhibit two general types of "linguistic behavior" that are related to their notions of space and time—assertions of connections between "words" and "things" and constructions of consistent languages. Thus, we have a continuum ranging from the Aristotelian law of identity at one end to mathematical consistency at the other. These linguistic procedures establish frameworks "within which 'knowledge' is presented, and in terms of which 'fact' is organized." Thus, "in the former case the 'existence' is assigned to the fact, and certified to by the word. In the latter case, so far as 'existence' enters at all, it is an existence that has its full locus *within* the consistency of the expression and its system of expansion" (BKF, 20). Since a consistent system of the sort exemplified by mathematics provides "richer and wider control of 'fact'" than Aristotelian realism, Bentley claims that "scientific" and "linguistic" are virtually synonymous. To the extent that physics is the "self-contained linguistic-mathematical formulation of physical experience and physical fact" it is a genuine science and serves as a model for psychology and the social sciences (LAM, 274; BKF, 23–24).

As a discipline, psychology contains two sorts of languages or vocabularies—a "physical language" of physiological or neurophysiological variables and a "mind language" of psychic entities, functions, processes, and faculties. Most of Bentley's attention is devoted to "mind language," for this language is pervasive in psychology. As we might suspect, a commitment to "mind language" in a psychology indicates that its linguistic behavior is likely to be located closer to the Aristotelian than the scientific end of Bentley's continuum. Even psychologists who employ a physical language typically claim to be able to explain in this language the phenomena presented in a mind language. Thus, there is a sense in which mind language is primary in conventional psychology even when behaviorism, for example, opposes mentalistic explanations.

Bentley then divides the properties of mind language into four "sectors": "immateriality," "apprehensionality," "isolationality," and "environmental" (BKF, 28–32). Without claiming that this is the best or only possible classification, Bentley asserts that each of his terms designates a major characteristic of mind language. With "immateriality" Bentley intends to identify all psychological terms or concepts connected with the notion that the facts of psychology are not physical facts. Some version of the mind/body or mind/matter dichotomy seems difficult to avoid in most psychological discourse. "Apprehensionality" refers to dichotomic relations between "sensation" and "thought" expressed in mind language. Psychological notions found in the "apprehensionality" sector are elements of the dubious legacy of empiricist philosophy. Bentley insists that we should not confuse mind/body and subject/object dichotomies. Such confusion is exhibited in behaviorism, which Bentley argues simply converts the "body" into the "subject" or agent of perception. This move simply relocates the problems of perception and our knowledge of the external world to the body. That is, the difficulties posed by the seeming necessity to link perceptions to immaterial mental properties or processes do not vanish when we substitute physiological properties or processes for them, for the question then beomes how "sensations" are to be linked with these proposed substitutes for mentalistic phenomena. We do not eliminate the explanatory difficulties raised by a mentalistic view of psychology by redefining mental processes as physiological processes.

The most important aspect of mind language is designated by "isolationality." "Minds," "personalities," and all their terminological equivalents are taken as isolated from an external world. Even the most intransigent behaviorist thinks that the physiological processes he invokes to explain mental phenomena have a distinct body as their locus. Psychologists who employ "social" variables do not avoid these difficulties, since they too understand mental phenomena as properties of individuals. The last sector includes terms or concepts having to do with relations between organisms and their environments, hence the label "environmental." What Bentley has in mind here are psychologies that trade on confusions of mind and physical language, with biological variables taken improperly as psychological variables. Psychologies which make claims about the "organism-as-whole" seem to have revived vitalist or organismic biology with all its problems. Although Bentley says relatively little about this sector, his targets may have included such doctrines as the "hormic psychology" of William McDougall.[7]

Bentley makes clear why he is concerned with the language of psychology and not with defending his own psychological theory. "The issue here is not merely one that concerns incidental uses of language in science, such as those of terminological specialization and precision; rather, we are here involved in the deepest constructional problems of knowledge itself" (BKF, 7). Our "contacts" with a science can only come "by way of its linguistic form" which increases in consistency as a science develops. As the most developed science, physics is "so completely organized in the frame of the most coherent of all languages—mathematics—that without this frame the science of physics would straightway vanish in large measure from knowledge." The "language" of a science is a "form of historically recorded activity or behavior" apart from which we are literally unable to bring any "presentation of knowledge" to our attention. As we have seen in the previous chapter, Bentley rejects any general distinction between "language" and "knowledge" in that he takes as conceptually untenable any notion of "extralinguistic" knowledge. Bentley has set up psychology for study in the same manner as he did foundational disputes in the philosophy of mathematics.

Critique of Behaviorism

Behaviorism is a "mechanistic" psychology employing what Bentley calls "movement-spaces" in its explanatory apparatus (BKF, 52–65).

It claims to explain psychological phenomena by the systematic observation of various sorts of "movements" which it takes to be isolated in "segments" of space and "successions" of time. The behaviorist simply accepts a Newtonian or classical understanding of space and time which leads him to theorize measurable stimuli, responses, physiological processes, and the like that possess position coordinates in a three-dimensional space and are connected temporally as successions of causes and effects.

Bentley's criticisms of behaviorism are unsparing. His arguments in *Behavior Knowledge Fact* were adapted from his attack on John B. Watson in the 1928 article "A Sociological Critique of Behaviorism."[8] A rehearsal of Bentley's arguments will allow us to understand his support for the psychological views of John Dewey, which appear more scientific than the influential doctrine of Watson.

In the 1928 article Bentley identifies several major problems posed by Watsonian behaviorism. First, can "observation" in Watson's naive empiricist sense be an adequate scientific procedure for the study of phenomena lying outside an experimental setting? Given the extravagant claims by behaviorists to have developed a foundational discipline for the study of all human phenomena, Bentley finds that behaviorist explanations cannot be extended to nonexperimental situations. Second, Watson's methodology is not compatible with that of the advanced sciences, since it is crudely inductivist and relies upon a distinction between "observation" and "theory" which simply has been made obsolete by contemporary physics. Third, Watson cannot explain social phenomena reductively as "complexes of stimuli" and indeed offers no reasons why a science of human behavior must employ only a stimulus-response model at all. Suppose, Bentley suggests, that a sociologist and a behaviorist set out to explain the action of a man who fires a gun. While the Watsonian behaviorist can provide a stimulus-response account, a "scientifically significant description," in contrast, requires us to know if the gun was fired at a target, a bird, or a king. If at a king, was the king understood by the agent as a private person against whom he had a grudge or as a symbol of an oppressive government, or what? A behaviorist account cannot allow such distinctions and thus is prevented from giving us knowledge of social phenomena.

Now the behaviorist may reply to the Bentleyan sociologist that the factors Bentley has listed are simply aspects of the "historical background" of an action that can be explained adequately in behaviorist terms. Bentley's rejoinder is that such a notion of "historical background" presupposes "isolationality" or the existence of an "individual" who can simply be abstracted from a "background." Although behaviorism makes a show of rejecting mind language and thus individual consciousness, it retains the "individual behavioristic agent" in its explanations. Moreover, behaviorism ignores one of the "general requirements of scientific analysis": systematic consideration of epistemological issues. The greatest scientists address in the idioms of many scientific disciplines the problem of an "objective" world of which we seem to be a "part," which is "known" or "experienced" by us in ways often called "subjective." By failing to reflect on this issue, behaviorism states the "equivalent of a fixed initial philosophical postulation" and is, in consequence, a metaphysical and not a scientific teaching.[9]

The behaviorist is like a man who tries to assemble a jigsaw puzzle from a few pieces to which he gives arbitrary emphasis. Watson's doctrine nowhere reveals its limitations more than when it is applied to language. When "language" is taken as subvocal speech or a form of movement, the result is to strip it of "all implications of thought and meanings" and thus to make it unintelligible as language (BKF, 58). Now Bentley has not rejected his long-held opinion that social science must dispense with mentalistic concepts. He has not advanced any substantive thesis about the nature or sources of the "meanings" which behaviorism cannot consistently study. What can be said with certainty, for Bentley, is that a science of behavior must not attempt to remove or simply ignore the constitutive features of the phenomena it claims to study.[10]

While the behaviorist emphasis on "movement" is defective, more suitable psychologies can be constructed around the notion of "action." Bentley's distinction between "movement" and "action" strongly resembles distinctions drawn between these notions by "post-Wittgensteinian" philosophers such as R. S. Peters, A. I. Meldon, and Richard Taylor who assert the conceptual impossibility of a causal account of "action" as distinguished from bodily motion.[11] Among the many paths taken by psychologists during the 1920s and 1930s, Bentley finds the study of "activity" a frequent choice (BKF, 66–73). As Paul F. Lazarsfeld has noted, a number of psychological themes could be structured around the notion of "action" or "activity."[12] A simple model of "action" taken as a unit encompassing initiation, conduct, and completion was employed in studies of motives, environmental influences on behavior, and the like.

For Bentley, a focus on "activity" defines "action-spaces" which are not segmented in behaviorist fashion and reveals a temporal structure of duration. The principal limitation of the "action psychology" of R. S. Woodworth and others was its continued use of mind language. "Activity" simply became another property of the "individual." Knight Dunlap's version of action psychology takes "awareness" as our primordial experience of ourselves as active creatures but theorizes awareness as a neurophysiological variable, which makes clear the extent of his confusion. The underlying difficulty with these and other similar approaches is that they take for granted that everyday and scientific concepts are continuous.

The "mind-language reconstructions" of the psychologist Madison Bentley and, more important, John Dewey, are significant improvements over the various psychologies Bentley has criticized (BKF, 74–83). Mind language cannot be ignored as behaviorists claimed to do. Nor could it be taken as a suitable basis for scientific psychology. Madison Bentley and Dewey recognized that the language of science is a reconstructed language. Thus, they avoid the illicit borrowings from physics and biology so typical in contemporary psychology. Their systems point toward but do not reach an "adequate psychological space-form" for psychology.

Bentley's comments on Dewey's psychology are his first published remarks of any length on the philosopher and reveal the deferential attitude he would always take to Dewey's work. He endorses Dewey's thesis, developed in *Experience and Nature* (1925), that such distinctions as subject/object, potency/act, and matter/form are not determinate prior to their connections. Thus, "organism" and "environment" are separated by our "analysis and selective abstraction," since "interaction is the primary fact, and it constitutes a *trans-action*."[13] Our experience presents an "unanalyzed totality" available for determinations through human action. For Dewey scientific concepts, in consequence, "are not a revelation of prior and independent reality. They are a system of hypotheses, worked out under conditions of definite test, by means of which our intellectual and practical traffic with nature is rendered freer, more secure and more significant."[14] "Interaction [is] the one unescapable trait of every human concern." Since Dewey's naturalistic metaphysics is a description of the "generic traits of existence," interaction or "transaction" is a fundamental metaphysical category. Failure to recognize interaction gives rise to views that isolate knowledge, interest, value, and the like from action. In turn, these views rest upon the obsolete notion that "there are things which can exist and be known apart from active connection with other things." The term "trans-action," which Dewey would later substitute consistently for "interaction" under Bentley's influence, appears in *Experience and Nature* as a characterization of the locus of an action when we cannot determine its "simple location."[15] Bentley doubtless noted that Dewey introduces "trans-action" in the course of remarks on how legal reasoning often unites events widely separated in space and time into a single "act" for purposes of regulation. Law is more advanced than philosophy in this respect, Dewey maintains, since philosophers often find problematic the loci of actions that pose no problems for legal thinking.

For Bentley, Dewey has established that "durational trans-action" is the object of psychological research. Dewey's understanding of the task of psychology is less than satisfactory. For Dewey psychology should concentrate on the "life-career of individualized activities." Why, Bentley asks, should psychology be defined so narrowly when the "direct data of psychology are 'trans-actions' across organisms and environment and . . . such trans-actions are 'changes' running in durations of time with respect to organism and environment alike?" Bentley's answer to his own question shows how he would come to handle basic disagreements between his own position and that of Dewey. First, Dewey has shown that we may speak legitimately of certain "discernible qualities" as "mental" for a specific inquiry. Moreover, we may employ such terms as "conscious" and "individual" as matters of "postulation" without making existence or truth claims. According to Bentley, Dewey "assigns" the act of "experienc*ing*" (where the italicized "ing" suggests activity) to persons in the scientific or semantic sense articulated in *Linguistic Analysis of Mathematics*. However, Dewey's scientific credentials are deficient since he understands "acts" in a Newtonian fashion. Bentley's explanation of Dewey's failure is that the philosopher's "dominant interest in ethics and logic has checked his psychological construction just at the point where it was about to expand into a wider form than, perhaps, the world has anywhere yet seen" (BKF, 79–81).

After Dewey had read *Behavior Knowledge Fact*, Bentley made clear in his correspondence with the philosopher the precise point on which they differed.[16] For Dewey, psychology was concerned with ethical conduct. As he put it to Bentley, he had been "impressed with how damn little we know about the behavior of *individuals* and consequently make such a terrible mess of our relations with each other." He conceded that Bentley's criticisms were valid but said he was more interested in the "improvement of human relations" than conceptual precision. Bentley agreed that Dewey's "broad theoretical position" permits the development of an ethical doctrine but remarked that he was "not interested in issues of that kind." "You," he wrote to Dewey, "have a range of practical interests and activities which I forfeit."

Bentley's "Floating Cosmology"

In *Behavior Knowledge Fact* Bentley is less hesitant to suggest some of the implications of his teaching than in most of his other writings. Despite his ritual disclaimers of tentativeness he believed he had formulated his position as forcefully as possible. In this section we shall examine several implications that are developed in Bentley's search for answers to the Kantian question of what the universe must be like if a "transactional" approach is the basis for scientific inquiry. The basic arguments of Part 2 of the book, "Knowledge and Fact," are already familiar from our study of *Linguistic Analysis of Mathematics*. The suspension of judgments about connections between words and facts recommended for psychology in Part 1 is now revealed as an application of a general "postulational" method (BKF, 132). The four regions of inquiry—fact, experience, knowledge, and language—are introduced as a field divisible only in terms of what Bentley now calls "scientific" analysis. He explains that the "semantic" analysis he had proposed earlier should be changed to "scientific" analysis because "semantics" has become identified with positions quite unlike his own, although Leon Chwistek and Alfred Korzybski are mentioned (BKF, 153–54). We cannot conduct a scientific inquiry without discovering that "whatever we touch in our exploration exhibits all four of these aspects, and in such a manner that we lose full contact whenever we ignore any one of them." To isolate any aspect requires an "explicit determination" that recognizes the "participation" of the other three aspects. There are no properties of anything whatever that cannot be studied in terms of the fourfold classification. As Bentley puts it, "I say in substance: 'These are the facts'" (BKF, 140–42).

Among the most important issues Bentley addresses is the nature of language (BKF, 146). Against behaviorism he argues that we cannot produce a purely "physical interpretation" of language that eliminates the "full system of interconnections" conventionally understood with the "terminology of 'meanings.'" It is "absurd" to restrict a theory of language to an "arbitrary and dogmatic physical basis." For Bentley most theories of language require a jump from physical to mind language, which means they are categorially ambiguous. For a "physical" theory of language, the ambiguity arises from our application of categories suitable for the theorizing of physiological processes required for the production of speech, for example, to the theorizing of the constitution of meaning.

Bentley's position may be made more clear if we compare it with that of Noam Chomsky. A rehearsal of Chomsky's views, let alone their evolution, is neither possible nor necessary for us to draw a clear distinction between his position and that of Bentley. For Chomsky, "grammar" is a "cognitive structure" or "system of rules and principles that determine the formal and semantic properties of sentences." "Universal grammar," then, is the "system of principles, conditions, and rules that are elements or properties of all human languages not merely by accident but by necessity—of course, I mean biological, not logical, necessity." Chomsky's view is that such a universal grammar is "an innate property of the human mind. In principle, we should be able to account for it in terms of human biology."[17] For Bentley, the thesis that a system of principles, conditions, and rules can be accounted for by "biology" reveals an immense amount of confusion about the nature of a scientifically appropriate explanation. While we may turn to "biology" to furnish an account of the neurophysiological structures that comprise the necessary condition for linguistic behavior, Bentley would find it quite problematic that such an account is thereby an account of the formal properties of language. Moreover, he would certainly reject as untenable Chomsky's thesis that such a grammar is an "innate" property of the human mind. Both the behaviorist positions Bentley criticizes and Chomsky's thesis claim to "localize" meanings in a physical space, a move Bentley challenges "on grounds of linguistic coherence." Instead, the proper locus for language lies in "many human beings interacting with all of their interconnecting materials and processes, not in some arbitrary space and time adopted from the procedures of other branches of investigation, but in such space and time as may be developed in the full range of the study," a notion Bentley designates as "behavioral space-time" (BKF, 149).

Although Bentley's vocabulary in *Behavior Knowledge Fact* is not the idealist idiom of classical German sociology, it is clear that his notion of the collective locus of language and thought has affinities with the "objective spirit" central to that tradition. While Bentley was at this time indifferent to any parallels between his teaching and idealist views, his friend J. R. Kantor was not. In 1936 he remarked in a letter to Bentley: "As I have told you many times, there is in your work a suggestion, which I hope is *only* a suggestion, of Hegelianism = general abstract monism."[18] Under Dewey's influence, Bentley would later agree that such British idealist philosophers as T. H. Green, F. H. Bradley, and Edward Caird had developed arguments similar to some of his own views.[19]

In his discussions of experience and fact, Bentley distances himself from philosophies of social science that claim to be based on the natural sciences. He doubts that an adequate case can be made for the primacy of "experience" over the other regions of inquiry since there is no dominant understanding of experience. "Fact," in contrast, has a powerful spokesman in modern natural science. If the cosmos of modern natural science is taken as the "hardest of hard Fact," Bentley believes his own teaching must be "rejected out of hand." That is, the realm of "facts" brought to light, organized, and explained by modern natural science should not be transformed into a criterion for knowledge. In Bentley's words:

> We have here to show that the extrapolated cosmos, the locus of human activity and the background of inquiry for all the modern sciences of nature, is the "local view" of the men who are "within" it and "part" of it. It is Fact under the qualification "as seen from a local point of view." Our factual cosmos itself is before us as arising from the "reactions" to it of the men who have evolved within it. The very insistence upon its "actuality" is before us in this way. In the course of their history men have come to orient themselves towards a cosmos, to recognize and "know" it, and to establish it as the locus of themselves and of their reactions. The cosmos in which they frame their reactions is the cosmos as viewed from their reacting positions—from the "human" position—and is itself qualified by all that that implies. (BKF, 170)

The scientist cannot properly object to the description of his cosmos as a "local view." In Bentley's opinion, as we have seen, methodical provisionality is built into the structure of scientific thinking. It is only when man elevates himself above his "local view" that he develops an "absolutist" position. In addition to traditional expressions of this tendency, Bentley criticizes the "more modern but no less 'magical' qualities that appear as place-holding substitutes for the older terms." It is difficult, Bentley believed, for the scientist, let alone the "man in the street," to understand that the cosmos of modern science is an "ordering of Fact" or a "technique" of inquiry rather than "massive factuality."

All sciences employ a postulate of "uniformity" whether implicitly or explicitly (BKF, 275−79). There are two ways in which scientific uniformity may be understood, based on the extent to which a science employs "transaction"; "One of these we may call the postulate of the *uniformity of nature*; the other, that of *uniformity of knowledge*. The first presents 'nature' as so thoroughly and uniquely 'known' that it is before us in transcendence of the limiting conditions of its 'being known'; the second retains this limiting condition in its statement." The postulate of the uniformity of nature depends upon the notion that man is simply a "part" of nature or is somehow "located" within nature in such a way that he can "report" on it or gain immediate knowledge of it. For Bentley it makes no sense to argue that there is a "part" that enjoys such a position. Indeed, on his grounds there is no correct formulation of the notion of the uniformity of nature. The uniformity of knowledge, however, does not depend upon the notion that "nature" is a container for "minds" mysteriously able to know it.

In the absence of any commitment to the contradictory thesis of the uniformity of nature we find that the "ranges of fact, experience, knowledge, and language are all included" and we "slide our interpretations around and among them in whatever way may seem desirable in order best to make them fit together in system."[20] The interpenetration of the regions of inquiry requires that any science, properly understood, must have a "circular" character. Circularity is required because language is the only vehicle for inquiry and yet it is a "phase" of the other regions of knowledge. The circle is unavoidable but not vicious, for it is only in traditional epistemologies that circularity is considered a "radical defect."[21] A mature science recognizes the "circle of interpretation" that characterizes its structure. "Parts" and "wholes," then, are mutually determining. There can be no room in this understanding for foundationalism. Increasingly consistent formulations unfold through the progressive elimination of "realistic" premises so that a mature science reaches a comprehensive or completely descriptive standpoint implicit in every partial standpoint.

Bentley realized that his teaching seemed to make impossible demands on his readers. Could even the most conscientious student of human behavior understand any apparently distinct phenomenon as a "phase" of the various domains of inquiry? The "man in the street," Bentley was convinced, will resist the substitution of "postulates" for the "real world" of everyday speech and thought (BKF, 172–73). His standpoint is the "small, prim, assertive, and tenacious view embodied in our practical, everyday language." In the face of the truths reached by science he is "driven from one defense after another" until there is "nothing left for him except to be sullen, and that is exactly the mood in which we are apt to find him." Modern natural science had contributed to the sense of homelessness that seemed pervasive to critics of modernity. Bentley does not claim that all men can accept the truth of a universe of process made intelligible by a science that can no longer speak of substance and that offers no safe haven. He does insist that this universe is intelligible and can be inhabited by those who choose to do so:

> I can deeply sympathize with anyone who objects to being tossed into such a floating cosmology. Much as I have stressed its substantiality, I can hardly expect everyone to feel it. The firm land of "matter" or even of "sense" or "self" is pleasanter, if only it stands firm. To anyone whose tasks can be performed on such ground, I have not the slightest thought of bringing disturbance. But for many of us tasks are pressing, in the course of which our firmest spots of conventional departure themselves dissolve in function. When they have so dissolved, and when we are so involved, there is no hope of finding refuge in some chance island of "fact" which may appear. The continents go, and the islands. The pang may be like that felt by a confirmed landsman at his first venture on the ocean, but the ocean in time becomes familiar and secure. . . . If such a cosmology seems fluid . . . still all of this fluidness is within knowledge. (BKF, 183–84)

In the face of the cosmos constructed by science many chose dogmatism or silence. The temptation to seek an island in the sea of flux was almost irresistible. While Bentley understood the failure of nerve that seemed to afflict men like Einstein, he insisted that it be identified for what it was. The distance between Bentley and his contemporaries who were confident that social science could be grounded in the natural sciences was immense. His understanding of the implications of the forward positions in natural science resembles that expressed by Hermann Weyl:

As scientists, we might be tempted to argue thus: "As we know" the chalk mark on the blackboard consists of molecules, and these are made up of charged and uncharged elementary particles, electrons, neutrons, etc. But when we analyzed what theoretical physics means by such terms, we saw that these physical things dissolve into a symbolism that can be handled according to some rules. The symbols, however, are in the end again concrete signs, written with chalk on the blackboard. You notice the ridiculous circle.[22]

For Bentley, however, what Gerald Holton has called the picture of the universe as "the labyrinth with the empty center" was neither absurd nor threatening.[23] The science that had brought this universe to light would in time learn to comprehend it. Our understanding, in turn, requires us to accept the truth that we are not privileged dwellers in a universe built for us. The advancement of knowledge will result from our efforts only if we "stay within our sphere" and do not claim to seek knowledge beyond the necessary conditions of knowledge. There is a sense in which Bentley's science is intended to teach humility. The task of science is continuous "reformulation" of itself in light of the recognition that while it may achieve consistency it cannot achieve certainty.

Observation and Theory

The scientific study of behavior cannot be limited to the study of individuals. As Bentley put it in "Observable Behaviors" (1940), psychology struggles with the "boundary-transcending characteristics" of its phenomena.[24] In *Behavior Knowledge Fact*, Bentley is disturbed by the tendency of psychologists who recognize this characteristic to account for it by employing the term "social" as a kind of residual category of analysis. If psychology is to become a science, it must arrive at a coherent account of the "social," the "psychological" and their connections. Bentley rules out any appeal to sociology since he does not think it can claim scientific status any more than psychology can. His task is to explore the question of whether or how we can speak scientifically about the "social." His inquiry is not a search for the "essence" of the "social" but is rather whether we can

in the specific case of the "social," select, under verifiable observation, definite presentations which, by the broadest tests of present-day technique and construction, are separable from those other presentations which are dealt with by the techniques and constructions of the physical and biological sciences? And if we do select such presentations, can they maintain themselves in scientific work in correlation with other presentations established through specialized psychological investigation and set forth in terms of the "individual" as separate from the "social"? (BKF, 195)

Bentley proposes to establish the "presence of specific behavioral facts" which we can properly consider "social facts." These facts must be observable, which raises the issue of "observability" in Bentley's teaching. In most of his work he had said relatively little about observation. He certainly seems to have regarded discussions of research techniques such as experimentation, survey research, and the like as secondary concerns for students of basic issues in social science. In my judgment the appearance of a discussion of observation in the text and in such articles as "Observable Behaviors" is intended to address the concerns of philosophers of science and social scientists who gave a prominent place to "verification" in scientific explanation. Bentley had never subscribed to the logical empiricist or logical positivist position that theoretical terms in scientific discourse have meaning only through processes of empirical verification. In "classical" logical positivism the "observation language" of science was a "*physicalistic language* or thing-language where one speaks of material things and ascribes observable properties to them."[25] Thus, "one merely observes and sees whether the thing has the claimed property; if it does, the assertion is verified; if not, it is falsified." Sociologists like Lundberg tried to adapt the verificationist criterion to social science with the doctrine that our response to phenomena such as beliefs, customs, and the like "consists of reactions of sense receptors to stimuli from outside or inside the organism as truly as our experience of a stone or a tree" so that sociological phenomena can be brought "within the framework of natural science."[26] As we might expect, Bentley's account of observation follows a rather different course.

The social must be visible if we are to study it (BKF, 198–215, 216–28). We typically believe, according to Bentley, that the social is invisible, that it is a concept or an abstraction or is somehow assembled from individuals. As he had done since his first writings, Bentley rejected methodological individualism. If we are to retain the state, for example, in a science of behavior, we cannot rest content with the claim that it is simply an invisible product of individual actions, or a legal abstraction or even the ultimately "real" entity of idealist political philosophy. As Bentley put it in his "New Ways and Old to Talk About Men" (1929), a description of Parliament as a "sum of individuals, or in some peculiar way as a sum of aspects of individuals" prevents us from speaking of its "trends in durations" and its "complex interactions with other institutions."[27]

Bentley develops seven theses about observation (BKF, 201–3). First, observation is not simply a matter of "sensation." The issue of observation is thoroughly muddled if we suppose that it can only be approached through some account of perception. The practice of science shows us that there are legitimate "observables" that are not directly given to human senses. Indeed, there are few propositions in well-developed sciences that do in fact refer to immediate sensory experience in spite of the philosophical strictures of logical positivism. Bentley's arguments here parallel J. L. Austin's rejection of the foundationalist doctrine that knowledge is a "structure the upper tiers of which are reached by inferences" while "the foundations are the *data* on which these inferences are based."[28]

Second, scientific observation properly employs tools or instruments of various sorts. We can hardly say that the objects of a science are nonobservable simply because specialized instruments are required. Under the influence of empiricism, scientists and philosophers alike tend to identify "observability" and "directness" or the absence of an instrumental intermediary. For Bentley there is literally no coherent defense for this view. Skepticism about the appropriateness of instrumental observation is linked to the view, rejected in Bentley's third thesis, that observation is an instance of the operation of a mental "faculty" isolated in the mind of the "individual." His argument here is that we must learn how to observe when we learn a science. Observation is possible, then, to the extent that we become members of a scientific community engaged in the practice of a science. While this argument does not show that we need not understand "observation" in terms of the operation of a mental faculty, it does counter the subjectivist tendency of the logical positivist notion of observation.

Bentley's next thesis carries his argument further by connecting "observation" with the necessity of employing "signs." That is, we cannot observe apart from our use of the language of a science. Moreover, our scientific language possesses "cultural-historical" dimensions which for Bentley means that the activity of observation cannot properly be isolated from its numerous spatial and temporal contexts. To speak strictly, there is no genuinely scientific observation that occupies a point in space and a moment in time. This thesis is related to Bentley's fifth claim, which is that since language reveals "ordering or pattern," observation must do the same. That is, a scientific observation, regardless of the delusions of empiricists, is never "about" particulars. The scientist is *not* interested in minimum sensibles located at a set of space and time coordinates as in the famous "here-now-a-red-patch" example of Otto Neurath. The scientist is interested in particulars only to the extent that they fit into intelligible wholes.

Against the empiricist notion that observation is linked with incorrigibility, Bentley argues that all observations lack finality. Most philosophers do not undestand that observations are always made in terms of an "Observation Base"—a set of notions, perhaps quite complex, about the "texture of the thing-observed in its observational setting." The scientist is never confronted with the demand that he begin with a complete absence of knowledge. Thus, it makes no sense to impose on science any minimum epistemological condition that must be satisfied before it can proceed. In a casual remark, which may put present-day readers in mind of Thomas S. Kuhn, Bentley says that the history of a science may be presented usefully as a series of transformations of its observation base.

Finally, in a move that parallels recent criticisms of the logical empiricist philosophy of science, Bentley rejects any fundamental difference between observation and theory. Once more, consideration of scientific practice makes it impossible to restrict terms to one or the other of these categories consistently, a point advanced in recent discussions by such philosophers of science as Hilary Putnam.[29] Unlike scholars who argue that either observations or theories determine each other, Bentley insists that observation and theory must be understood transactionally, that is, as phases of the field of inquiry.

Most scientists and philosophers of science draw a firm line between visibility and construction. In a number of articles which appeared during the mid-1930s and early 1940s Bentley argues against writers who suppose that, since it is impossible to observe certain phenomena directly, they must treat such phenomena as concepts.[30] A decision to take "electron" or "state" as a "concept" reflects a needless submission to philosophical positions descended from traditional empiricism and Kantian idealism. For Bentley, the combined effects of these traditions led scientists to understand scientific theories as collections of statements that report the beliefs or mental states of scientists. Beneath this understanding rests a distinction between direct observables (empiricist "sense data" in various disguises) and nonempirical "concepts" (Kantian ideas given a non-Kantian subjectivist interpretation). Even for the contemporary physicist, the task of establishing intelligible connections between an external world of facts and internal world of thought is as hopeless as ever it was for traditional philosophers. If the scientist can dispense with his philosophical prejudices he will no longer need to distinguish between direct observations such as instrument readings and the concept of an electron. While Bentley skirts the edge of operationism, he makes a rather different argument. The notion of "observability" must be altered to permit us to say without fear of epistemological difficulties that an elementary particle is observable as an intelligible component of a scientific system. That is, the electron is observable because it has a place within physics demarcated by a constellation of theories, measurable values such as electrical charge, a mathematical formalism, and the like. There is no a priori reason why the mode of observation designated as "direct" should serve as a criterion for determining that a scientific object is "visible."

Indeed, observation in earlier scientific theories must be understood in the same way. For Bentley, earlier theories had no more direct contact with some of their objects than did contemporary theories. Bentley's teaching makes it meaningless for us to rank the objects of a science in terms of their "distance" from our ordinary experience as W. V. Quine has suggested.[31] Any such ranking presupposes that we can step outside our experience and observe objects apart from their linguistic constitution as objects of experience. The propositions of classical mechanics, for example, which seem to involve simple observables, are actually as abstract or as concrete, depending upon our constructional frame, as the propositions of quantum theory. Intelligibility is primary, not observability. Thus, the visibility of the social will depend upon the possibility of rendering it intelligible within a coherent system.

Bentley's Behavioral Science

We now have the most important philosophical underpinnings of Bentley's behavioral science. He did not attempt to examine such complex terms as the "social" directly but instead turned to a range of phenomena he believed was more accessible to analysis as a starting point for his behavioral science. Throughout Part 3 of *Behavior Knowledge Fact* he develops and uses a complex and awkward terminology intended to allow us to speak in an idiom freed from the ontological contamination of ordinary language. Now he was hardly the first or last philosopher to propose a novel vocabulary. In defense of his strategy we may refer to various efforts with which he was familiar: the coinages of the pragmatists, especially Peirce and Dewey, the vocabularies of German social science, the specialized terminology of contemporary physics and, less obviously, the literary experiments in structure and language of his favorite writers, Proust, Joyce, and Gertrude Stein.[32] In most of his work Bentley seems to be straining against the boundedness enforced by ordinary language, a trait that connects him with a number of otherwise quite dissimilar thinkers. His system of neologisms in *Behavior Knowledge Fact* is his most explicit attempt to free the language of science from ontological claims about persons, things, and processes. His intention is to avoid all terms "implying discreteness of separate fact and bare succession in time," for they "mutilate observation where they are forced upon phenomena which they cannot properly frame" (BKF, 318, 370). We may shed additional light on Bentley's behavioral science by referring to a later formulation of its transactional methodology made with Dewey's assistance: "A system of naming and description are employed to deal with aspects and phases of action, without final attribution to 'elements' or other presumptively detachable or independent 'entities,' 'essences,' or 'realities,' and without any isolation of presumptively detachable 'relations' from such detachable 'elements.'"[33]

Through an analysis of a conversation between two men, Bentley unfolds his terminology and thus the basic categories of his behavioral science. What he claims to show through his exhaustive account of the many aspects of the conversation is the utter failure of our conventional realistic language or any of the scientific languages unwittingly built upon it to present the "full behavioral situation." In non-Bentleyan language, the multidimensional character of the conversation is expressed in the complex structures of space and time which are, so to speak, occupied by the event. Bentley's description may be understood as an attempt to map the conversation onto an appropriate set of subspaces in the infinite dimensional Hilbert space of scientific inquiry.

The notion of "communicational event" is central to Bentley's system because even in ordinary language communication has con-notations of process (BKF, 249−57). Any aspect of the full system is an event in the sense of relativity theory, that is, with specifications of space and time positions incorporated as inseparable from the as-pect in question. Each of Bentley's neologisms is intended to draw our attention to an aspect of the communicational event. The term *Communact* designates the general situation of "men seen in com-munication" with any reference to the " 'what' that the communica-tion is 'about' " systematically excluded. Under this heading are in-cluded three principal classes of events, along with an additional class about which Bentley says little. The *Dicaud* or "speaking-heard," compounded from the Latin *dico* and *audio*, designates the conversation with which Bentley's analysis begins. Like any other subset of the *Communact*, the *Dicaud* is a "whole" since it is spatio-temporal event, but in the absence of attention to its referent it is still a "part." While various disciplines may study the parts of the *Dicaud*, such as the physiology of speech production, the motives of the speakers, their social backgrounds, and the like, any reduction of the event to any of these parts is forbidden. Accordingly, there is no privileged explanatory idiom for the study of the *Dicaud*. The terms *Scriptilect* and *Gest* refer to "writing-reading" and gestures, while *t-phenomena* designates "thought transference," an issue Bentley never considers.

One of Bentley's own examples will suggest what he wants to do with this peculiar terminology (BKF, 254−55). The facts that "Plato wrote" and "John Smith reads Plato" are combined into the *scrip-tilect* "Plato-writing-Smith-reading." This combination identifies what Bentley takes as an intelligible event amenable to study by be-havioral science. Bentley's science would be able to distinguish, for example, between Smith, who is reading the Platonic text carefully, and Jones, who merely has his eyes fixed on a page. For Smith, there is likely to be a sense in which Plato's location in history is irrele-vant, while Jones, if he considers the matter at all, may well regard the text as a product of a past not connected with him in any way. For Bentley, these modes of attentiveness demarcate distinct events that require distinct accounts. Moreover, it is arbitrary to speak of the "same" text that is read with various degrees of care. Bentley's behavioral science agrees with the thesis of hermeneutic philoso-phers such as Hans-Georg Gadamer that the text and the reader con-stitute a whole.[34]

Bentley's discussion of the referents of the various classes of the

Communact (BKF, 258–81) is lengthy and complex. He introduces terms for the referents of each class. Thus, we have the following: *Dicaud/Dicaudane, Scriptilect/Scriptilectane, Gest/Gestane,* and *t-phenomena/Tn-phenomena*. The term *Communicane* encompasses both sets of classes and designates the "full behavioral situation" that behavioral science studies. *Communicane* must designate a "specific presentation" or an "observable" in Bentley's extended sense of the term. He insists that it is not an "additive combination" of a *Communact* and a referent. Any application of the notions of part and whole to *Communact* and *Communicane*, while not simply incorrect, is at best provisional since the notions of "part-ness" and "whole-ness" are themselves problematic. Bentley warns moreover against any temptation to turn the *Communact* into a set of phenomena with extension and duration and the *Communicane* into a set of nonextensional and nondurational "meanings." The study of *Communicane/Communact* must be fully behavioral, which requires modes of analysis that take into account the properties of behavior.

While Bentley has used the term "behavior" freely, his explication of "behavior" is not presented until he has introduced the terminology of his approach. To use a distinction Bentley regarded as dubious, "behavior" designates both a subject matter and a scientific discipline. Bentley's definition reads as follows:

> that specifically separate field of scientific inquiry, set over against the physical and vital, within which both "social" and "psychological" research must be carried on. It is that great type of activity which cannot be held within a physical description and technique, nor within a vital, but which requires a directly psychological and social form of research, with whatever better descriptions and techniques we may secure to replace the two very imperfect words "psychological" and "social." (BKF, 268)

"Behavior" in Bentley's sense has little to do with psychological behaviorism. As he put it in an article in 1940, no "summation of physics and physiology has ever yet shown signs of yielding behavioral knowledge."[35] The use of "behavior" by biologists or physicists to refer to observable characteristics or motions of cells or electrons is an example of categorial confusion. In other words, "behavior" is a term of distinction for Bentley that carries in his work the connotations possessed by "action" in the writings of present-day philosophers of action.

In order to describe the *Communicane* we must develop the notion of "behavioral space-time" (BKF, 308–21). We cannot ask "*What are space and time?*" in the fashion of metaphysics, but must recognize that space and time "present themselves as objectivized forms of experience, communicatively developed in the manner of all other objectivizations." Bentley's use of "objectivized" and his claim that space and time present themselves as "communicatively developed" make clear his rejection of any notion that space and time are subjective constructions. That is, any notion of space and time employed in our effort to theorize some aspect of experience is necessarily "public" in character. Moreover, while we must employ behavioral space-time in our study of the *Communicane*, the latter provides our only access to knowledge of behavioral space-time. The *Communicane* is both a "representation within the general constructional frame of knowledge" and that which "conditions that frame itself" (BKF, 281). Bentley's claim here as elsewhere is that circularity simply *is* the form of a mature science.

Bentley distinguishes the space-time framework of behavioral science from those of physical and "vital" sciences. Physical science may be understood as employing a space-time framework that both eliminates from its consideration any "nonphysical" phenomena and does not restrict the "physical" to the "material." That is, physical space-time predicates a categorially distinct inquiry. Bentley is less certain that categorial clarity is a characteristic of the vital sciences. For some biologists the purposive character of living organisms or "vital" phenomena means that they cannot be studied in terms of the physical space-time framework, while others propose various forms of reductionism. For Bentley the only merit of reductionist doctrines is the destructive effect they have on mentalistic positions. He gives the palm to advocates of categorial distinctions between physical and vital space-time frameworks for having introduced temporality into scientific thinking. Behavioral science will refine the study of temporality.

As he had argued in *Relativity in Man and Society*, Bentley insists that the structure of behavioral time cannot be grasped as the asymmetric repetition of the sequence "past-present-future." The purposive character of behavior is the key to behavioral time and thus to the behavioral space-time framework. Bentley does not wish to smuggle into his behavioral science any "subjective" teaching that encourages us to refer to the contents of individual minds when we speak of "purpose." "Purposiveness," in Bentley's view, is not a property we can ascribe to individual minds. He prefers to speak of "purposing" in transactional fashion, taking into account intentions, processes of action, and outcomes as parts of the whole of "behavioral duration." As he put it in an article from 1941, "In all purposing there is a 'look before and after,' perhaps likewise a dream of 'what is not.'"[36] Thus, man "acts 'at a distance' in the sense that 'connective' processes of Newtonian types cannot be precisely traced in research, however they may be indicated or believed to be collateral."[37]

Bentley offers an account of the temporal structure implicit in the behavior of a boy planning to attend college as an illustration of the limits of Newtonian temporal frameworks. The boy's behavior includes past, present, and future as "phases" and not as determinants of his actions. While we may acquire data about the origins of his attitudes and motives, these data can only supplement and not be the sole constituents of an appropriate explanation of his behavior. Any such evidence must be integrated into a larger description of the behavioral situation, which would include the boy's multiple locations in his society, his aspirations, connections between his aspirations and those of others, and so on. The boy's purposive activity of planning for college is inseparable from what Bentley calls spatial and temporal "spreads." None of the data we may abstract from these "spreads" can be employed to produce a causal or functional explanation of the boy's behavior as the "result" or "product" of some combination of "factors." Bentley's point is that while we may produce such accounts they are not appropriate explanations within behavioral science.

Even behavioral space-time is not the last word in the study of behavior. Bentley explicitly rejects the notion that it is a "perfected form" of construction when compared with physical and vital space-time frameworks. A future physical space-time framework may well make his own behavioral space-time obsolete. However, such a notion of space-time will not resemble present-day views. Thus, "when the time comes that the 'physical' and the 'behavioral' could be brought together into adequate scientific organization, it would be in a form which would not claim pure descent from either the physical or the behavioral of today" (BKF, 316–17). Bentley's speculations do not amount to a projection of a reductionist science, since what we view as a reductionist strategy in the present day, whether for good or ill in the study of behavior, is indissolubly linked to present-day understandings of the scope, objects, and foundations of physical and behavioral science. As these understandings change, so will our notions of connections between these sciences. Bentley's view resembles that of Charles Taylor, who reported his "hunch" about a "future science of human behaviour" with the remark that "I look forward to something at present unimaginable."[38] For Bentley, as we have seen, even physical science, regardless of its achievements and degree of consistent formulation, was much closer to its infancy than its maturity. Any understanding of the character and limits of science could only be, in his idiom, a reflection of the local view of the scientist or philosopher.

Objects and Individuals

Bentley was more aware of at least some fundamental problems with his teaching in *Behavior Knowledge Fact* than in many of his other writings. In this section I will consider two issues, both of which are raised by Kress.[39] The first issue, which Kress calls the "crisis of the object" in Bentley's science, is an issue Bentley addresses directly through his own internal criticism of his views. The second issue has to do with the possibility or intelligibility of Bentley's arguments against the role of the "individual" in social science explanation. Kress claims that the latter thesis, which we have seen in numerous versions in virtually all of Bentley's writings, is a mistake which signals the failure of Bentley's program.

The *Communact* and *Communicane*, together with their various subclasses, constitute the set of "communicative behaviors" with which behavioral science is concerned. Bentley, however, goes on to require names for "whatever is capable of scientific observation and inquiry in all those situations to which the words 'person' and 'thing' more commonly apply" (BKF, 265–66). If we can speak of the referent of some aspect of communicative behavior, have we not allowed into our inquiry something very like the "object" of which we have direct knowledge according to the tenets of traditional epistemology? This is the problem Kress identifies as the "crisis of the object." He argues that the difficulty of determining the identity and thus the intelligibility of any particular faces any "process" philosophy. In turn, Kress connects this problem with what he takes to be a central issue in twentieth-century philosophy: to find a "point at which reason might plausibly enter the flux of nature." The gulf between reason and nature opens up when we face seriously the task of making the world of flux presented to us by contemporary science discursively accessible. In particular, Kress is concerned that the teaching that the making of any qualitative distinctions or that the identification of "parts" is fundamentally arbitrary amounts to a surrender to irrationality. In his view, Bentley's later books "may be read as chronicles of a lost mariner, a man who has thrown the compass of reason over the side as so much excess ballast."[40]

I believe that a study of Bentley's effort to surmount the crisis of the object shows at the very least that whatever may be the case with respect to the status of the object in the doctrines of other philosophers of process, Bentley's teaching does not require concessions to irrationality. Bentley coins the term *Perceptane* to designate the observable behavior of any organism in an environment, where the special sense of "observability" must always be kept in mind. *Perceptane* is cognate with *Communicane* as a general term. It includes *Personan*, which designates the "behavioral participation" of nominally separate "individuals" in the behavioral situation of perception, and *Objectan*, which designates the behavioral referent of *Communicane* or *Perceptane*. *Personan* and *Objectan* may be taken as "phases of specialized inquiry with respect to *Communicane* and *Perceptane*, separately or together." When *Personan* is investigated as a phase of *Communicane*, Bentley labels it *C-personan*, while *P-personan* designates *Personan* as a phase of *Perceptane*. *Objectan* is similarly divided into *C-objectan* and *P-objectan*. If we are concerned with "object" and "person" as conventionally understood, Bentley labels these *Objectane* and *Personane* respectively. Finally, if we are concerned with "communicational and perceptional processes," we refer to *Communican* and *Perceptan*.

It is important not to let Bentley's baroque terminology conceal his intention. This elaboration of his system of neologisms is supposed to permit us to determine the modes in which we wish to speak about an object without claiming to be able to speak about the object as such. Thus, in his behavioral science we must always make clear precisely in what sense we propose to talk about an object. For Bentley there is no reason why we cannot or should not employ a different idiom in referring to an object in connection with perception than we would use in referring to an object in connection with communicative behavior. The notion that we are simply employing different vocabularies to refer to the "same" object is for Bentley a metaphysical doctrine. Although I do not think that an extended comparison is plausible, Bentley's treatment of the object resembles in a general way J. L. Austin's treatment of the variety of acts we may be understood as performing when we speak.[41] For

Bentley there is no a priori or privileged notion of "object" which is or should be taken as fundamental in relation to all other possible notions.

From this account of Bentley's strategy I conclude that on his own terms he solves the problem Kress identifies. For Bentley we do not encounter "objects" as such in science. He sets no minimum epistemological conditions that must be satisfied for us to speak about "objects." We are never actually faced with a situation in which we encounter objects directly, a claim that follows from Bentley's rejection of foundationalism. *Some* determination of both the identity of the object and the criteria something must have to count as an object can be found when we analyze even so-called elementary or fundamental sorts of experience. It is not Bentley but rather the traditional epistemologist who must try to explain how we gain knowledge of particulars. To his own satisfaction Bentley has shown that we are conceptually confused when we believe we can encounter particulars apart from their membership in systems.[42] We do not usually recognize systems when we employ ordinary language, which is permeated by notions of the primordial reality of particulars. When we are engaged in scientific activity we are, so to speak, methodically aware of relations between particulars and systems. The language of a science makes articulation of these relations possible. Within a science, identification of something as an "object," then, has little or nothing to do with Kress's concern about "how something undergoing change can be detected in the first place."[43] For Bentley's transactional methodology there is no *general* way in which this problem can be formulated and thus no *general* solution. Accordingly, Bentley does not contradict himself when he refers freely to both "ordinary spans of human discrimination of temporal and spatial changes" and a postulated "range of plasticity" in events (KK, 70, 63−64). Our method of detecting objects embedded in the flux of reality cannot be abstracted from the sort of inquiry in which we are engaged.

The problem of the "individual" in Bentley's teaching takes us to the heart of his understanding of scientific inquiry. While I agree with Kress's assessment of the importance of this issue in the study of Bentley, I am not convinced that Bentley's program must be judged a failure from Kress's criticisms. Kress employs arguments developed by Strawson in *Individuals: An Essay in Descriptive Metaphysics* (1959) and, to a lesser extent, positions taken by Peter Winch, A. R. Louch, and John G. Gunnell, to make a case against the intelligibility of Bentley's proposals to reject the primacy of "individuals" as units of analysis in social science. His criticisms of Bentley are intended to show that Bentley's "process philosophy" threatens to impoverish both empirical political or social science and political philosophy by abolishing all units or particulars. Bentley's teaching fails to "provide a mode of inquiry and discourse appropriate to our sense of what political matters are all about." Bentley's efforts to "substitute an ontology and methodology of process for a world of particulars" contribute to what Kress takes to be the "malaise afflicting political theory" in the twentieth century.[44]

In order to assess these claims I will begin with a brief sketch of Kress's principal arguments. Bentley's program, in his view, sought the "replacement of person-based concepts and the elimination of consciousness from scientific discourse," moves required by his "radical hostility to mental states as sources of explanation." What philosophers such as Strawson have shown is that we cannot eliminate "mentalistic" concepts from any attempt to understand human action, nor can we reduce these concepts to or translate them into a scientific language in which their essential character is ignored. The concept of a "person" or "individual" is "irreducible" or "primitive." Accordingly, a social or behavioral science based on the elimination of such concepts is categorially absurd. Recognizing that for Bentley the notion of "individuals" as ultimate units of analysis in social science was connected with his criticism of "ideas as causes," Kress believes that the elimination of "persons" was "not only unnecessary but impossible, given a faith in the integrity of our conceptual and linguistic systems."[45]

Since Strawson is Kress's principal source for arguments against the elimination of "individuals" from scientific discourse, I will turn to some of the theses presented in *Individuals*. In the first place, Kress reads Strawson incorrectly when he assumes that the latter's arguments for the priority of "persons" and "material bodies" are intended as ontological arguments. Instead, Strawson claims that we must employ some basic categories and that embodied persons and material bodies are such categories if we are to be able to make identifying references to mental states. Moreover, basic particulars permit us to reidentify elements in our experience. There is a "single system of relations" in which particulars are located and in which identifying references are made which we "always and essentially" possess and which is a spatio-temporal framework consisting of three spatial dimensions and one temporal dimension.[46]

Now since we cannot intelligibly be understood to lack the capacity to make identifying references, Strawson's claim is that the referential priority of basic particulars cannot be denied. In its application to "persons" and "material bodies," this transcendental argument shows that we cannot identify particular mental states without referring both to a "something" of which they *are* states and to the "same thing" to which we ascribe "corporeal characteristics, a physical situation" and the like. Thus, "person" is a more "primitive" concept than the "mental" or M-predicates and "physical" or P-predicates we necessarily ascribe to it. Since "individuals" have these predicates ascribed to them, it is in turn possible to distinguish "individuals" from one another as subjects of these predicates, which makes possible our own correct ascription of such predicates to ourselves. In addition, I will mention two of Strawson's theses, which are relevant to a study of Bentley, upon which Kress does not rely.[47] First, since Strawson claims that things undergo processes, there is no need to develop a category of "process-things." Little effort would be required to expand this view into a full-fledged criticism of Bentley's process orientation. Second, given the referential priority of individuals, it is a categorially confused fantasy to suppose that individuals can be absorbed by groups. Philosophers who propose what Strawson calls a "no-ownership" theory of consciousness are in error.

I am less concerned with defending Bentley than in making clear why Strawson's positions and those of Winch and other post-Wittgensteinians are not entirely applicable to him. The most important reason why Bentley is not as vulnerable to ordinary language philosophers as Kress believes is that for him there is no reason why social science must develop a mode of inquiry that is, in Kress's words, "appropriate to our sense of what political matters are all about" if by "our sense" Kress means everyday understandings. That is, Kress ignores what I have called Bentley's discontinuity thesis. I believe Bentley would have had few reservations about accepting most of Strawson's claims as long as those claims were expressly limited to ordinary language. If we are interested in making references to and reidentifying mental states then we must have some notions of basic particulars, including "individuals." For Bentley the crucial question would have to do with whether we need to perform similar operations in the practice of scientific inquiry. Bentley would have been at least sympathetic to, if not convinced by, Strawson's argument that his basic particulars need not involve existence claims and his effort to distinguish a "person" in his sense from a pure epistemological subject or an "individual consciousness." He would have been firmly opposed to Strawson's claim that the concepts he presents and defends are necessary features of a necessary conceptual structure or categorial scheme.[48]

From Bentley's standpoint it is doubtful that we can even speak intelligibly of a single fundamental conceptual scheme of the sort proposed by Strawson and other conceptual analysts. We may indeed describe the features of a conceptual scheme embedded in ordinary language which requires us to adopt a "mentalistic" vocabulary, locate objects in a particular spatio-temporal system, speak of "causes" and "effects" and the like. What conceptual analysts do not show is that this scheme is or can be the foundation for scientific conceptual schemes. If we find upon examining a scientific language that it draws distinctions not found in ordinary language or even fails to draw distinctions typically or even necessarily drawn in ordinary language, we have not, for Bentley, thereby made any argument against the intelligibility of that scientific language. The distinctions drawn or not drawn in a scientific language derive their intelligibility from their places in a structure of discourse, not their correspondence with features of ordinary language. If the conceptual analyst—who is from Bentley's standpoint simply an advocate of a version of foundationalism—claims that ordinary language and its categorial scheme are primary, then he must be prepared to show precisely how the meanings of scientific terms depend upon meanings found in ordinary language. As we have seen, Bentley himself argued that such connections existed, but that the maturity of a science could be gauged by the extent to which it both recognized and methodically severed these links. Indeed, in *Linguistic Analysis of Mathematics* this line of criticism was expanded to the thesis that a mature science does not appeal to any extrasystemic discourse or foundational discipline, including formal logic. While both the merits and the possibility of scientific discourse thus conceived will be considered in my concluding chapter, it should be clear at least that Bentley's position constitutes a challenge to the views of philosophers who give primacy to ordinary language.

Kress has also misunderstood Bentley's criticisms of mentalistic explanations when he claims that Bentley sought to eliminate "consciousness from scientific discourse." Bentley was vehemently opposed to all mechanistic and reductionist explanatory strategies. Kress fails to note that in his insistence on the purposive character of behavior Bentley develops criticisms of reductionist approaches similar to those made by several of the post-Wittgensteinian philosophers he uses against Bentley. As early as *The Process of Government*, Bentley insisted that his own approach was not intended to eliminate "conscious" phenomena from social science but rather to account for them more adequately. In very general terms, the strategy followed in most of Bentley's writings is to argue that we do not understand such phenomena correctly if we "localize" them in the "minds" (or, as in classical behaviorism, the "bodies") of the "individuals" with whom we are acquainted in and through ordinary language. For Bentley, Strawsonian M and P-predicates, whatever their status in ordinary language, should be taken rather as indicators of matters requiring further inquiry. There are, from the standpoint of Bentley's science, no genuine first-person statements or experiences. Even self-knowledge, as he argues in *The Process of Government*, is a public affair since I must use extrapersonal linguistic forms in order to introspect at all. Once again, Bentley does not deny that there are phenomena ordinarily designated in "mentalistic" terms. He is perhaps most easily understood on this issue as calling for a fundamentally different notion of what should be meant when we make such designations. For example, he proposes to understand "person" as a "specialized description" of "behaviors" which are "more adequately reported" in "situational" terms.[49] Bentley's criterion for "adequacy," in turn, is inseparable from the scientific inquiry in which we are engaged. He remarks that we fail to understand him if we assume that sciences are the "portraiture of 'realms of reality'" rather than "levels of description." We can only settle what some "mentalistic" term means after we have settled the question of what sort of description we seek.

As if in anticipation of Kress's criticisms, Bentley says that his approach does not reduce "person" and "thing" to "mere ghosts in the field of knowledge" but instead provides the best way of understanding their true factuality (BKF, 287–88). That "factuality" eludes us if we insist upon making ontological claims about the priority of "individuals." Bentley does not say that his science, which takes individuals as theoretically composed localizations, can or should replace ordinary language with its ontological and epistemological claims. His position is not the same as that of displacement theorists like Paul Feyerabend who argue that there is no conceptual impossibility in the notion that some future science might show that our mentalistic vocabulary is in fact without application and hence false.[50] He proposes rather, to use Richard J. Bernstein's words, to "change the criteria for the employment" of such terms as "action," "reasons," "intention," and the like. Unlike proponents of the possibility of radical criterial changes, Bentley does not have to be able to "give a satisfactory answer to questions like, 'Well, what was I talking about when I said that I did x for the following reasons?'"[51] A philosopher who wants to replace our mentalistic vocabulary with a scientific vocabulary purged of such terms must be prepared to answer these kinds of questions. For Bentley, I believe, ordinary language remains intact but confined to its appropriate domain. Within that domain we may indeed be concerned with questions of the sort asked by Kress. Bentley's behavioral science, however, recognizes that it is a part of the domain with which it is concerned. The embeddedness of the behavioral scientist in the behavioral situations he studies is an element of both the situations themselves and his scientific accounts of them. Thus, the "two-fold construction of the observation, in terms, on the one side, of what is observed, and, on the other, of the position from which the observation is made, is essential to any dependable knowledge of the kind we call scientific" (BKF, 381). The double vision required by science, its methodological awareness of its own conditions, was beyond the resources of any conceptual scheme Bentley could accept as residing in ordinary language.

8

Pragmatism as Behavioral Naturalism

I am participating in a great movement and search. For any important progress I must orient myself within that movement.

Memorandum, 1939

The most important dimension of the final chapter of Bentley's intellectual career is his relationship with John Dewey. The Dewey-Bentley correspondence and collaboration is remarkable for what it reveals about the last years of both men. Bentley was sixty-five years old and Dewey a decade older when the latter, at the suggestion of his teaching assistant, Ernst Nagel, began to read *Linguistic Analysis of Mathematics* and *Behavior Knowledge Fact*. In spite of their advanced ages, neither thinker was willing to remain content with his own positions. As always, Bentley treated his books as provisional rather than complete statements of his views. Dewey had already produced what would have served as final statements for many philosophers, *Experience and Nature* and his Gifford Lectures, *The Quest for Certainty* (1929). Still, he continued to produce a stream of books on social and political concerns, including *Individualism Old and New* (1930), *Philosophy and Civilization* (1931), *A Common Faith* (1934), and *Liberalism and Social Action* (1935). His intention to write a general treatise on pragmatic epistemology led to *Logic: The Theory of Inquiry* (1938) and conditioned his first exposure to Bentley's views.

The most distinctive feature of the Dewey-Bentley correspondence as it increased in volume and intellectual scope is the absence of any sense of dogmatic certitude. As Sidney Ratner put it: "From 1935 to 1952, each showed he had a rare capacity for self-renewal and self-development. They were as intellectually original and powerful in meeting and solving problems in the last two decades of their lives as they had been in their most productive earlier years. Each could revise or reject an old position ruthlessly and formulate a new position if such a change seemed justified in the light of new analyses and evidence."[1] Although Bentley was the more energetic and polemical of the two men, neither dominates the correspondence.[2] Dewey brought to their dialogue his knowledge of the history of philosophy, which was greater than Bentley's, while Bentley contributed his superior grasp of contemporary logic and mathematics, philosophy of science, and the social sciences. The identification of intellectual problems emerges slowly in their various exchanges, but for the most part it is Bentley who first formulates problems. He encouraged Dewey to join him in "linguistic" inquiry and it is doubtful that Dewey would have taken up the search for a language of scientific inquiry devoid of ontological premises apart from his friend's urgings. Dewey provided the larger intellectual framework for their collaboration with his pragmatism. The theory of language Bentley began to develop was to be built upon the foundations of Dewey's *Logic: The Theory of Inquiry*. For Dewey their joint work eventually seemed a complement to his own and he wrote of Bentley's fruitful impact: "I hadn't expected at my age (I'm 85 in October) to get a 'refresher course' that really refreshed. I feel I've got it through this contact with you, and that I can restate my own mode of approach and its results with my feet more on the ground than in the past. . . ."[3] For Bentley, one of the most important results of his relationship with Dewey was that he was encouraged to explore the pragmatic roots of his own thinking with greater care than he had ever done before. While he had known the works of the pragmatists for nearly half a century, he had never considered his own teaching as part of an identifiable philosophic tradition. Indeed, he had tended to avoid any effort to locate his own position in any broader context. Dewey spurred Bentley to undertake, in his early seventies, a voyage of intellectual self-discovery.

After nearly a decade of correspondence, Bentley and Dewey produced a series of articles that was published in several philosophical journals during the period 1945–1947.[4] The articles are a systematic study of "inquiry" undertaken in light of current tendencies in philosophy of science and logic. The principal thesis of the series is that pragmatism furnishes the best point of departure for the development of an adequate understanding of inquiry. Pragmatic epistemology is defended against what are taken as the fundamentally confused views of logical positivism. The two thinkers aspire to rectify the philosophic vocabulary by systematically purging it of ontological premises as the necessary prelude to the working out of a general theory of inquiry. Such a theory of inquiry, in turn, will permit the development of appropriate understandings of the various sciences.

Bentley's Critique of Logical Positivism

A great deal of the Bentley-Dewey enterprise was critical and destructive. As they saw it, logical positivism or empiricism was the emerging orthodoxy in philosophy of science. The savage attacks on logical positivism in the collaborative project have their roots in Bentley's own criticisms of the new movement. His brief contact with Friedrich Waismann in Vienna may have given him his first exposure to the views of the Vienna Circle philosophers but no notes have survived from his study with Waismann.

During the late 1920s some of the Vienna Circle members began to become aware of the American intellectual scene. Herbert Feigl notes that along with exposure to a few American philosophers who visited Vienna and some familiarity with James and Dewey, the Circle members were convinced by their discovery of behaviorist psychology and Bridgman's operationism that the American *Zeitgeist* "was thoroughly congenial to our Viennese position."[5] While there was no massive emigration to the United States at this time, Feigl, Karl Menger, and Moritz Schlick held various visiting and research appointments at American universities in 1929 and 1930. In 1929, Rudolf Carnap, Otto Neurath, Hans Hahn, Waismann, and Feigl issued the Circle's manifesto, *Wissenschaftliche Weltauffassung: der Wiener Kreis*. Feigl and the American philosopher Albert Blumberg gave the movement its English label in their article "Logical Positivism: a New Movement in European Philosophy" in the *Journal of Philosophy* in 1931. Bentley had begun to read some of the products of Circle members and their growing number of followers at this time. From his earliest acquaintance with logical positivism he accepted the view that philosophers like Carnap had of their own enterprise, which emphasized its dependence on Russell and Wittgenstein. Although he seems to have believed that a decisive criticism of these philosophers was sufficient to undermine their Viennese disciples, it became clear to him by the mid-1930s that the new movement required separate consideration.

In his criticisms Bentley concentrated on the central claim of logical positivism to have furnished the definitive account of the nature and structure of scientific theories.[6] This move was unusual since many philosophic criticisms of logical positivism tacitly accepted the positivist view of scientific theories and concentrated their attack on the verification theory of meaning, which the positivists expanded into a standard for all cognitively significant discourse. Bentley's position does him honor, for, as Frederick Suppe noted in 1973, most criticisms of the positivist explication of scientific theories have left "essentially unchallenged" the assertion that all genuinely scientific theories can be reformulated axiomatically.[7] He took for granted the notion, advanced in recent years in various ways by such philosophers of science as Peter Achinstein, Dudley Shapere, and Hilary Putnam, that an adequate analysis of scientific theories must characterize theories as they are used in the practice of science.[8] Philosophers had usually been all too willing to legislate the character of scientific theories and Bentley thought the logical positivists had simply continued this reprehensible practice.

Bentley's criticism in "The Positive and the Logical," which appeared in *Philosophy of Science* in 1936, is presented as "one phase of a wider inquiry undertaken to appraise the present status of the interpretation of science."[9] He could agree with the logical positivist goal of eliminating "metaphysics" from science and aligned himself with the positivists in giving science a central role in philosophy. The most important philosophic issues were, in his view, ultimately issues in philosophy of science. Bentley was skeptical of the logical positivist claim that it had succeeded in eliminating metaphysics, however, because he saw in the recourse to a supposedly atheoretical "observation language" a thoroughly traditional materialist metaphysics. The positivists believed that we have immediate access to a world of things with directly observable physical properties. As always, Bentley considered this thesis not only unacceptable but completely discredited by the actual course of development in the advanced sciences. Since the positivist understanding of the meaningfulness of theoretical notions in science stressed the foundational role of the deliverances of the observation language, that understanding was dubious.

What seemed even more problematic to Bentley was the logical positivist reliance on the logical doctrines of Russell, Wittgenstein, and their numerous disciples. Bentley found conceptual confusion at the heart of the logical instruments employed by the Viennese philosophers. Philosophers who claim to be "logical" must be judged by more stringent standards of consistency than the metaphysicians they criticize. As Dewey noted, Bentley tried to hold his opponents "up to a strictly mathematical level of coherency."[10]

Carnap seemed to exhibit most of the failings of logical positivism and Bentley would direct extravagantly sarcastic criticism at him throughout the late 1930s and 1940s. In *Der logische Aufbau der Welt* (1928), Carnap attempted to create a "construction system" (*Konstitutionssystem*) of definitions and theorems that would employ the modern logic of relations to devise a hierarchical ordering of all areas of knowledge or types of "objects," including sociocultural, other minds, physical, and introspective objects. In Bentley's view, Carnap's reliance upon a division of sentences into "real-object" and "syntactical" types was misplaced. That is, Bentley rejected the notion that there can be a logical syntax that is cognitively neutral with regard to the objects whose relations it reconstructs. Carnap's logic of relations is itself completely embedded in a variety of cognitive contexts.

The deeper difficulty in Carnap's enterprise, which was shared by logical positivism as a whole, was its acceptance of the analytic/synthetic distinction, reflected in the ease with which the positivists claimed to distinguish between theoretical and observational statements and terms. For Bentley, reflection on the practice of physics made clear that this distinction had little or nothing to do with the actual structure or use of physical theories. As we have already seen in chapter 7, Bentley had worked out an understanding of "observation" that did not require any commitment to a natural division of terms into those directly observable and unobservable.[11] Although he did not make his argument especially clear on this point, Bentley evidently thought that Carnap's acceptance of the observational/theoretical distinction was linked to his decision to base his epistemology on an account of subjective experiences. While Carnap did not claim that the sense data of traditional empiricism had epistemic priority, his recourse to a doctrine of "elementary experiences" linked by relations of similarity from which we can assemble the hierarchy of concepts was not an advance over the earlier empiricists. Indeed, Bentley finally claimed that logical positivism was best understood as an extension of German idealist philosophy. Although he was familiar with the positivist or empiricist background of the Vienna Circle which supported Ernst Mach's philosophy of science, Bentley believed he could see the buried outlines of the Kantian tradition.

The secret of Carnap's system lay in what Bentley called the "operator" of the logical apparatus central to the methodology of logical positivism. The "operator" is the "mind," taken unproblematically by the positivists as a collection of faculties or powers. That is, the positivists saw no difficulty in ascribing to the "subject" the same status as that accorded by traditional epistemology. Carnap's *eigenpsychische* or private-psychical domain of subjective experience is as dubious as any version of this doctrine Bentley had ever criticized. Logical positivism took the subject's constitution of concepts as a sort of Kantian ordering of the flux of experience. As such, the subject makes liberal use of "concepts." Bentley finds examples in Carnap where material and formal modes of speech, scientific terms, and even the "objects" of science are treated as "concepts." The mind as "itself concept and bearer of concepts" is the basis for logical positivism's "two language" doctrine exhibited in the observational/theoretical distinction, which is essentially a version of Kantian dualism. Bentley indicts Wittgenstein for his use of formal logic to mask his traditional ontological views, with the remark that "Wittgenstein's attempted rigor is the historical source from which the degeneracy of logical positivism stems."[12]

Logical positivism's reliance on the epistemological subject posed for it the significant problem of explaining the public or intersubjective character of science. How could this character be built up from the separate experiences of isolated subjects? Herbert Feigl and Carnap had explicitly resorted to "methodological solipsism." Otto Neurath's proposal to refer scientific propositions to acts of perception accessible to behaviorist investigation, which was intended to avoid the problem of solipsism, hardly sufficed. The logical positivists failed to understand that the language of science, like any other sort of language, was necessarily public. Accordingly, they posed for themselves the pseudoproblem of how to arrive at reliable reports about the content of subjective experiences. Reliance on such reports, moreover, plays no part in the conduct of the sciences.

The Defense of Pragmatism

From 1936 onward, Bentley's critique of logical positivism links up with his deepening study of pragmatism. He had read widely in the posthumous collections of G. H. Mead's writings, *The Philosophy of the Present* (1932), *Mind, Self and Society from the Standpoint of a Social Behaviorist* (1934), *Movements of Thought in the Nineteenth*

Century (1936), and *The Philosophy of the Act* (1938). His reading notes for the 1934 collection express his uneasiness with Mead's "social behaviorist" thesis that "mind" and "self" emerge from communicative behavior. If "mind" is a suitable scientific topic at all, it should be treated as an "indication" of behavioral processes.[13] Both *Mind, Self and Society* and *The Philosophy of the Act* were edited by Charles W. Morris, who assimilated pragmatism to logical positivism. Dewey was deeply disturbed by these efforts at bridge building, writing to Bentley in 1939 that the "attempt to make a mechanical union of Mead and Carnap is doomed. If Morris gave up his pragmatism entirely, he could at least be more consistent. . . . I am more and more impressed as far as most of the logical positivists are concerned by their practically total lack of any historic, cultural interest or sense."[14] Bentley had been thinking along similar lines. He replied that Morris, like so many contemporary philosophers, viewed pragmatism in terms of the issues central to logical positivism. Pragmatism was not simply an early and immature version of the doctrines of the Vienna Circle. Moreover, Bentley had begun to think of his own work as a continuation of pragmatism and was now able to see why Dewey could link his work with that of Mead and Peirce.

Peirce began to move to the center of Bentley's thinking when he first studied him closely in 1939. Bentley planned a book-length study called "Peirce the Forerunner" which would establish the importance of the neglected pragmatist in modern philosophy.[15] Although he got no further on this project than reading notes and an outline, his view of Peirce is quite clear. For Bentley, Peirce had decisively criticized the "subjective turn" in modern philosophy which originated with Descartes. The related doctrines of mind/body dualism, immediate knowledge of sense data or some equivalent, and subjective verification were simply untenable. After Peirce, it could no longer be held that "ideas" are somehow mental "objects," much less located in or possessed by individual minds. Certainly the fact that Peirce made thinking inseparable from language and thus necessarily collective and historical in nature was not lost on Bentley. Scientific activity was for Peirce an exhibition of the character of inquiry in general which revealed itself as a continuous process of self-correction conducted by a "community of inquirers." As a philosophy of "process," Peirce's teaching showed the futility of any a prioristic doctrines such as Bentley took traditional empiricism and idealism to be. Bentley was not an uncritical disciple, however, for he found in Peirce's ethical and religious views the remnants of a

naive belief in the ontological primacy of "persons." Peirce's epistemological and logical doctrines were in conflict, according to Bentley, with his unexamined premises.[16] Peirce had written "thought
. . . is more without us than within. It is we that are in it, rather than
it in any of us"; if this were so, philosophy had to account for reality
"independent of the vagaries of me and you," and this insight must
penetrate into every part of Peirce's system.[17]

The stage was set for Bentley to explain his own relation to Peirce.
He knew that Peirce's original master had been Kant and proposed to
characterize himself as standing in relation to Peirce as the latter
had to Kant. Just as Peirce had believed his categorial scheme and
complex classification of the branches of knowledge were improvements on Kant, Bentley claims that his own work will go still further along these lines. In his notes he felt free to rank his own efforts
more explicitly than in his published writings. While Dewey has developed Peirce's teaching through his various attacks on conventional logic and epistemology, he has failed to offer a theory of linguistic behavior. This next step is Bentley's own task. The true heir
of Peirce the forerunner is Bentley himself.[18]

By the end of the 1930s Bentley was prepared to regard his work
as the next stage in the development of pragmatism. His relationship with Dewey had reached the point where collaborative activity
seemed possible. With Dewey he would develop the theory of language that was the core of the advance in pragmatism he sought.
Bentley's role in the correspondence became even more active as he
urged Dewey to cooperative work, explicated Dewey's writings, and
tried to show that Dewey's philosophical growth pointed toward the
joint project, the outlines of which were still only dimly visible.
Bentley took on the defense of pragmatism in his published work
and proved an intransigent advocate of pragmatism against contemporary misinterpretations of it.

Bentley's articles of the early 1940s are the products of a writer eager to defend his newly discovered masters from the philistines.[19] He
had never been in better form as polemicist as he was when he pa-
tiently searched contemporary philosophical writing for pragmatic
echoes, uncovered incorrect or careless interpretations of the great
pragmatists, and scored points off the logical positivists. His targets
are excoriated with such phrases and adjectives as "enormous con-
ceit," "confused camp-followers," "antiquated mentalism," "delu-
sional," and "verbal chaos."

The finest of these articles is "The Jamesian Datum" from the

Journal of Psychology (1943), which warrants attention for the light it sheds on Bentley's views as his joint project with Dewey began in earnest. The presentation of a number of papers by various philosophers at the James Centenary meeting of the Conference on Methods in Philosophy and the Sciences at Columbia University in 1941 was the stimulus for Bentley's study of James.[20] He discovers a number of ways in which James is typically misread by scholars through an extraordinary survey of the James literature. Where misinterpretations are not the result of ignorance they often result from failure to consider both the evolution of James's thinking and what Bentley calls James's "rhetoric." Unlike contemporary philosophers, who write for a select professional audience, James addressed a wider audience and, according to Bentley, presented his views in a number of ways, some of which may seem to contradict each other. Where the casual philosophic reader sees confusion, the careful reader finds intellectual consistency. One of Bentley's most sensitive pieces of scholarship is his scrupulous tracing of the contexts and meanings of such Jamesian terms as "pure," "immediate," "neutral," "concrete," "datum," and "experience" through virtually the entire Jamesian corpus.

Bentley argued that James was neither a subjectivist theorist of immediate experience, nor an incoherent metaphysician, nor yet a crude forerunner of behaviorism. The "Jamesian datum" is the "pure experience" that figures so prominently in his teaching taken in its totality and, thus, prior to such determinations as subject/object, knower/known, and the like. Even James's concern with religion in *The Varieties of Religious Experience* (1902) reflects a willingness to remain open to the totality of experience rather than an eccentric dogmatism. For Bentley, the internal development of James's views led from the notion of a "stream of consciousness" as an appropriate metaphor for the flux of psychic life or experience to the "flow of the neutral datum in a natural world of organism-environment," that is, to the notion of "activity" as such without ontological foundations or privileged interpretive standpoints.[21] Bentley rejected the view that James's "radical empiricism" was evidence of metaphysical contamination by Bergson late in James's life. Instead, he found impressive continuity in James's leading ideas. James had tried to avoid both the reductionism of traditional empiricism and the speculation of idealism by trying to bridge what he called the "epistemological gulf" in ways Bentley found suggestive of his own postulational or semantic doctrine.

The larger intellectual context for the study of James is the pragmatic philosophy understood primarily as an effort to reflect on the new world created by Darwin.[22] Pragmatism is not simply another philosophy but a mode of thinking structurally similar to both the natural process and the theory of evolution. Evolutionary theory was concerned with processes requiring time to take place and its units of analysis were not individual organisms but populations. Moreover, it was clear that evolutionary theory understood the properties of genotypes and chromosomes as the result of their structures and was in consequence nonreductionist.[23] In the same manner, the major pragmatists

all survey human behaviors in durations; they agree that thought "requires a time"; they agree in holding knowings among the durational behaviors; they agree in rejecting the spaceless-timeless pattern . . . typical of pre-Darwinian and pseudo-Darwinian inquiry, which insists on having a "doer," knows such a doer only from his "doings," defines him, nevertheless, as an entity apart from his doings, and endows the entity (which is to say, the definition) with powers of *fiat*—the pattern which, when once embraced, seems to make a full durational inspection (in other words, modern science) eternally incomprehensible to the embracer.[24]

According to Bentley, James took Peirce's discovery of the temporal structure of thought and in *Essays in Radical Empiricism* (1912) expanded it into the thesis that "experience as a whole" can only be a "process in time." Our participation in this process can never be other than "social." Bentley's effort to weave together the threads of pragmatism follows:

No one has known better than Peirce or felt more strongly how deeply social our knowings are. No one has made a more brilliant raid into the social field than James in his analysis of the "selves." Either of them . . . was far ahead of the academic sociologies of today, but neither followed this lead in systematic development. It was Dewey who broadened the study of knowings into a full cultural form. "Transaction," for Dewey, underlies "action," and the "indeterminate" underlies the "determinate" in a way similar to that in which, for James, the factual datum underlies the purportedly independent subjectives and objectives. In each of these cases a view in full system is offered as a vastly richer approach to knowledge than any of the dualistically split views have ever yielded. . . . Where Darwin places nature beneath organism and environment to bring them into system, Peirce by a great vision extrapolates this approach across the full field of knowings, and identifies durational "sign" as the procedural unit. James, placing his microscopic observation upon the phenomena called "conscious," and holding doggedly to his task, brings the datum naturalistically to view. Dewey maps the wide cultural procedures of knowing—the prospectings, the testings, and the stabilizings of warranted assertion—with never a break away from the natural universe. For all four there is a common denominator of formulation—indicated, if not yet advanced in use. The immediacy of Darwin, literally present in the treatment of organism-environment as system, is the frame of the behavioral immediacy which James identified by name, which Dewey has organized and established for inquiry, and to which Peirce supplied the key.[25]

To continue with Bentley's own metaphor, Peirce's key cannot be turned without a theory of language that conforms to the "behavioral fact" of the spatial-temporal structure of language. Such a theory will be part, then, of behavioral science. In turn, behavioral science requires the method of postulation. What is needed, in other words, is an instrument of inquiry that conforms to the necessary conditions of inquiry.

Bentley finds the textual warrant for his program in Dewey's *Logic: The Theory of Inquiry* where he speaks of the need for a "general theory of language in which form and matter are not separated."[26] The Bentley-Dewey correspondence in the early 1940s gradually came to center on exhaustive analysis of the connotations, merits, and ontological commitments of such words as "proposition," "judgment," "meaning," "name," "fact," and "knowledge," among many others. Bentley's search was for a "firm terminology" that avoids the problems inherent in both the casual usage of everyday language and the specious clarity afforded by the philosophical vocabulary. In its intention the Bentley-Dewey program resembles Carnap's logical reconstruction, but claims to be more radical in that it refuses to base itself upon the presumed stability of formal logic, which Bentley had questioned in *Linguistic Analysis of Mathematics*. Beginning in May 1943, the two thinkers exchanged letters almost daily. Each made lists of key terms with appropriately "trans-

actional" interpretations which were then subjected to minute analysis. By early 1944 some of these seemingly endlessly revised lists had
grown into full-fledged manuscripts. Bentley was aware that he had
done the bulk of the work on the early stages of the project and that
the emerging product was "a specialization of my own type of procedure" rather than an example of philosophy in Dewey's idiom.
Dewey minimized the importance of his own contribution and suggested that his name be omitted as co-author out of "common de-
cency." Bentley prevailed, writing to Dewey, "We need big artillery.
You're it."[27] For him, if not for Dewey, the battle lines had been
drawn.

Behavioral Naturalism and the Theory of Inquiry

The collaborative articles assembled as *Knowing and the Known*
contain little not found in the earlier works of their authors. I can
find in Bentley's contributions no major theme not already treated
in his works of the 1930s, while Dewey's efforts amount to rehearsals of some of his most characteristic views. The finished project
resembles Bentley's work much more than Dewey's, especially in
what Arnold Brecht has aptly described as the "iconoclastic fury"
with which opposing positions are criticized.[28] For the most part,
Bentley was responsible for the microscopic analyses of a number of
contemporary works in logic, semantics, and philosophy of science,
while Dewey provided historical reflections and graceful summaries
of various parts of the Bentley-Dewey position.

   Knowing and the Known is of great importance for a study of
Bentley because in it he finally addresses directly the question of
his own philosophical views. The position of the joint work is identified as "behavioral naturalism."[29] As a naturalist Bentley holds that
there is nothing beyond "nature" or that "nature" properly understood is the absolute horizon for all human concerns. Nature thus
constitutes the limiting condition for "inquiry," which is the theme
of the joint work. Bentley's naturalism is quite similar to that of W.
V. Quine who, as a student of Dewey, writes: "With Dewey I hold
that knowledge, mind, and meaning are part of the same world that
they have to do with, and that they are to be studied in the same
empirical spirit that animates natural science. There is no place for a
prior philosophy.[30] Like other naturalist philosophers such as J. H.
Randall, Jr., and Y. H. Krikorian, Bentley took "science" as paradigmatic for the conduct of inquiry, but differed from them in his

awareness that the method of science was not simply or even primarily experimentation.[31] An "experimentalist" notion of science, which could be found in Dewey as well, doubtlessly seemed to Bentley to resemble too closely the verificationism he found unacceptable in logical positivism. From Bentley's standpoint, experimentalism was no different from any other epistemology that deploys a method to obtain knowledge that presupposes either the possession of knowledge or at least an adequate understanding of what will count as or furnish the criterion for knowledge. Accordingly, Bentley and Dewey do not claim to offer another epistemology but to theorize "inquiry" on a more fundamental level than can be found in epistemology.[32]

The core of Bentley's naturalism is his understanding of behavior. He suggests that "behavior" can and should replace "experience" in the philosophic vocabulary because the latter cannot be stripped of its traditional subjective connotations. As we have seen, "behavior" in Bentley's sense is intended to encompass and dialectically supersede traditional notions of objectivity and subjectivity. Thus, in the "trial group of names" that Bentley and Dewey propose to replace the confused vocabulary of philosophy, "experience" appears only to indicate the unity of internal and external properties needed to warrant assertions about the "existence" of something. The linguistic reformation of behavioral naturalism will prohibit us from asking with philosophical propriety such questions as "whose experience is this?"

"Behavior" in Bentley's sense designates one of three scientific "subject matters"—the physical, the physiological, and the behavioral. "Behavioral subject matters" encompass but are not reducible to the domains of psychology and sociology. Reflection on "behavior" reveals what Bentley had long identified as its "boundary-transcending" properties, which may be summarized as its spatio-temporal structure. In his vocabulary we can understand behavior only in terms of its durations and extensions, which means that it is unintelligible to apply the term "behavior" to any isolated "thing" or "person." Moreover, "inquiry" is itself a form of behavior, and thus a theory of inquiry must be a theory of behavior.

A distinctive mode of discourse is required for both the study and conduct of inquiry. Bentley and Dewey chose "transactionalism" to identify the conceptual framework they believed had to be employed. "Transaction" designates the "knowing-known" as "one process" prior to any determinations of "knowing" which may contain epistemological theses or of "knowns" that contain ontological claims.[33] In the notion of "transaction" we have Bentley's final candidate for the status of the basic unit of analysis in social science. For him to speak of a "transaction" is to employ an idiom free of tacit assertions about the primacy or even the reality of subjects or objects. Any determinations of subjects or objects are "specifications" that involve Bentleyan postulation.

Transactionalism is the foundation of scientific thinking. Bentley identifies three ways in which we may speak about "naming and knowing" and "named and known," which correspond to three decisive steps in the self-corrective evolution of science. "Self-action" designates modes of speaking and thinking that identify "things" in terms of essential properties and explain their actions in terms of these properties. Following Dewey, Bentley claims this was the teaching of classical philosophy, which modeled the entire natural world on what it thought was the truth about the actions of living beings. "Interaction" finds "causal interconnection" among things and leads to mechanistic teachings such as Newtonian physics. As we have seen, Bentley claimed that these views had been incorrectly extended to psychology and the social sciences. Finally, "transaction" is a mode of speaking and thinking in which "systems of descriptions and naming are employed to deal with aspects and phases of action, without final attribution to 'elements' or other pre-sumptively detachable or independent 'entities,' 'essences,' or 'realities,' and without isolation of presumptively detachable 'relations' from such detachable 'elements.'"[34] Neither "elements" nor "relations" can be given priority in Bentley's teaching. By "systems of description and naming" Bentley means the formalism toward which science moves as it gives up any foundationalist or priority thesis. The world understood by science is one of "action," which, as I suggested in chapter 6, may be understood as if it could be modeled by an infinite dimensional vector or Hilbert space.

According to Bentley, "interactional" inquiry was the "dominant pattern of scientific procedure up to the beginnings of the last generation" and affected all notions of inquiry in all scientific disciplines. Even the "isolation" of logical terms and concepts from their contexts in language and thus in human behavior is a result of the interactional standpoint. Logicians have treated their own "units" of analysis as if they were the conceptual equivalents of elementary physical particles.

As always, contemporary physics is wiser than philosophy or

logic. Bentley associates his position with Niels Bohr's notion of "complementarity" in physical theory.[35] For Bohr, there was no need to choose between the classical "wave" theory of light and the contemporary "particle" theory of quantum mechanics. Rather than reduce one explanatory theory to another, he proposed the principle of "complementarity" which permitted acceptance of both theories, where the choice between them was related to the purposes of a specific inquiry. Bohr elevated this notion into a larger philosophical thesis: "The integrity of living organisms and the characteristics of conscious individuals and human cultures present features of wholeness, the account of which implies a typically complementary mode of description. . . . We are not dealing with more or less vague analogies, but with clear examples of logical relations which, in different contexts, are met with in wider fields."[36]

According to Bentley, who was for once rather cautious in claiming anything more than a family resemblance between his views and Bohr's, the underlying issue of complementarity has to do with the formal organization of scientific theories. In the transactional mode of inquiry, philosophical terms can be given "specified" meanings. Bentley contrasts "specification" with "definition" by showing that philosophers have no clear understanding of "definition" and thus employ it inconsistently. What disturbs Bentley is that many philosophers speak as if one could define *things* and establish connections between words or terms and things. There is a sense in which even the most stringent logical positivist becomes a metaphysical realist when he begins to speak of definitions. What is presupposed, Bentley claims, in any notion of definition is some doctrine of immediate knowledge.

The traditional distinction between "mind" and "reality" survives in conventional views of definition that requires "third-realm insertions" such as "propositions" or "concepts" to bridge the supposed chasm. "Specification," in contrast, suffers from none of these difficulties. The atom has been "specified," for example, so that it is no longer the smallest possible material object but is rather a "descriptive name as a kind of expert's shorthand for a region of carefully analyzed events." The physicist no longer asks what the atom "really is" in any fashion similar to that we might use in ordinary language when we ask about the nature of something. Bentley claims that "specification" is virtually identical with "science."[37] Again, a comparison with Quine may be illustrative. According to him, there is no adequate scientific account of our ordinary notion of "similarity," which is closely linked with our ordinary notion of "natural kinds." For example, a thing is soluble in water, even if it has never been immersed in water, if we determine that it is similar to other things known to be soluble. In turn, we have defined solubility in terms of kinds. For the chemist, however, solubility is understood by describing the structural conditions or mechanism of this disposition, which for Quine is an example of how similarity proves to be unnecessary in a mature science.[38] Bentley would, I think, not only agree with Quine's handling of this example, but would take the additional step of dispensing with talk about mechanisms. What is specified is the interwoven collection of scientific theories which, taken as a whole, allows us to describe the structural conditions of solubility.

Bentley explicitly rejects the view that science is concerned with material objects only, for it is evident that specification is not confined to the physical. It "yields the veritable object itself that is present to science" as "one aspect of the process in which the object appears in knowledge," while the object as a spatio-temporal event "yields the specification." This does not mean that we constitute the objects of scientific inquiry in idealist fashion. Rather, we can know them only as phases or aspects of our inquiry. Indeed, for Bentley it is absurd to suppose that we can know them in any other way whatever, for while our inquiry does not constitute its objects it is a condition of their appearance to us. The "scientific object," Bentley says, is "that which *exists*" where "existence" means "that which stands forth," which Bentley derives, as Heidegger did, from the Latin *exsistere*.[39] Anything that "exists" demarcates a spatio-temporal "spread," recognition of which must be incorporated into its scientific specification. Moreover, Bentley remains open to the possibility of "scientific objects" which in no way possess material characteristics.[40]

In a mature science we find systems of specifications rather than isolated instances of specification. A mature science is a semantic or formal system, the elements of which constitute a whole in that none of their "meanings" is controlled externally. When transactional inquiry is "deliberately comprehensive" in this sense Bentley suggests the description "full system" for it.[41] Since Bentley's notion of formalism does not include any general model of a formal system to which the sciences should conform, the process of formalization is identical with the maturation of a science. A highly developed science is both formal and perspectival. We should not be surprised that Bentley was distressed at Einstein's "realistic" metaphysics. The greatest pioneer in twentieth-century physics could not enter the promised land he had discovered.[42]

Logic and Truth

Most of Bentley's polemical vigor is exercised on the writings of contemporary logicians. Among the philosophers he subjects to criticism are Charles W. Morris, Carnap, C. I. Lewis, Ernest Nagel, Morris R. Cohen, Russell, Stephen Pepper, Quine, and Alfred Tarski. His criticisms usually involve the uncovering of "realistic" presuppositions, terminological vagueness, and dogmatism. The inconsistencies of the pragmatists, unlike those of the logicians, can be defended, explained, or resolved.[43] Only Tarski is singled out for praise. His work is "like a breath of fresh air after the murky atmosphere we have been in," primarily because he "seems free from that persistent, malignant orientation towards the kind of fictive mental operator" whose presence haunts the work of most logicians. Bentley's view of Tarski allows us a rare opportunity to glimpse his understanding of "truth."

Tarski's "semantic" theory of truth claims to be epistemologically and metaphysically neutral, i.e., independent from any doctrine about either the acquisition of knowledge or the nature of things.[44] Thus, to use Tarski's famous example, the *meaning* of the sentence "'Snow is white' is true" is that snow is white. We can know the meaning of this sentence, however, without having to decide whether or how the sentence is verifiable. All terms that have to do with relations between the sentences of a language S and the objects to which these sentences are supposed to refer belong not to S but rather to a "metalanguage" M, in terms of which we can determine the conditions for specifying a "true" sentence of S, now called the "object language." The "languages" with which Tarski is concerned are formal languages and any definitions of "truth" and "reference" must be made for a particular S. Since Bentley was not interested in the formal languages constructed by logicians, his enthusiasm for the semantic theory of truth may seem curious. For him, the strength of Tarski's doctrine lay in its recognition that we cannot speak of "truth" or "reference" in general but must instead specify conditions under which such determinations are to be made. The semantic theory of truth, then, was completely compatible with the practice of empirical science as Bentley understood it. In eliminating epistemological and metaphysical issues from the theory of truth, Tarski eliminated as well any need to speculate about the cognitive processes of Bentley's despised "fictive mental operator." Bentley's understanding of the implications of Tarski's work bears a striking resemblance to that of Karl Popper, who opposes Tarski's "objective theory of truth" to all "subjective" or "epistemic" theories "which can conceive of knowledge only as a special kind of mental state, or as a disposition, or as a special kind of belief. . . ."[45] Popper's syllabus of subjectivist doctrines includes positions against which Bentley had argued for decades. I believe Bentley would have objected to Popper's designation of the Tarskian teaching as an "objective" view of truth, since this adjective would have suggested some notion of immediate knowledge. While Bentley recognized that Tarski himself had intended to rehabilitate a correspondence theory of truth, the semantic view broke decisively with traditional theories because it required that we specify both the formal and material conditions for the use of such notions as "facts" and "correspondence." Although he makes no effort to connect them, Bentley considers as acceptable notions of truth only Tarski's semantic theory and Dewey's familiar understanding of "true" as "warrantedly assertible."[46]

Most logicians fail to realize that logic is inseparable from inquiry as a whole. In Bentley's words, they and their logics are "in the world." "Pre-Darwinian" logic retains the untenable traditional view of logic as the "laws of thought," in spite of heroic efforts to escape from this trap. The doctrines of Boole and Frege, continued and developed by Russell and his followers, are "mind-steeped" because they ignore the behavioral context of the rules and operations of logic. As we have already seen in chapter 6, the general form of this ignorance is exhibited in appeals to "intuition" in logic and mathematics. "Post-Darwinian" views of logic, such as those of Dewey, understand logic as the "theory" or reflective reconstruction of historically specific modes of inquiry, not as an a priori foundation for inquiry. Accordingly, the traditional canons of logic such as the laws of identity and contradiction are neither intuitively obvious nor authoritative, but rather the products of the process of inquiry. Bentley makes clear that "naturalistic" logic has nothing to do with "materialism." Rather, the adjective "natural" designates a "single system of inquiry for all knowledge with logic as free to develop in accordance with its own needs as is physics or physiology."[47] When logic is freed from external controls, logical theory becomes, in Dewey's words, the "systematic formulation of controlled inquiry" where "controlled" refers to the "methods of inquiry that are developed and perfected in the processes of continuous inquiry."[48]

The antithesis of the Bentley-Dewey view of logic could be found in the claim of Cohen and Nagel that the principles of logic are "inherently applicable because they are concerned with ontological traits of utmost generality."[49] Equally objectionable to Bentley was Russell's warning that "complete metaphysical agnosticism is not compatible with the maintenance of linguistic propositions."[50] While Bentley approved of Nagel's later search for a "logic without ontology," he patronizingly claimed that this was no more than a restatement of Dewey's own "instrumental" logic.[51] Both Bentley and Dewey found tendencies in Otto Neurath's work that were closer to their own position. From his reading notes for Neurath's *Foundations of the Social Sciences* (1944), we can see that Bentley saw no need to accept a materialist interpretation of Neurath's "physicalism." Indeed, physicalism ran counter to Neurath's own effort to purge scientific language of substantive or "metaphysical" assertions.[52] His survey of contemporary work in logic convinced Bentley that his own position was a decisive improvement on the doctrines of thinkers influenced by either traditional or logical positivist views. He was prepared, however, for the hostile reception he was certain his views would encounter.

For Alonzo Church and Arthur F. Smullyan, among others, the Bentley-Dewey view of logic was simply a revival of "psychologism."[53] Bentley and Dewey were charged with having claimed that logical propositions are in some way dependent upon or even identical with propositions belonging to an empirical science of human behavior. Bentley responds to this criticism with the remark that he and Dewey have been aware of the "academic and pedagogical" distinction between logic and psychology from "early youth."[54] What they reject is any "rigid *factual* difference" between logic and psychology in the process of inquiry. He challenges the critics to describe a "pure" logic intelligibly in any way except as a form of "knowing behavior." The Bentley-Dewey program does not claim to "reduce" logic or psychology to one another, but rather to study "certain phases of the system" of human behavior in which they may be found. Bentley sees no reason why logic cannot be studied with the "general field of behavioral inquiry."

In addition to the charge of psychologism, Church had argued that the list of "firm names" in *Knowing and the Known* had nothing in common with the practice of logicians when constructing a formal system. Bentley cheerfully admitted that his system was not a conventional axiomatic system. Axiomatization rests upon philosophical views he refuses to take for granted. Accordingly, the Bentley-Dewey system, which was never intended as an axiomatic doctrine, cannot properly be criticized as an unsuccessful attempt to develop such a system.

Bentley's Last Years

Bentley was unable to produce any large-scale works after *Knowing and the Known*. His health began to fail by the late 1940s although he continued to refine his views. His correspondence with Dewey shows that he was not satisfied with *Knowing and the Known* and contains proposals for revisions of the Bentley-Dewey positions. His dialogue with Dewey continued until the latter's final illness. As the stream of correspondence began to falter, Bentley's energies diminished. As he put it in one of his last letters to Dewey: "I haven't heard from you in some time. In much the same figure of speech, however, I might say that I have not heard even from myself."[55]

In 1949 Bentley attempted another restatement of his views in an unpublished essay "Logic and Logical Behavior," which he intended as a sketch for a larger work to be entitled "Nature and Logic."[56] He knew that "nature" could not be ignored. Scientific inquiry requires a way in which we can speak of nature without resorting to any of the discredited epistemological and metaphysical doctrines of philosophers. The study of "knowledge" raises the question of whether we can bring "knowing" and the "known" into a "common system of observation, description and interpretation." As he had done in *Behavior Knowledge Fact*, Bentley distinguishes between the notions of the "uniformity of nature" and the "uniformity of knowledge." We cannot take the "knower" as a privileged "part" somehow able to know the larger "whole" or "nature" in which the knower is located. From this arrogant premise flow all the contradictions of philosophy. Bentley's teaching claims to point toward, but has not yet reached, a way of speaking that brings into indissoluble unity "knower," "known," and the conditions of "being known." "Nature" is a "name for the world in course of being known." According to this understanding, nature is not an unchanging horizon that sets limits on what can be known. We must be able to study man as a "locus of knowing" in the "system of nature" and nature in the process of being known together. Bentley has thus formulated his central position in a familiar way. "Knower" and "known" are not self-sufficient particulars but phases of a process or parts of a whole. "Transaction" designates the "togetherness" of knowing behavior and the known. Accordingly, "behavior" need not be attributed to individuals as agents or to any internal properties of individuals. "Behavioral events" are arranged along a continuum from the sensory to the symbolic. "Behavioral inquiry," in consequence, does not begin with, nor are its propositions reducible to, propositions about physical or physiological processes.[57] Bentley moves to defend his position against the criticism that it is a "process" philosophy incapable of analytic precision or clarity by repeating his familiar thesis that any categorial distinctions can be used in a transactional framework when they are taken as perspective from which problems can be investigated rather than "authoritarian" doctrines that contain a priori solutions.

The advanced sciences do not make assertions about "reality" nor do they assume a correspondence between words and things apart from specifications intelligible in terms of a given inquiry or mode of inquiry.[57] Thus, the sciences recognize that the "whole is life-in-process on an earth-in-cosmos." They do not explain or account for "things" but rather for "thing-ing." Bentley's ontological teaching is that the "thingness" of a "thing"—its determinate form or that which allows us to know it *as* one thing rather than another—simply is the "growth" of the "thing" so that there can be no description of it apart from its spatio-temporal structure. Implicitly, Bentley has excluded any things without such a structure from the domain of what is. In more traditional philosophical terminology, we may say that the "being" of anything whatsoever is its spatio-temporal structure. In turn, this structure is known to us only as a "phase" or "aspect" of behavior. Bentley warns that "aspect" and "phase" are not equivalents to "property" or "quality." Instead, they designate "differentiations in the activity of the joint knowings-known."[58]

Bentley's transactionalism takes human activity, including inquiry, as an exhibition of the whole. Indeed, any activity, when properly understood, exhibits the whole. "Circularity," then, is a fundamental feature of Bentley's teaching. He had always held that the world is known only to man as inextricably in the world, so that inquiry is concerned with "world-being-known-to-man-in-it."[59] We may concentrate our inquiry on any phase of this process. Thus, a transactional statement is a "statement about the kind of report the cosmos gets for itself and about itself from one portion of its own activity which in its celebrated linguistic human form reports itself tentatively as the most interesting part of the cosmos."[60] The circle of Bentleyan inquiry is both logical and temporal. The inquirer must look in both directions. "In all stages of behavioral activity new processes are seen developing out of old, and turning back upon the old for their further strengthening. This *turning back* is what needs to be glimpsed."[61] Traditional epistemology arbitrarily arrests the retrospective moment of inquiry or theorizes it incorrectly in terms of historical "backgrounds." When we move forward along the circle of inquiry, our activity appears as the development of form or system. From the cosmic point of view, retrospection and the development of form are themselves aspects of the whole. The inquirer, who must work from within the process, is thus enabled to grasp the whole with increasing comprehensiveness.

In his final years, Bentley's influence among political scientists grew, but we have seen that he believed that social science was quite poorly developed. He found David Easton's *The Political System* (1953), which praised him lavishly, a fundamentally confused work that showed little understanding of scientific inquiry.[62] He was much more interested in the growth of "transactionalism" in psychology, exemplified in the work of Hadley Cantril and Adelbert Ames, Jr., and of "general systems theory" in the work of the biologist Ludwig von Bertalanffy. As we shall see, Bentley was convinced that general systems theory, transactional psychology, and a number of other contemporary positions marked the beginning of the convergence of the sciences he had so long projected. The basis of this convergence was the growing recognition that the "knower" could no longer be isolated from the "known" and that fundamentally new forms of theorizing were needed for the complex organized systems that constituted the domains of the sciences.

By early 1957 Bentley's health had failed. He died on May 22, 1957, after a brief illness, leaving a draft of his final manuscript, an essay for *The Humanist* on the meaning of "transaction."

9

Conclusion:

Inquiry and the Limits of Form

The characteristic behavioral process is the process of knowing. . . . Its study constitutes the primary behavioral science.

"Kennetic Inquiry"

The conclusion of my study of Bentley's teaching will begin with a comprehensive account of his views that connects his teaching with a number of major issues in social science and current philosophy. This summary will be followed by a criticism of what I believe are the crucial defects of Bentley's position.

Social Science and Philosophy

As I have shown in chapter 2, Bentley's reflections on social science began with a belief that social science should be grounded in psychology. Regardless of their philosophical opinions, such a view was shared by most contemporary social scientists. The biologism of many Anglo-American social scientists and the spirit of Bentley's German masters were both presented as offering a suitable foundation for social science because they provided accounts of the mind. Bentley's views resembled those of the proponents of the *Geisteswissenschaften* in his insistence that social science had to concern itself with "meanings." He developed and retained throughout his career the thesis that there were fundamental or categorial differences between the phenomena of the natural sciences and those of the social sciences. His belief in the irreducibility of "purposes" or "intentions" resembles, as we have seen, the basic position of post-Wittgensteinian philosophy of mind. Indeed, I would suggest that apart from variations in philosophic idioms there is little to distinguish the teaching of analytic philosophers who argued against a naturalistic social science on categorial grounds from the teaching of the founders of interpretive social science. Unlike either of those schools of thought, however, Bentley sought, even in his earliest work, to arrive at a unified science. He came to doubt that science as such had been adequately understood. Accordingly, he did not propose to establish a boundary between things that could be understood in or through science and things that could not. Rather, he sought to enlarge and transform science so that the sorts of accounts considered categorially sound by interpretivists and conceptual analysts could be understood as appropriately scientific.

Bentley's first efforts at synthesis revealed something of the differences between his thinking and that of most present-day social science. He sought to unite the analytic power of marginalist economics with the empirical richness of historical sociology. Neither theory nor description was to be sacrificed. Unlike recent proponents of a social or political science grounded in economics, Bentley saw no reason to choose between the two.[1] Put generally, Bentley began his thinking with considerable skepticism concerning the self-imposed limitations that social scientists tended to transform into necessary distinctions. Bentley did not accomplish his synthesis and was diverted from pursuing it because his deepening reflection disclosed a substratum of problems which could not be ignored having to do with connections between everyday and scientific understandings.

In chapters 3 and 4, I examined *The Process of Government* as a record of Bentley's journey from social science to philosophy, although in his opinion it was simply an attempt to think through the problems of social science. Although the book's coherence is severely affected by its author's numerous intentions, it allows us to bring to light most of the major differences between Bentley and present-day social science, as well as some of the positions that have larger philosophic importance.

Under the influence of Dewey's pragmatism, Bentley had come to doubt the necessity of grounding social science in psychology. This development is among the most important themes in his teaching. The principal defect of contemporary social science, regardless of its philosophical premises or substantive claims, lay, in Bentley's opinion, in the notion that explanation in social science must ultimately refer to mental properties or conditions or dispositions. Against the interpretive tradition in social science, this meant that explanations in terms of the "values" supposedly operative in the actions of individuals had to be taken as fundamentally confused. Against the emerging psychological orientations in Anglo-American social science that culminated in behaviorism, this meant that explanations in terms of inferences from observed variations to mental processes had no place in social science. The presuppositions of psychological explanation in general could be found in our everyday understanding. Social science had thus far failed to recognize its relation to this understanding and was in consequence largely dominated by it. The source of the ontological contamination Bentley criticized in social science is our everyday understanding of reality. As we have seen, Bentley rejected causal explanation in social science primarily because, in his opinion, it was a product of everyday modes of thinking and, moreover, was inextricably connected with the notion that an understanding of human action had to be based upon psychological considerations.

From Bentley's standpoint, the so-called behavioral revolution in social science was hardly revolutionary, since it was based firmly upon the foundational role of psychological explanation.[2] Because Bentley was so clearly opposed to psychological explanation, he has often been misinterpreted as a behaviorist in the Watsonian or Skinnerian sense. This interpretation fails to consider the philosophical position he began to articulate in *The Process of Government*. While he was opposed to psychological explanation, he resisted reductionist views with equal vigor. Social science explanation based upon the study of objective determinants of human action was unacceptable because, like its subjective rival, it rested on the epistemological dualism Bentley believed was pervasive in modern thought. The critique of epistemology which dominates much of his later work is a central feature of his first book. On the basis of his tentative criticism of epistemological dualism, we should see that his teaching parts company with that of analytic philosophers of mind in addition to social scientists. The post-Wittgensteinians are, I believe, rightly understood as dualists.[3] Bentley did not wish to dispense with "meanings," "purposes," or "intentions" in social science. Instead, he sought a radically different account of them that would not depend upon any claim that they were properties or processes or contents of the minds of individuals. That is, he agreed that such terms suggested a categorial difference between natural and social science but denied that the difference had to do with any traditional version of distinctions between subjects and objects.

Finally, *The Process of Government* develops a critique of any doctrine of immediate or direct knowledge. That is, Bentley criticized what present-day philosophers call "foundationalism." The opinion that we have or indeed can intelligibly be supposed to have immediate knowledge is carried into science from ordinary modes of thinking or is a premise of everyday understanding. As such it has no appropriate place in science. Well before his systematic reflection on science, Bentley was convinced that a central feature of science is perspectivism. For social science, perspectivism meant that there can be no standpoint that claims authoritative status on the basis of any privileged connection with immediate experience. This thesis serves to distinguish Bentley from social scientists who believe that quantification provides a foundation for their enterprise. The basic mistake of what we may identify as inductivism is that it fails to realize that the homogeneous units it counts and assembles into explanations have a theoretical and not a natural articulation. Put briefly, quantitative social science rests upon a premise Bentley had already rejected early in the twentieth century: there is no cognitively or theoretically neutral domain of facts to which quantitative methods give privileged access and which as such serve as pretheoretical foundations for the theories of social science.

Bentley's perspectivism reveals once more his relation to the interpretive tradition, but unlike some proponents of the *Geisteswissenschaften*, he did not argue that intellectual rigor must be sacrificed to impressionistic or poetic illumination. The notion that social science was inherently perspectivist or that no foundational position was possible required instead that the articulation of a diversity of perspectives be conducted as an exhibition of formal structures. Any foundational doctrine was, in Bentley's terminology, "realistic." Once foundationalism is rejected, social science can become formalist.

In chapter 5, I followed Bentley's path beyond conventional social science. His understanding of science amounted to a "postpositivist" philosophy of science before the fact. Put concisely, Bentley's study of the new physics convinced him that the practice of science disclosed the nature of science. Unlike logical empiricists or positivists, Bentley never accepted any version of the notion that there is a radical distinction between the process of scientific thinking and the structure of scientific theories and explanations.[4] Thus Bentley rejected what Stephen Toulmin has identified as the central axiom of logical empiricist philosophy of science:

at any stage in its historical development, the established intellectual content of a science or scientific theory can be exhaustively represented as a "logical system"—that is, that the theoretical concepts and conclusions of the science are related to one another, and to the observational evidence on which they are based, in a formal network of logical relations—and that the consistency, richness, and logical structure of this network determine the validity, and/or degree of establishment, of the theoretical concepts and conclusions in question.[5]

As critics of the logical empiricist doctrine have noted, this understanding of science rests upon both the opinion that there is or should be a general logico-mathematical model or structure in terms of which a scientific theory should be constructed and that there is a fundamental distinction between observation and theory. This latter distinction may be identified simply as the foundationalist premise of logical empiricism. We have seen that Bentley was already prepared to reject such a premise. As I have suggested at various points in the previous chapters, his understanding of science resembles that of historians of science such as Kuhn who emphasize connections between scientific thinking and its larger intellectual contexts. "Problems," "facts," and "theories" appear linked systematically in some versions of this position. Physicist-philosopher David Bohm's formulation of this orientation is quite close to Bentley's own teaching: a scientific theory "is itself a whole, in which analysis into disjoint components or elements is not relevant . . . because all terms in such a theory can have their meanings and their criteria of factuality and truth only in the total context given by that theory."[6]

Bentley's study of science convinced him that each science articulated its own categorial framework. As far as I can tell, this claim, which forms a major theme in his teaching, distinguishes him from any other philosopher of social science. One of the basic lessons of the new physics was that a plurality of categorial frameworks was not only possible but necessary. Traditional philosophy, everyday understanding, and unreflective science all agreed that there must be a single categorial framework to serve as a neutral matrix for knowledge. The practice of physics as the most advanced natural science provided, Bentley claimed, refutation of this dogma. The perspectivism Bentley had taught as indispensable in social science appears as the thesis of categorial diversity in his mature work. The opinion that there is a single spatial and temporal framework, after all, has a determinate origin in the conjunction of modern philosophy and classical physics. It is a foundational claim just as any other doctrine of immediate knowledge is such a claim, and is vulnerable to the same criticism.

I presented Bentley's critique of logico-mathematical discourse in chapter 6 as his most radical venture. He was certainly aware of the deeply rooted doctrine that mathematics and logic simply were the basis for science or indeed for any exhibition of human rationality. That doctrine had united ancients and moderns (or Plato and Russell) and had survived the most profound changes in logic and mathematics themselves. Nonetheless, Bentley tried to show that such discourse was inherently unstable. The source of its instability lies in the connections between ordinary language and formal discourse. Bentley's recognition of the importance of the context of analytic speech or logico-mathematical discourse is still not widely shared by philosophers and, it need hardly be added, is absent from the thinking of social scientists. Bentley's linguistic analysis showed that the concepts employed in logic and mathematics derived their intelligibility from nonlogical and nonmathematical contexts. His "semantic" methodology, unlike that of formal semanticists in present-day philosophy, is not merely modeled on logic and mathematics. Rather, it was intended to exhibit the *emergence* of formalism or to identify formal discourse with the processes of formation of formal discourse. Such an account both recognizes the link between the contexts of analysis and the methods of analysis on the one hand and claims to contribute to the formalization of these connections on the other hand. Formal discourse depends, so to speak, on the achievement of complete clarity by formalists concerning the emergence of formalism. That is, Bentley's semantic methodology calls for the elimination of all presuppositions that might lie beneath formal discourse. The development of modern natural science toward formalism shows, in Bentley's opinion, how this goal may be reached.

The themes of chapters 7 and 8 were Bentley's behavioral science and his attachment to pragmatism. Unlike later behavioralism, Bentley's behavioral science is not based upon some understanding of the foundational role of natural science. That is, Bentley had no intention of creating a "natural science" of society or of human behavior. Such a project, he had argued, was inherently confused. A science was a full or presuppositionless account of its own domain or subject matter. Relations among the sciences simply could not be properly understood in terms of hierarchical imagery. Thus, behavioral science was a new sort of science. It may be understood as an advance over interpretive social science in that it rejects the psychological basis of its predecessor. The characteristics of human things that had led interpretive social scientists to propose their unique status had never been properly understood. In other words, Bentley takes the thesis of categorial difference more radically than most interpretivists. Thus, behavioral science requires its own categorial framework, its own notions of space and time, in order to account for its phenomena. Its objects are theoretically articulated, as Bentley shows in *Behavior Knowledge Fact*. That is, our everyday understanding of behavior is woefully inadequate for a behavioral science. A science of behavior must begin with recognition of what William James had identified as the boundary-transcending features of psychological phenomena. *Behavior Knowledge Fact* bears more than a passing resemblance to James's *Principles of Psychology* refracted through Bentley's own formalism.

Bentley was convinced that a general theory of inquiry was needed in view of the defects of prevailing philosophical positions. With the exception of pragmatism, he was convinced that all understandings of inquiry failed because they took the form of epistemologies, that is, of efforts to anchor knowledge in a determinate ontological condition, cognitive state, or mode of action. In contrast, Bentleyan naturalism understands "knowings" and "knowns" as "concrete instances of organic-environmental action in behavioral space and time," which means that there are neither "pure knowers" nor "pure reals." In Bentley's view, any epistemology comes down on one side or the other of such a distinction. Accordingly, the "what" with which knowledge is concerned is neither a "demand made by a 'thing'" on the knower nor a "determination" or construction of the knower. Bentley's "transactionalism" requires that inquiry be seen as reflexive. Thus, any scientific theory must have the character of a unified field theory in physics, which should "show itself to be a process of knowing, as clearly as it shows itself to be a system of the known."[7]

The pragmatism that emerged in Bentley's teaching brings his position into the forefront of present-day philosophical debates that rest in part on a revival or creative development of pragmatism. That a crucial part of pragmatism consists in a radical criticism of the modern epistemological tradition or of the complex role that epistemology plays in modern philosophy can be seen in a number of recent works of philosophy.[8] The pragmatic rejection of foundational thinking, when understood radically, leaves no room, however, for the authority of science. While Bentley believed that scientists and philosophers would be "shocked at the statement that science is a specific form or mode of cultural trans-acting instead of an exclusive and hence pure approach to Reality or Truth or some equivalent term—doing for nature what theology used to do for super-nature," we have seen the paradigmatic role science plays in his teaching.[9] I believe that the central problems of Bentley's teaching have to do with his understanding of science. It is to these problems that I shall now turn.

The Limits of Form

In an earlier chapter I considered the argument of one of Bentley's critics, who claimed that Bentley is "engaged throughout in a dispute with the view that thought rules the world."[10] I am inclined to say instead that Bentley's teaching is defective because he is ultimately unable to distinguish decisively between thought and the world. My criticism of Bentley will concentrate on four closely related themes in his understanding of science and thus of inquiry as such. In order, these are: the soundness of his rejection of foundationalism and his criticism of realism; the intelligibility of his understanding of language; the crucial issue of his formalism; and his rejection of any version of the epistemological subject.

Bentley's attack on foundationalism is, I have shown, intended to be comprehensive. Any candidate for the role of foundational belief, condition, or procedure can be challenged as problematic. For Bentley, as for such present-day philosophers as Richard Rorty, Wilfrid Sellars, and Donald Davidson, the notion of an atheoretical basis for a class of "privileged representations" of reality is hopelessly confused.[11] Bentley argues in virtually all his writings some version of the thesis, adapted to the problems of whatever field he was studying, that we cannot step outside of *some* conceptual framework to inspect the connections between representations and objects. Accordingly, I believe Bentley would oppose recent efforts by such philosophers as Saul Kripke to rehabilitate epistemological and metaphysical realism with a theory of reference that purports to show that and how we can move from intuitions to knowledge of "natural kinds."[12] In Bentley's view, science, properly understood, neither has nor claims to have knowledge of the "essences" of things.

What Bentley does not adequately explain, however, is the character of the account a science provides of something within its domain. That is, while Bentley's case against any *general* foundationalism is intelligible, his understanding of the practice of science is less intelligible. He seems to have sought to combine the view that science does not arrive at knowledge of how the world really is with the view that a scientific account is superior to any other account. For many philosophers of science, such as Frederick Suppe, "accepting science as a paradigm knowledge-yielding enterprise commits one to a realistic philosophical analysis of scientific knowledge and truth."[13] A realist position need not be identical with a traditional empiricist understanding of the foundational role of sense data. Bentley's strictures against realism are most effective when he is concerned with empiricist positions. His opposition to realism, however, lies deeper than any criticism of empiricism. Whatever is the case with present-day rejections of foundationalism, Bentley's criticism cannot be understood apart from his view of language.

It is apparent that Bentley never completed his general theory of language. I have shown that for him it is unintelligible to claim that we have or can have any prelinguistic knowledge of anything whatsoever. Since language is for him the most general condition of knowledge, one might turn his position around to characterize him as a linguistic foundationalist. Certainly in *Linguistic Analysis of Mathematics* he comes very close to claiming that there is no difference between "logic" and the language in and through which logicians "do logic." For him, demonstration of this claim serves to overthrow the authority of logic for science. Since logic is inextricably linked with language, there is a sense in which it is, so to speak, the object of a science of language. When we connect this view with Bentley's thesis that the scientific character of a discipline is an emergent feature of that discipline, we have, in my opinion, his answer to the charge that his account of science is relativistic. It is not the case that "anything goes" in Bentley's understanding of science. Instead, notions of "truth," "rationality," and "objectivity," to list several characteristics often ascribed to scientific knowledge, are themselves subject to development or evolution. This familiar pragmatic argument rests, at least in Bentley's version of it, on the view that there is no language that provides us with direct access to any part of the world. Thus, the language of theoretical physics, at any point in its development, is no more directly linked to reality than is any other language. The terms of theoretical physics do not refer to entities in any way about which we can speak apart from the language of theoretical physics.

Bentley's understanding of language allows him to recharacterize such issues as that of reference. We mistakenly concern ourselves with whether or how scientific terms refer to extrascientific things because we do not realize that the understanding of what it means to refer to something is itself drawn from natural or everyday language. Bentley's semantic doctrine may be understood as holding that a well-developed science possesses a specific understanding of reference which is unlike that to be found in natural language. We will recall that Bentley's view of "truth" comes closest to that of Tarski. Bentley's pragmatic extension of Tarski's theory of truth is, put simply, that there is no universal condition answering to the word "truth." A science contains, whether explicitly or implicitly, a collection of notions that specify what such terms as "truth" mean within that science. We can now see why Bentley insists upon consistency as a feature of scientific languages. Well-developed sciences are bundles of practices that have at their cores sets of agreements having to do with truth and other matters. To ask whether we can step outside the domain of a science to answer the question of whether a scientific theory is "really" true is to exhibit a defective understanding of the scientific enterprise. Bentley may be read as challenging us to explain coherently how to ask, let alone how to answer, such a question.

Nevertheless, Bentley does have a candidate for the role of an indicator of the extent to which a science is well developed. That candidate, of course, is "formalism." At the risk of seeming repetitious, I must state again that Bentleyan formalism is not the formalism of axiomatization or of hypothetico-deductive models of scientific theories. Rather, formalism for him is best understood as the methodical elimination of ontological claims. What remains in scientific language when it has been rendered presuppositionless is "form." In chapter 6, I suggested that Bentley's formalism can be understood as analogous to a phase space or Hilbert space permitting the mapping of any scientific theory onto it without any privileged location. An ontological claim, then, is an assertion about a privileged mapping. Bentley's frequent criticisms of the damaging effects of the presuppositions of Newtonian mechanics on psychology and sociology may be read as criticisms of precisely such assertions. Coherence becomes the basic feature of a scientific theory. Unlike many present-day proponents of "coherentism" against foundationalism, Bentley is more radical, for he rejects a stable model of coherence drawn from logic. A Bentleyan formal or consistent science is, so to speak, a purely semantic affair.

Bentley's semantics establishes two important requirements for science. First, we have seen that a science is a system of "specifications," as Bentley put it in his work with Dewey. This means that all aspects of the scientific enterprise must be specified. Such matters as the identification and formulation of scientific problems, choices of research methods, determinations of what will count as explanations, and relations between a given science and other sciences are all supposed to be completely visible. The view that a scientific theory must rest on at least some assumptions which are held to be unproblematic is for Bentley an admission of failure in science.[14] The second characteristic is that all such matters are decidable. Scientists must be understood as choosing or deciding to employ any and all concepts in their science and, more radically, choosing what categorial frameworks are appropriate for their science.

Specifiability raises the question of whether it is possible for a science to achieve what may be called complete self-awareness. Certainly the goal of a presuppositionless science has been a part of the programs of such philosophers as Hegel and Husserl. Bentley insists that there can be no dark corners in the scientific enterprise. If presuppositions can be identified in science, they can be eliminated. The burden Bentley thus places on scientists is immense. Not only must they engage in what a conventional philosopher of science would recognize as scientific practice, but they must also undertake Bentleyan semantic or linguistic analysis as well. That analysis discloses the connections between the language of science and its complete contexts. It is this inquiry, I believe, that *generates* form in Bentley's sense.

Decidability raises the issue of whether Bentley's science is not ultimately a poem or an expression of human creativity. A science exhibits a greater amount of form as it brings more matters under the heading of decidable questions. A completely formal science would be a science that had no room for undecidable matters. Thus, science is constructed, a conclusion that follows from Bentley's insistence that realism and science are opposed. Now if science is a construction, it would seem that there is no difference between Bentley and Nietzsche, or between science and poetry. Indeed, when we consider the enormity of the task of the Bentleyan scientist, we may at least raise the possibility that the development of a pure semantics of science rests as much upon the resolution or will of scientists as upon their technical ingenuity.

Bentley would reject the criticism that science as he understands it is simply or even primarily an invention of the scientist. He explicitly rejected the notion that science provided or intends to provide certain knowledge of anything. We must recall that science aims at complete description. Such description is not an exhaustive inventory of facts nor yet, in the fashion of realist philosophers of science such as Rom Harré, an account of "ultimate entities."[15] Complete description is achieved when a science arrives at recognition of the diversity of standpoints from which problems may be formulated and theories or explanations developed. What is descriptive, then, is the phase space onto which these standpoints can be mapped. In this connection we should recall Bentley's distinction between the problematic metaphysical thesis of the "unity of nature" and the thesis of the "unity of knowledge." Any standpoint from which we claim to speak of the unity of nature may be challenged or cannot conceivably be taken as self-evident. This possibility suggested to Bentley that the ground of unity cannot be understood to lie in nature but rather in knowledge, a move that restates in his own idiom the methodological premise of modern philosophy. To revert to the analogy from *The Process of Government*, any domain of knowledge may be carved up or subdivided in as many ways as the possible standpoints scientists may choose and, thus, the sorts of questions they choose to ask. Bentley would have agreed with Donald Davidson's remark that nature has no preferred way of being represented.[16]

Although Bentley's own metaphysical views are difficult to make clear, we are, I believe, warranted in asking what a world is like that has no preferred way of being represented. Such a world would be constructable but not literally "made up" by human intentions. The central focus of science becomes potentiality rather than actuality. Bentleyan formalism, we may say, is compatible with a world of flux or of possibilities because it is agnostic with respect to the ranking or ordering of possibilities. Bentley would have been sympathetic to the use of "possible worlds" by present-day proponents of essentialism but would have turned this device against any argument of the sort advanced by Kripke and others to the effect that an essence is that which we rightly understand to remain unchanged in a number of possible worlds. He would have been quick to note that such a doctrine must rest upon a determinate understanding of "nature," which returns us to his belief that such an understanding cannot be articulated coherently.[17] For Bentley, the proper self-understanding of science must recognize the diversity of what Nelson Goodman calls "ways of worldmaking." Indeed, Goodman's summary sketch of the location of his own views in the history of philosophy is reminiscent of Bentley's own journey. Kant "exchanged the structure of the world for the structure of the mind," a move followed by the exchange of the structure of the mind for the "structure of concepts." Goodman proposes to exchange the structure of concepts for the "structure of the several symbol systems of the sciences, philosophy, the arts, perception, and everyday discourse."[18] In none of these systems can one find, for either Goodman or Bentley, some incorrigible or preferred way of representing what is. None of them answers the question of what foundation knowledge should have. Instead of understanding concepts within a system in terms of their links with some extra-systemic reality, Bentley insists that the only genuine issues have to do with consistency and coherence.

What Bentley owes his reader is an account of "form" that will address the numerous questions that must be asked about the core of his teaching. In the first place, Bentley never makes clear how the process of formalization is carried out. His destructive criticism of the ontological premises of theories or, for that matter, of entire sciences is not, despite his protestations, identical with the construction of an increasingly formal science. Put concisely, we have, as far as I can see, no Bentleyan way of knowing how far we have come along the path of formalization in any science. If we cannot make this determination, we cannot possess the sort of complete knowledge of the current condition of a science that Bentley requires in order for further formalization to take place. That is, Bentley offers no account of how we know what we are doing in the construction of science. Bentley claims that "good" science can be distinguished from "bad" or inadequate science by virtue of the distance it has traversed from the realist presuppositions attached to ordinary understanding and embedded in everyday or natural language. This claim is what I have called the discontinuity thesis. It is crucial that Bentley provides some indication of how to measure this metaphorical distance. He cannot rely upon our intuition of, say, the completeness of description or the consistency of scientific discourse, because our understanding of what it means to intuit something is embedded in the fabric of the sort of experience from which science must be decisively dissociated.

I believe a more general formulation of this issue will enable us to understand more clearly why Bentley's formalism fails. It would seem that in order to know that a scientific theory or the condition of a science is an exhibition of emergent formalism, we must be able to identify formalism by its look or appearance. For the proponent of conventional axiomatization, this task is made simple by virtue of the use of a general or standard notion of form. Bentley rejected this standard notion. Although I find the basis of his criticism illuminating, I am not convinced that he can explain the distinguishing features of form. Now it might be argued that my criticism presupposes what Bentley has rejected—that there are fixed features of form which permit us to say that a theory is more or less formal. I do not claim that Bentley must produce such fixed features. Even if form evolves or develops, we must be able in some fashion Bentley does not clarify to assert that physics is more advanced than sociology. Bentley makes precisely this assertion throughout his work.

Let me be as clear as possible about the significance of Bentley's failure to explicate his notion of form. We may grant to him that science is not continuous with ordinary experience or that the practice of science requires recognition of this discontinuity. If this is so, Bentley's problem is still urgent, for we need to know when we are engaged in science and when we are not. The source of this knowledge must lie, so to speak, either in science or outside science. If it lies within science, Bentley must show that there is a correlation between the evolving practice of science, in which the movement from realism to formalism takes place unconsciously, and the self-knowledge of science. If it lies outside of science, then Bentley has permitted an extrascientific source of knowledge about science, which he opposes. Now I do not think that Bentley's thesis that the structure of science is circular saves him from this dilemma. For him, any science has the characteristics Hegel saw in philosophical science or logic. In Hegel's opinion, all other sciences begin with a distinction between content and method, while logic cannot take for granted either its procedures or the thesis that the "material of knowledge is present in and for itself in the shape of a finished world apart from thinking. . . ."[19] The goal of absolute knowledge, which is intelligible as Hegel's version of the project of modern philosophy as a whole, is achieved through the exhibition of the Whole or the first principle of all things in the activity of the philosopher whose comprehensive conceptualization unites subject and object or discloses the ground on which they may be shown to be united. The structure of Hegelian philosophic science is circular because the origin and the result of comprehensive conceptualization must be the same.[20] Because Bentley has no counterpart for the Hegelian Whole or Absolute, his own formal science, which we must remember possesses a circular structure, seems less an exhibition of rationality than a dispensation of fate or history. Whatever problems we may find with Hegel's teaching, it claims to show not merely that formalization takes place but that its emergence is not accidental. I do not believe Bentley can show why we cannot argue that his formalism is accidental.

It is ironic that the intuition or spirit of the scientist, shared by a community of inquirers, appears to be the only support for the emergence of form. After all, Bentley insisted that the power of social science theories to illuminate their subject matter is accidental or a product of the delicacy and power of the mind of the social scientist. Bentley hoped to dispense with such arbitrariness in science. What we may call the "political" dimension of the modern doctrine of method is the notion that method allows science to dispense with reliance on the knowledge or wisdom or judgment of those who by nature may be superior to other men. Science does not depend upon the natural superiority of one mind to others. While Bentley accepted this modern doctrine in both its political and its scientific senses, he nowhere shows precisely how the achievements of science follow from the method of science apart from consideration of the achievements of scientists. He shows that Einstein or Simmel inherited and transformed problems, learned from others, and took part in the on-going practice of a science. What he does not show is that the achievements for which he admires Einstein or Simmel are intelligible as the collective product of a community of scientific practitioners.

Bentley insisted that science or knowledge is not properly understood if our account of it turns upon an account of the mind. He urges us to understand the "individual" and his mental properties as "decidable cases." There is no reason why the mind or anything predicated of the mind should be taken as logically or epistemologically primary. Bentley seems to have understood the role of the subject as historically specific in the way in which Michel Foucault views the role of "man" in modernity. In Foucault's words, "man" appears as the "being such that knowledge will be attained in him of what renders all knowledge possible."[21] Bentley was convinced that knowledge was radically misunderstood if it was viewed as having to do with relations between subjects and an external world. We are inextricably in the midst of what we seek to know. In Bentley's words, "Man is a bit of the cosmos inspecting itself."[22] For Bentley, the "individual" is a kind of indicator of the underlying flux or process and not the source of the significance of that process. The science Bentley was convinced would emerge would have nothing to do with knowledge claims of the sort made by present-day science or philosophy. Those claims are ultimately based on some version of foundationalism and inevitably refer to the contents or operations of the minds of subjects. What Bentley does not explain is the character of this science. For whom will this science be a practice? Even if, to use Bentley's poetic idiom, man is that part of the cosmos or the whole whose activity is to engage in inquiry, man is thereby a part unlike other parts not engaged in inquiry. Bentley does not reflect, that is to say, on the significance of the possibility of reflection. The science of the future may well be radically unlike that of the past or present. On Bentley's own doctrine, however, it will not lie any closer to reality and will still require the uncovering of dogmatic presuppositions. Bentley relies upon the practice of science as his key to the authority of science. The practice of science is the practice of scientists. The critical reflection that both generates and exhibits the formalization of science is also the practice of scientists. Bentley's implicit reliance upon superior examples of that practice inclines me to the conclusion that his methodological teaching does not liberate itself successfully from the subject with which it contends.

Finally, Bentley's teaching calls for a radical recharacterization of science that points beyond the modern doctrines with which his views are at bottom compatible. As pure construction, science would appear to be fundamentally contemplative, if not of a stable world then of our own constructive activity. I believe Bentley's understanding of science suggests that it is not primarily concerned with practice or with the relief of man's estate. The task of science was so immense and its development was so tentative that questions of its application virtually disappear in Bentley. Certainly a great distance separates him from social scientists who pushed for the application or asserted the political relevance of their findings. One example from Bentley must suffice to illustrate this difference. He did not propose to resolve the fact/value dichotomy with which social scientists wrestled by reducing "values" to "facts" or transforming "facts" into "values." Instead, both "facts" and "values" as conventionally understood were for him crude indications of matters that warranted further exploration. Science at present could not make sense of or clarify either term sufficiently to theorize connections between them coherently. Moreover, there was no guarantee that the form in which they would or could be theorized by science would have anything to do with the form in which they were originally presented.

A social science that follows Bentley's path has little in common with the protodiscipline that may be understood as having originated in modern political philosophy. However inadequately, social science preserved with some hesitation the question of the best way of life or best social order. For Bentley the origins of that question in everyday experience barred it from being taken as a scientific question. Until or unless the problems with which social science is concerned are determined entirely by the formal considerations of social science, there will simply be no genuine social science.

My criticism of Bentley turns on issues of coherence or consistency. I believe he set out to show how science could be understood by attempting to distinguish more sharply than most modern philosophers between everyday and scientific experience. His teaching is an attempt to work out more coherently the implications of this modern distinction. Unfortunately for him, even his behavioral science exhibits dependence upon everyday views. Regardless of its technical ingenuity, Bentleyan behavioral science rests upon the thesis that there is a categorial difference between behavior and everything else. This distinction, while capable of complex explication, has to do with such notions as "meanings" and "purpose." No matter how a well-developed behavioral science may eventually understand these notions or the aspects of the whole which they imperfectly designate, the categorial differences involved do not originate in or with that mature science. When Bentley chooses to explain or justify his science, he must appeal to features of "behavior" that have at least some intelligibility apart from the transformations they must undergo in his science. While it may be the case that we lack comprehensive knowledge of behavior unless we practice Bentley's science, we do not thereby lack a sufficient familiarity with its subject matter to begin to construct a science that may prove able to comprehend it.

For Bentley's science to be complete, it must be more than a doctrine of method. It must present an account of what it proposes to study that permits us to understand why method makes this study possible or how method illuminates its objects. Bentley's writings contain abundant evidence of how he understood his subject matter. His understanding could have been connected with his formalist semantics to show why his procedures were necessary. His failure to make this connection cannot be attributed to a failure of nerve. Instead, it must be attributed to his agreement with the modern doctrines he criticized. Perhaps the contemplative resignation he sought to substitute for moral philosophy has larger importance as an admission that there were some presuppositions he did not choose to explore.

Appendix

The Arthur F. Bentley Manuscript Collections

The two Arthur F. Bentley Manuscript Collections are held by The Lilly Library, Indiana University. The Arthur F. Bentley Manuscripts 1 collection or MSS 1 consists of manuscript drafts of published and unpublished writings and reading notes. The Arthur F. Bentley Manuscripts 2 collection or MSS 2 consists of correspondence and miscellany. I have benefited from Jules Altman's chronological list of Bentley's published and unpublished work which is included with the Bentley collections.

MSS 1 contains approximately fifteen thousand items. I have selected published and unpublished material for listing which in my judgment sheds light on Bentley's intellectual development. In those cases where the material was published, I have provided publication information. I also have included significant collections of Bentley's reading notes because they often contain critical reflections of some length, and thus deserve study.

1891–93. "The Condition of the Western Farmer as Illustrated by the Economic History of a Nebraska Township" (840 pp. including survey instrument, responses, tally sheets, manuscript drafts, and final version). Published in The Johns Hopkins University Studies in Historical and Political Science, Eleventh Series, nos. 7–8. Baltimore: Johns Hopkins University Press, 1983. 92 pp.

1894. "On the Relation of the Individual to Society in the Social Sciences" (46 pp.).

1895. "The Individuality as the Basis for Reasoning in the Social Sciences" (80 pp.).

1895. "Phenomenal Monism as the Basis for the Theory of Society" (45 pp.).

1895. "The Units of Investigation in the Social Sciences." Publications of the American Academy of Social and Political Science 149 (1895): 87–113.

1896. "'Causational' and 'Valuational' Sciences of Society" (61 pp.).

1896. "Lecture Notes. Sociology Department, University of Chicago" (767 pp.).

1904–7. "Municipal Ownership Interest Groups in Chicago: A Study of Referendum Votes, 1902–7" (376 pp.). This work is identified in MSS 1 as having been published by Principia Press in 1935, but it does not appear on Altman's list and I have been unable to find a copy.

1905–6. "The Play of Interests in Legislative Bodies" (136 pp.).

1905–7. The Process of Government: A Study of Social Pressures. Chicago: University of Chicago Press, 1908. 501 pp. Second edition, Bloomington, Indiana: Principia Press, 1935. Third edition, Bloomington, Indiana: Principia Press, 1949. Re-

236 · Language, Form, and Inquiry

print of the first edition. Edited, with an introduction by Peter H. Odegard, Cambridge, Massachusetts: John Harvard Library, Harvard University Press, 1967.

1910. "Knowledge and Society" (790 pp.). Published in *Inquiry into Inquiries: Essays in Social Theory*. Edited by Sidney Ratner, pp. 3–26. Boston: Beacon Press, 1954. Reprint. Westport, Connecticut: Greenwood Press, 1975. All references to this collection will appear as "Published in *Inquiry*" with page numbers.

1919–20. *Makers, Users, and Masters* (2,278 pp. including notes, data, and drafts). Edited by Sidney Ratner. Syracuse: Syracuse University Press, 1969.

1924–26. *Relativity in Man and Society* (1,047 pp. including notes and drafts). New York: G. P. Putnam's Sons, 1926. 363 pp.

1926. "Remarks on Method in the Study of Society." *American Journal of Sociology* 32, no. 3 (1926): 456–60. Published in *Inquiry*, pp. 27–30.

1926–27. "Sociological Studies and Papers: Six Essays" (454 pp.).

1926–28. "Perry's Theory of Value" (62 pp.).

1928. "A Sociological Critique of Behaviorism." *Archiv für systematische Philosophie und Soziologie* 31, nos. 3/4 (1928): 334–40. Published in *Inquiry*, pp. 31–37.

1928–30. "The Postulates of Operational Physics" (314 pp.).

1928–32. *Linguistic Analysis of Mathematics*. (3,200 pp. including notes and drafts). Bloomington, Indiana: Principia Press, 1932. 315 pp.

1929. "Individual and Social—Terms and Facts" (186 pp. including notes and drafts). Translated by Jeanne Duprat and Arthur F. Bentley as "L'individuel et le social: les termes et les faits." *Revue Internationale de Sociologie* 36 (March–June 1929): 243–70.

1929. "New Ways and Old to Talk About Men" (113 pp. including notes and drafts). *Sociological Review* 21, no. 3 (1929): 300–14. Published in *Inquiry*, pp. 37–52.

1929. "Eine Dreifache Annäherung des Kontinuumproblemes" (171 pp.).

1929–31. "The Psychic and the Social" (25 pp.).

1930. "Number One and Number Ought" (135 pp.).

1930–31. "The Linguistic Structure of Mathematical Consistency" (53 pp. including notes and drafts). *Psyche* 12 (1932): 78–91.

1931. "Examination of Einstein's Term 'Space'" (65 pp.).

1931. "Sociology and Mathematics" (160 pp. including notes and drafts). *Sociological Review* 23 (1931): 85–107; 149–72. Published in *Inquiry*, pp. 53–101.

1931. "Analytic Sociology," with Jacob R. Kantor (227 pp.).

1932–35. *Behavior Knowledge Fact* (2,358 pp. including notes and drafts). Bloomington, Indiana: Principia Press, 1935.

1932. "A Visual Illusion Affecting Mathematical Reasoning" (25 pp.).

1933. "Preliminary Essays on Psychology" (507 pp.).

1934–38. "Physics Reading Notes" (504 pp.).

1936. "Scientific Behavior versus Logical Misbehavior" (168 pp. including notes and drafts).

1936. "Conceptual Reliance in Logical Construction" (196 pp. including notes and drafts).

1936. "Bridgman's Concepts in Operation" (459 pp. including notes and drafts).

1936. "The Positive and the Logical" (50 pp.). *Philosophy of Science* 3 (1936): 472–85. Published in *Inquiry*, pp. 101–13.

1937. "The Concept" (132 pp.).

1937–38. "Physicists and Fairies" (188 pp. including notes and drafts). *Philosophy of Science* 5 (1938): 132–65. Published in *Inquiry*, pp. 113–41.

1937–40. "The Human Skin: Philosophy's Last Line of Defense" (377 pp. including notes and drafts). *Philosophy of Science* 8 (1941): 1–19. Published in *Inquiry*, pp. 195–212.

1938–39. "Situational vs. Psychological Theories of Behavior" (2,258 pp. including notes and drafts). *Journal of Philosophy* 36 (1939): 169–81; 309–23; 405–13. Published in *Inquiry*, pp. 141–75.

1939. "Peirce" (319 pp.).

1939–40. "Observable Behaviors" (360 pp. including notes and drafts). *Psychological Review* 47 (1940): 230–53. Published in *Inquiry*, pp. 175–95.

1939–40. "Memoranda on Dewey's Logic" (125 pp.).

1940. "The Behavioral Superfice" (244 pp. including notes and drafts). *Psychological Review* 48 (1941): 39–59.

1940. "Decrassifying Dewey" (49 pp.). *Philosophy of Science* 8 (1941): 147–56.

1940. "Unity of Science" (116 pp. including notes and drafts).

1940–41. "L. Bloomfield" (95 pp. including notes and drafts).

1940–41. "The Factual Space and Time of Behavior" (151 pp. including notes and drafts). *Journal of Philosophy* 38 (1941): 477–85. Published in *Inquiry*, pp. 214–33.

1941–42. "The Phenomena Called 'Conscious'" (149 pp. including notes and drafts).

1941–42. "Language" (876 pp. including notes and drafts).

1942. "As Through a Glass Darkly" (150 pp. including notes and drafts). *Journal of Philosophy* 39 (1942): 432–39.

1942. "Subjects and Objects" (129 pp. including notes and drafts).

1942–43. "Truth, Reality and Behavioral Fact" (288 pp. including notes and drafts). *Journal of Philosophy* 40 (1943): 169–87.

1942–43. "The Jamesian Datum" (537 pp. including notes and drafts). *Journal of Psychology* 16 (1943): 35–79. Published in *Inquiry*, pp. 230–67.

1943–44, 1950. "Process of Vision" (776 pp. including notes and drafts). A ms. dated 21 August 1943, "The Fiction of 'Retinal Image,'" appears in *Inquiry*, pp. 268–85.

1943–49. *Knowing and the Known*, with John Dewey. Boston: Beacon Press, 1949. The original articles that were included in this volume appear below:
"A Search for Firm Names." *Journal of Philosophy* 42 (1945): 5–6.
"On A Certain Vagueness in Logic: I, II." *Journal of Philosophy* 42 (1945): 6–27, 39–51.
"A Terminology for Knowings and Knowns." *Journal of Philosophy* 42 (1945): 225–47.
"Postulations." *Journal of Philosophy* 42 (1945): 645–62.
"Logicians' Underlying Postulations." *Philosophy of Science* 13 (1945): 3–19.
"Interaction and Transaction." *Journal of Philosophy* 43 (1946): 505–17.
"Transactions as Known and Named." *Journal of Philosophy* 43 (1946): 533–51.
"Specification." *Journal of Philosophy* 43 (1946): 645–63.
"Definition." *Journal of Philosophy* 44 (1946): 281–306.
"Concerning a Vocabulary for Inquiry into Knowledge." *Journal of Philosophy* 44 (1947): 421–34.
"The New 'Semiotic.'" *Philosophy and Phenomenological Research* 8 (1947): 107–31.
"Signs of Error." *Philosophy and Phenomenological Research* 10 (1949): 99–104.

1945–51. "Mathematics" (131 pp. including notes and drafts).
1947. "The Behavioral Fact" (115 pp. including notes and drafts).
1947. "Sketch on Pavlov" (116 pp. including notes and drafts).
1948–49. "Logic and Logical Behavior" (508 pp. including notes and drafts). A ms. dated June 27, 1949, with this title appears in *Inquiry*, pp. 286–319.
1950. "Kennetic Inquiry" (344 pp. including notes and drafts). *Science* 112 (1950): 775–83. Published in *Inquiry*, pp. 337–54.
1951. "Seeing and the Seen" (164 pp. including notes and drafts).
1951–52. "Skinner Comments" (81 pp. including notes and drafts).
1953. "An Epilogue." In *Life, Language, Law*, edited by Richard W. Taylor, pp. 210–12.
1956. "The Word 'Transaction'" (94 pp. including notes and drafts). *The Humanist* 5 (1957): 17–21.

Notes

Preface

1 My criticisms of this work are not intended to minimize its influence on the present study. Kress's book led me to take Bentley seriously as a social theorist and philosopher of social science.
2 Kress, *Social Science and the Idea of Process*, p. 204.
3 Henry S. Kariel, *Open Systems*, p. 97. Kariel's view of Bentley is based, as he makes clear, on Norman Jacobson, "Causality and Time in Political Process," pp. 15–22. Jacobson's understanding of Bentley is a superb version of the "process" interpretation of his work.

1 Introduction

1 Thomas S. Kuhn, *The Structure of Scientific Revolutions*.
2 Leo Strauss, *Natural Right and History*, p. 76.
3 Karl Mannheim, *Ideology and Utopia*, p. 226.
4 Michel Foucault, *The Order of Things*, p. 344.
5 Keith Michael Baker, *Condorcet*, p. x.
6 For typical examples of this view see: Russell Keat and John Urry, *Social Theory as Science* and Arnold B. Levison, *Knowledge and Society*.
7 See Jacob Klein, *Greek Mathematical Thought and the Origins of Algebra*, pp. 46–49, 119–23, 308–9.
8 The "invention" of method is ignored or becomes obscured when the Cartesian understanding of mind is neglected. The connection may be made more generally with the remark that epistemology and modern doctrines of the mind are correlative.
9 Hans Jonas, "The Practical Uses of Theory," in *Philosophy of the Social Sciences*, ed. Maurice Natanson, p. 133.
10 In saying this I am not unaware that Machiavelli takes the aims of ordinary men as the limits within which the prince, regardless of his superiority, must work. See Leo Strauss, *Thoughts on Machiavelli*, p. 297.
11 The movement of reflection is replaced in Hobbes by the doctrine that we can construct what Strauss suggestively calls an "island that is exempt from the flux of blind and aimless causation." The notion that science is ultimately a construc-

tion is the logical counterpart to the notion that the best social order is a construction. See Strauss, *Natural Right and History*, pp. 172–73.

12 Alvin W. Gouldner, *The Two Marxisms*, pp. 363–73.

13 See, for example, G. W. F. Hegel, *Philosophy of Right*, paras. 19, 184–86.

14 For Max Weber's view see Strauss, *Natural Right and History*, p. 40. For Dilthey's views see Hans-Georg Gadamer, *Truth and Method*, pp. 211–13.

15 Hans Jonas, "The Practical Uses of Theory," in Natanson, *Philosophy of the Social Sciences*, p. 139.

16 G. W. F. Hegel, *Phenomenology of Spirit*, p. 18.

17 Stanley Rosen, *The Limits of Analysis*.

18 Strauss, *Natural Right and History*, p. 77.

2 The Intellectual Matrix of Bentley's Social Science

1 Arthur F. Bentley to Joseph Ratner, 6 May 1948.

2 Bentley's juvenilia are contained in a single folder in the MSS 2 collection. They
consist of undated pages from a diary and slips of paper with quotations from
Goethe, Hegel, popular works on Eastern religions, radical political literature,
and remarks by Bentley.

3 For a brief account of Charles Bentley's career, see Sidney Ratner, "Arthur F.
Bentley's Inquiries into the Behavioral Sciences and the Theory of Scientific Inquiry," in *Life, Language, Law*, ed. Richard W. Taylor, pp. 54–55.

4 Sidney Ratner, "Introduction," in Arthur F. Bentley, *Inquiry into Inquiries*, p. ix.

5 See biographical material Bentley prepared for Sidney Ratner in a folder dated October–December 1951, MSS 2.

6 Sidney Ratner, "Arthur F. Bentley: Behavioral Scientist," in John Dewey and
Arthur F. Bentley, *John Dewey and Arthur F. Bentley: A Philosophical Correspondence*, p. 23.

7 Paul F. Kress, *Social Science and the Idea of Process*, p. 22.

8 Arthur F. Bentley to John H. Randall, Jr., 6 November 1953, MSS 2.

9 A fragment of a letter from her father to Bentley's first wife, Anna Harrison
Bentley, dated 13 February 1908, expresses the opinion that Bentley should enter a
sanatorium (MSS 2).

10 Arthur F. Bentley to Joseph Ratner, 7 September 1948, MSS 2.

11 See H. Stuart Hughes, *Consciousness and Society*, pp. 296–300, and Hans S.
Gerth and C. Wright Mills, "Introduction," in Weber, *From Max Weber: Essays in
Sociology*, pp. 28–31.

12 Max Weber cited in Gerth and Mills, "Introduction," *From Max Weber*, p. 12.

13 Sidney Ratner, "Arthur F. Bentley's Inquiries into the Behavioral Sciences and the
Theory of Scientific Inquiry," in Taylor, *Life, Language, Law*, p. 54.

14 Hughes, *Consciousness and Society*, p. 300.

15 Ibid., pp. 299–300.

16 Robert H. Wiebe, *The Search for Order, 1877–1920*, pp. xiii–xiv.

17 I have relied on the following works for information about Grand Island, Nebraska: Frederick C. Luebke, *Immigrants and Politics*, pp. 17, 39–41, 94–99,
160–62; James C. Olson, *History of Nebraska*, pp. 196, 252; Federal Writers Project of the Works Progress Administration for the State of Nebraska, *Nebraska: A
Guide to the Cornhusker State*, pp. 162–68.

18 See Louis Hartz, *The Liberal Tradition in America*, chap. 9.

19 Barry D. Karl, *Charles E. Merriam and the Study of Politics*, p. 7.
20 Undated note in Folder 15, 1948–49, MSS 2.
21 Arthur F. Bentley to Joseph Ratner, 7 September 1948.
22 Joseph Schumpeter, *History of Economic Analysis*, ed. Elizabeth Boody Schumpeter, p. 807.
23 Donald Fleming, "Social Darwinism," in *Paths of American Thought*, ed. Arthur M. Schlesinger, Jr., and Morton White, p. 134.
24 See Fritz K. Ringer, *The Decline of the German Mandarins*, pp. 143–62.
25 For a useful study of Patten see Daniel M. Fox, *Simon N. Patten and the Transformation of Social Theory*.
26 Lester Frank Ward, "The Political Ethics of Herbert Spencer," pp. 582–619.
27 Simon N. Patten, "The Failure of Biologic Sociology," pp. 919–47.
28 Richard Hofstadter, *The Age of Reform*, pp. 55–58.
29 See Bentley's drafts of the preface to his thesis in Carton 1, MSS 1 collection. All references to material in the MSS 1 collection will include, where possible, the carton and folder numbers in which material is found.
30 From a note dated 16 June 1953, attached to the thesis material (MSS 1).
31 See Albert Somit and Joseph Tannenhaus, *American Political Science*, pp. 30–41.
32 Hutchins Hapgood, *A Victorian in the Modern World*, pp. 84–85. There are a number of excerpts from the Bentley-Hapgood correspondence reprinted in Neith Boyce and Hutchins Hapgood, *The Story of an American Family*.
33 Arthur F. Bentley to Hutchins Hapgood, 28 January 1894.
34 Hapgood, *A Victorian in the Modern World*, p. 112.
35 Folder 66 in the MSS 2 collection contains Bentley's *Ameldbuch*, #3251, 14 October 1893, which lists his courses and professors.
36 Schumpeter, *History of Economic Analysis*, pp. 814–15.
37 Ringer, *The Decline of the German Mandarins*, pp. 152–53.
38 Hayden V. White, "Translator's Introduction," in Carlo Antoni, *From History to Sociology*, p. xv.
39 Guy Oakes, "Introductory Essay," in Max Weber, *Critique of Stammler*, p. 6.
40 Dilthey made these remarks in his copy of Mill's *System of Logic*. See Hans-Georg Gadamer, "The Problem of Historical Consciousness," p. 15.
41 Hans-Georg Gadamer, *Truth and Method*, pp. 55–63.
42 See Antoni, *From History to Sociology*, pp. 10–11.
43 Georg Simmel cited in Gadamer, *Truth and Method*, p. 62.
44 See Talcott Parsons, *The Structure of Social Action*, vol. 2, *Weber*, pp. 482–86. For a lucid formulation of this position, see Alfred Schutz, "Concept and Theory Formation in the Social Sciences," in Schutz, *Collected Papers*, vol. 1, *The Problem of Social Reality*, pp. 48–66.
45 Two excellent studies of Dilthey's unpublished system are Manfred Riedel, "Einleitung," in Wilhelm Dilthey, *Der Aufbau der geschichtlichen Welt in den Geisteswissenschaften* and Peter Krausser, "Dilthey's Revolution in the Theory of the Structure of Scientific Inquiry and Rational Behavior," pp. 262–80.
46 The literature on *Verstehen* is enormous and of uneven quality. For Dilthey's complex position see Wilhelm Dilthey, *Gesammelte Schriften*, 5:172–80 and 7:84–85, 148. For a simple account of the issue see Hughes, *Consciousness and Society*, pp. 187–88, 310–14.
47 Max Weber, *Roscher and Knies*, pp. 142, 170.
48 Georg Simmel cited in *Georg Simmel, 1858–1918*, ed. Kurt H. Wolff, p. 106.

49 Georg Simmel, "The Problem of Sociology," in Simmel, *On Individuality and Social Forms*, pp. 27–28.

50 Arthur F. Bentley, "Epilogue," in Taylor, *Life, Language, Law*, p. 211.

51 Carl Menger, *Untersuchungen über die Methode der Sozialwissenschaten und der politischen inbesondere* (Vienna, 1883), p. 36. See also George J. Stigler, "The Development of Utility Theory," in Stigler, *Essays in the History of Economics*, p. 94.

52 Arthur F. Bentley to Joseph Ratner, 7 September 1948.

53 Franklin H. Giddings to Arthur F. Bentley, 8 January 1895.

54 All Bentley's unpublished essays discussed in this section can be found in various drafts in Carton 1, 1891–1904, MSS 1. See "On the Relation of the Individual to Society."

55 See "The Individuality As the Basis for Reasoning in the Social Sciences" and "Materials for a Comparison of Organisms and Societies." Bentley's peculiar term "individuality" is not simply a synonym for "individual." It is intended to permit us to distinguish between the properties and the experiential reality of the "individual." When Bentley writes "individuality" he usually is referring to the former.

56 "The Individuality As the Basis for Reasoning in the Social Sciences," p. 31a.

57 "Phenomenal Monism as the Basis for the Theory of Society." This is perhaps the best of Bentley's early unpublished essays. By "phenomenal monism" Bentley means any theory that claims to be grounded in some self-evident fashion, e.g., by appealing to the reality or "matter" or the primacy of "mind."

58 Arthur F. Bentley, "The Units of Investigation in the Social Sciences," pp. 87–113; see esp. p. 89.

59 Georg Simmel, "Über eine Beziehung der Selectionslehre zur Erkenntnistheorie," *Archiv für systematische Philosophie und Soziologie* 1 (1895): 34–35. It is unlikely that Bentley could have seen Simmel's article before completing his dissertation manuscript for publication.

60 More precisely, Bentley agrees with Dilthey that a subject-object unity underlies all "higher" determinations and thus disagrees with Simmel's teaching that the subject-object division is itself primordial. See Dilthey, *Gesammelte Schriften*, 5:152. For Simmel, see Rudolph H. Weingartner, *Experience and Culture: The Philosophy of Georg Simmel*, pp. 41–42.

61 Bentley, "The Units of Investigation in the Social Sciences," p. 103.

62 Herbert Baxter Adams to Arthur F. Bentley, 15 February 1896 and 18 May 1896.

63 Adams to Bentley, 10 July 1895.

64 Bentley did not consider the extent to which Smith was indebted to Locke for this view.

65 Arthur F. Bentley, "'Causational' and 'Valuational' Sciences of Society," in Carton 1.

66 See Bentley's note dated 8 February 1941, attached to "On the Relation of the Individual to Society."

67 This is one of Dewey's later formulations. See John Dewey, *The Quest for Certainty*, p. 107.

68 John Dewey, "The Present Position of Logical Theory," *Monist* 2 (1891): 1–17. See also Dewey, *The Quest for Certainty*, pp. 62–63. Dewey intends his social theory to resemble Hegel's in its "glorification of the here and now," which amounts

to "an invitation to the human subject to devote himself to the mastery of what is already contained in the here and now of life and the world."

69 John Dewey, "The New Psychology," in Dewey, *Philosophy, Psychology and Social Practice*, pp. 50–51.

70 Dewey, *The Present Position of Logical Theory*, p. 13.

71 John Dewey, "Psychology as Philosophic Modeel," in Dewey, *Philosophy, Psychology and Social Practice*, p. 129. Cf. John Dewey, "The Reflex Arc Concept in Psychology," in *The Philosophy of John Dewey*, vol. 1, *The Structure of Experience*, p. 147.

72 Bentley cited in Ratner, "Arthur F. Bentley: Behavioral Scientist," in Dewey and Bentley, *Dewey and Bentley: A Philosophical Correspondence*, pp. 27–28.

73 See Darnell Rucker, *The Chicago Pragmatists*, p. 3.

3 The Process of Government and the Reconstruction of Social Science

1 Charles A. Beard reviewed PG in *Political Science Quarterly* 23 (1909): 739–41. For documentation of Beard's assignment of PG in his seminars at Columbia University see Sidney Ratner, "Arthur F. Bentley's Inquiries into the Behavioral Sciences and the Theory of Scientific Inquiry," in *Life, Language, Law: Essays in Honor of Arthur F. Bentley*, ed. Richard W. Taylor, p. 33. Morris R. Cohen expressed his praise of PG in a letter to Bentley, 4 December 1932. Bentley had sent Cohen a copy of LAM on 17 November 1932, but in his letter Cohen said nothing about the book. In his reply of 8 December 1932, Bentley thanked Cohen for his praise of PG. He added that the backwardness of American social science was shown by the fact that Durkheim's *Les règles de la méthode sociologique* had only been translated into English recently, whereas he had taught it at the University of Chicago in 1895–96. Karl N. Llewellyn's enthusiasm for PG is noted in his "The Constitution as an Institution," pp. 1–40.

2 The most important case studies include: Peter H. Odegard, *Pressure Politics: The Story of the Anti-Saloon League* (New York: Columbia University Press, 1928); Pendleton Herring, *Group Representation Before Congress*; Harwood L. Childs, *Labor and Capital in National Politics*; E. E. Schattschneider, *Politics, Pressures and the Tariff* (New York: Prentice-Hall, Inc., 1935); Bette Zeller, *Pressure Politics in New York* (New York: Prentice-Hall, Inc., 1937); Oliver Garceau, *The Political Life of the American Medical Association* (Cambridge: Harvard University Press, 1941).

3 Peter H. Odegard's remarks on this point are instructive. Reflecting on his experience as a research assistant for a property-tax relief organization, he writes: "As I watched our staff operate and listened to spokesmen for the railroads and the lumber interests, for labor and various farm organizations, for chambers of commerce and manufacturers' associations, for civic clubs and a wide variety of reform groups, it seemed to me that Bentley's description of the process of government was not only eminently reasonable but almost self-evident. . . . My own early encounter with this process of government gave me a pro-Bentley bias from which I have never quite recovered. No one else, I believe, has so effectively cut through the verbal and ideological thicket that tends more to conceal than to reveal the political process for what it really is" ("Introduction," in Arthur F. Bentley, *The Process of Government*, pp. viii–ix).

4 Bertram Gross, review of PG, *American Political Science Review* 44 (1950): 742–48. Gross had first read PG during the 1940s and became personally acquainted with Bentley in 1949. After Bentley read a draft chapter from Gross's *The Legislative Struggle*, which claimed to be based upon Bentley, he cautioned Gross to refrain from invoking the authority of physics and objected to the latter's claim that "standards" are not the proper concern of social science. Bentley suggests that a resolution of "is" and "should be" statements is conceivable (Arthur F. Bentley to Bertram Gross, 31 May 1949).

5 The most important of these works are: David B. Truman, *The Governmental Process*; Bertram M. Gross, *The Legislative Struggle*; Earl Latham, *The Group Basis of Politics*.

6 See Heinz Eulau, *The Behavioral Persuasion in Politics*. Among efforts to connect Bentley's work with behavioral political science are: Richard W. Taylor, "Groups and the Political Process: A Study of the Methodology of Arthur Fisher Bentley" (Ph.D. diss., University of Illinois, 1950) and "Arthur Bentley's Political Science," pp. 214–30; Heinz Eulau, Samuel Eldersveld, and Morris Janowitz, *Political Behavior*, p. 7; Robert T. Golembiewski, William A. Welsh, and William J. Crotty, *A Methodological Primer for Political Scientists*, p. 122.

7 Robert T. Golembiewski, "'The Group Basis of Politics': Notes on Analysis and Development," pp. 965, 967.

8 Robert T. MacIver, *The Web of Government*, p. 220.

9 Louis Hartz, *The Liberal Tradition in America*, pp. 30, 250.

10 Leo Weinstein, "The Scientific Study of Groups," in *Essays on the Scientific Study of Politics*, ed. Herbert J. Storing, p. 222.

11 Myron Q. Hale, "The Cosmology of Arthur F. Bentley," pp. 955–61. For an account of the conservatism within which Hale proposes to assimilate Bentley, see Carl J. Friedrich, "The Political Thought of Neo-Liberalism," pp. 509–25.

12 See R. E. Dowling, "Pressure Group Theory: Its Methodological Range," pp. 944–55; Floyd W. Matson, *The Broken Image*, pp. 102, 105–6; Bernard Crick, *The American Science of Politics*, pp. 123–25.

13 Crick, *The American Science of Politics*, pp. 129–30.

14 See H. Stuart Hughes, *Consciousness and Society*, p. 74.

15 Arthur F. Bentley, "Epilogue," in Taylor, *Life, Language, Law*, p. 211.

16 Paul F. Kress, *Social Science and the Idea of Process*, p. 18.

17 Bentley, "Epilogue," in Taylor, *Life, Language, Law*, p. 211.

18 Ratner, "A. F. Bentley's Inquiries into the Behavioral Sciences and the Theory of Scientific Inquiry," ibid., p. 31.

19 Theodore Dreiser cited in Richard Hofstadter, *The Age of Reform*, p. 191.

20 Hofstadter, *The Age of Reform*, pp. 196–97.

21 See the first complete draft for "The Western Farmer."

22 Barry D. Karl, *Charles E. Merriam and the Study of Politics*, pp. 50–53, 59, 54.

23 The data and drafts for these studies fill seventy-five and twenty-five folders respectively in MSS 1.

24 I am unaware of any similar use of these techniques among American political scientists at this time.

25 Sidney Ratner, "Arthur F. Bentley—Fashioner of Social Tools," in *A Great Society?* ed. Bertram M. Gross, p. 287.

26 Arthur F. Bentley, "Sociology and Mathematics," in *Inquiry into Inquiries*, p. 53.

27 The only discussion of Bentley's original aims in PG I have discovered is Sidney

Ratner, "Arthur F. Bentley—Fashioner of Social Tools," in Gross, *A Great Society?*, p. 288. The notes and drafts for PG fill Cartons 3–5 (101 folders) in MSS 1.

28 Robert H. Wiebe, *The Search for Order, 1877–1920*, pp. 150–53.

29 See Carton 4, especially Folders 56–61 for Bentley's notes.

30 See Wilfrid Sellars, "Philosophy and the Scientific Image of Man," in *Science, Perception and Reality*.

31 Kress, *Social Science and the Idea of Process*, p. 45.

32 I have been unable to find more than fragmentary evidence to suggest that Bentley was familiar with Hegel except in the most cursory way. I believe that any Hegelian influence on Bentley is traceable to John Dewey. For a representative text exhibiting Hegel's position, see G. W. F. Hegel, *Phenomenology of Spirit*, pp. 48–49.

33 Arthur F. Bentley, *Relativity in Man and Society*, pp. 73–90. For a suggestion that Hegel's understanding of philosophy shows how "mind is made ready to comprehend that everything in its universe, including, most importantly, the structure of consciousness itself, is contingent; it discovers that there is no Archimedean point from which it might get at the truth," see Kenley Royce Dove, "Hegel and Creativity," p 9.

34 Immanuel Kant, *The Critique of Pure Reason*, B197.

35 This is a central teaching of Immanuel Kant, *Prolegomena to Any Future Metaphysics*.

36 For a superb study of Hegel's understanding of language see Hans-Georg Gadamer, *Hegel's Dialectic*, pp. 75–99.

37 Max Weber, *Roscher and Knies*, p. 185.

38 On this problem see Thomas Burger, *Max Weber's Theory of Concept Formation*, pp. 111, 114.

39 Weber, *Roscher and Knies*, pp. 177–78.

40 Weber, *Max Weber on the Methodology of the Social Sciences*, p. 81.

41 A classic statement of this view is Charles Taylor, *The Explanation of Behaviour*.

42 There are few good studies of Albion Small's views. See Harry Elmer Barnes, "Albion Woodbury Small: Promoter of American Sociology and Expositor of Social Interests," in *An Introduction to the History of Sociology*, ed. Harry Elmer Barnes, pp. 409–36.

43 Albion Small, *General Sociology*, pp. 196–200, 441–81.

44 Bentley discusses this analysis in PG, 32–35.

45 Karl R. Popper, "Three Views Concerning Human Knowledge," in *Conjectures and Refutations*, p. 105.

46 Kress, *Social Science and the Idea of Process*, p. 64.

47 Lewis Henry Morgan, *Ancient Society* (New York: Henry Holt and Co., 1877), pp. 3–4, 424.

48 Franklin H. Giddings, cited in PG, 131.

49 Franklin H. Giddings, *Descriptive and Historical Sociology* (New York: Henry Holt and Co., 1904), p. 523.

50 Hale, "The Cosmology of Arthur F. Bentley," p. 956.

51 Crick, *The American Science of Politics*, p. 129.

52 See Michael Oakeshott, "The Activity of being an Historian," in *Rationalism in Politics and Other Essays*, pp. 164, 153–59.

53 Hans-Georg Gadamer, "The Problem of Historical Consciousness," pp. 8–9. See Bentley, *Relativity in Man and Society*, pp. 296–97.

54 Kant, *Critique of Pure Reason*, A553=B581, A34=B50.

55 Hughes, *Consciousness and Society*, p. 16.

56 See Max Weber, *Basic Concepts in Sociology*, pp. 49, 65; Reinhard Bendix, *Max Weber*, pp. 474–76. For a description of Weber's study see Paul F. Lazarsfeld, "Historical Notes on the Empirical Study of Action: An Intellectual Odyssey," in *Qualitative Analysis*, pp. 90–96.

57 G. David Garson, "On the Origins of Interest-Group Theory: A Critique of a Process," p. 1513.

58 Graham Wallas, *Human Nature in Politics*, pp. 144–60.

59 John B. Watson, *Psychology from the Standpoint of a Behaviorist* (New York: Henry Holt, 1919), p. 10 (this book appeared over a decade after Bentley's first book); *Behaviorism* (London: Victor Gollancz, 1925), pp. 6, 11.

60 Merriam's address was originally published as "The Present State of the Study of Politics," *American Political Science Review* 15 (1921): 173–85. For an analysis of Merriam's views see Karl, *Charles E. Merriam and the Study of Politics*, pp. 105–9.

61 See the reports of the conference proceedings in the *American Political Science Review* 17 (1923): 268; ibid. 19 (1925): 107–8, 735–61.

62 L. L. Thurstone cited in *American Political Science Review* 19 (1925): 112.

63 Floyd Allport, "The Psychological Nature of Political Structure," *American Political Science Review* 21 (1927): 612.

64 L. L. Thurstone, "Attitudes Can Be Measured," *American Journal of Sociology* 33 (1928): 520. An indispensable study of the development of the notion of "attitude" in modern theoretical psychology is Donald Fleming, "Attitude: The History of a Concept," in *Perspectives on American History*, ed. Donald Fleming and Bernard Bailyn, 1:287–369.

65 Charles E. Merriam, *New Aspects of Politics*, pp. 325–28, 315, 289.

4 The Group Interpretation of Politics

1 Arthur F. Bentley, "Kennetic Inquiry," in *Inquiry into Inquiries*, p. 348. See also Bentley to Dewey, 18 August 1950, John Dewey and Arthur F. Bentley, *John Dewey and Arthur F. Bentley: A Philosophical Correspondence*, p. 634.

2 Paul F. Kress, *Social Science and the Idea of Process*, p. xi.

3 See Marx's letter to Joseph Weydemeyer in 1852: "No credit is due to me for discovering the existence of classes in modern society nor yet the struggle between them. Long before me bourgeois historians had described the intellectual development of this class struggle and bourgeois economists the economic anatomy of the classes" (Karl Marx and Friedrich Engels, *Correspondence, 1846–1895*, p. 57).

4 David B. Truman, *The Governmental Process*, p. 47. Truman refers to John Dewey, *The Public and Its Problems* (New York: Henry Holt, 1927), p. 151.

5 Leo Weinstein, "The Scientific Study of Groups," in *Essays on the Scientific Study of Politics*, ed. Herbert J. Storing, p. 218.

6 R. E. Dowling, "Pressure Group Theory: Its Methodological Range," p. 949.

7 Weinstein, "The Scientific Study of Groups," in Storing, *Essays on the Scientific Study of Politics*, pp. 172–75.

8 Paul F. Lazarsfeld, "Historical Notes on the Empirical Study of Action: An Intellectual Odyssey," in *Qualitative Analysis*, p. 100.

9 Clark L. Hull, *Principles of Behavior*, pp. 25–26.

10 Charles Taylor, *The Explanation of Behaviour*, pp. 107–8.
11 Max Weber, *Roscher and Knies*, p. 63.
12 See Folder 61, *The Process of Government*, Bentley MSS 1.
13 Peter A. Winch, *The Idea of a Social Science and Its Relation to Philosophy*, p. 82.
14 Although Bentley was never a genuine disciple of Comte, he often made casual use of the Comtean distinction between "metaphysics" and "positive" science.
15 Weinstein, "The Scientific Study of Groups," in Storing, *Essays on the Scientific Study of Politics*, pp. 217–19.
16 Georg Simmel cited in *Georg Simmel, 1858–1918*, ed. Kurt H. Wolff, p. 106.
17 For a competent study of connections between the "group theory" and opposition to "legalism" among political scientists see G. David Garson, "On the Origins of Interest-Group Theory: A Critique of a Process," pp. 1505–20.
18 For these criticisms see Peter H. Odegard, "A Group Basis of Politics: A New Name for an Old Myth," pp. 689–702; Joseph LaPalombara, "The Utility and Limitations of Interest Group Theory in Non-American Field Situations," pp. 29–49; Stanley Rothman, "Systematic Political Theory: Observations on the Group Approach," pp. 15–33.
19 Weinstein, "The Scientific Study of Groups," in Storing, *Essays on the Scientific Study of Politics*, pp. 183, 221–22.
20 Ibid., p. 182.
21 Karl Mannheim, *Ideology and Utopia*, pp. 292–306.
22 Weinstein, "The Scientific Study of Groups," in Storing, *Essays on the Scientific Study of Politics*, pp. 194ff., 179.
23 Ibid., pp. 197–205.
24 See Folder, Correspondence 1951–52, ms. draft dated 8 August 1951, Bentley MSS 2 collection.

5 Social Science and the Problem of Knowledge

1 Bentley to Joseph Ratner, 7 September 1948. See also Carton 5, Folder 101, draft for a preface to *The Process of Government*.
2 Bentley had discussed Lane briefly in PG, 93, 250.
3 A. Lawrence Lowell, "The Physiology of Politics," p. 1.
4 Paul F. Kress, *Social Science and the Idea of Process: The Ambiguous Legacy of Arthur F. Bentley*, p. 161.
5 *Sophist* 249.
6 Bentley refers to Dewey's *The Influence of Darwin on Philosophy* (1910) to establish the connection between pragmatism and evolutionary theory. The declaration of war of the New Realists against idealism appears in William Pepperell Montague, "Professor Royce's Refutation of Realism," pp. 43–55, and in Ralph Barton Perry, "Professor Royce's Refutation of Realism and Pluralism," pp. 446–58.
7 In 1910 Bentley was evidently either unable or unwilling to distinguish clearly between Bergsonian and Darwinian "evolution." Although he does not mention it in "Knowledge and Society," he was familiar with William James's affinity with Bergson as revealed in *A Pluralistic Universe* (1909).
8 See John Passmore, *A Hundred Years of Philosophy*, pp. 218–23, 235.
9 Bruce Kuklick, *The Rise of American Philosophy*, pp. 348–49.
10 Ludwig Wittgenstein, *Philosophical Investigations*, paras. 258, 261.

11 Bentley's position parallels Peter Winch's controversial thesis in "Understanding a Primitive Society," pp. 307–24.

12 See Carton 7, Folder 4.

13 This feature of his argument was noted by the anonymous reviewer in the *Times Literary Supplement*, December 16, 1926, p. 62.

14 See Gerald Holton, "On the Origins of the Special Theory of Relativity," in *Thematic Origins of Scientific Thought*, p. 166.

15 A useful historical study of the physical and philosophical issues concerning relativity theory is A. D'Abro, *The Evolution of Scientific Thought from Newton to Einstein*. For more technical studies see Lawrence Sklar, *Space, Time and Spacetime* and Adolf Grünbaum, *Philosophical Problems of Space and Time*. Bentley's belief that relativity theory had dealt the final blow to any possible metaphysics of substance resembles the position of Richard Burton Viscount Haldane, *The Reign of Relativity*.

16 Holton, *Thematic Origins of Scientific Thought*, pp. 166, 170–71.

17 Ernst Cassirer, *Substance and Function* and *Einstein's Theory of Relativity*, p. 445.

18 One of the few summaries of von Wiese's sociology available in English is J. Milton Yinger, "The Systematic Sociology of Leopold von Wiese: The Origin and Structure of Interhuman Relations," in *An Introduction to the History of Sociology*, ed. Harry Elmer Barnes, pp. 294–306.

19 The Bentley-von Wiese correspondence covers 1926–1932. Von Wiese initiated the exchange on 1 July 1926 with a letter praising *Relativity in Man and Society.*

20 Leopold von Wiese and Howard Becker, *Systematic Sociology*, pp. 103–4.

21 See Leopold von Wiese's review of RMS in *Kölner Vierteljahrshefte für Sozialwissenschaften* 4 (1926): 186–90.

22 Richard S. Rudner mistakenly attributes this intention to all proponents of interpretive social science. See his *Philosophy of Social Science*, pp. 69–70.

23 J. J. C. Smart, "Time," in *Encyclopedia of Philosophy*, ed. Paul Edwards (New York: Macmillan and The Free Press, 1967), 8:128.

24 Charles Taylor, "The Explanation of Purposive Behavior," in *Explanation in the Behavioural Sciences*, ed. Robert Borger and Frank Cioffi, p. 55.

25 See Gerald Holton, "Mach, Einstein, and the Search for Reality," in *Thematic Origins*, pp. 224–25.

26 Kress, *Social Science and the Idea of Process*, p. 88.

27 Arthur F. Bentley to Joseph Ratner, 7 September 1948.

28 Carton 8, 1926–28, contains nine folders of "Sociological Studies and Papers." Folders 1 and 2 contain the reading notes and three drafts of "'Individual' and 'Social' in Recent American Studies." Approximately ninety articles were surveyed. Folder 5 contains a shorter manuscript, "The Individual and the Social with Reference to Space" based on the same research. A general statement, "Space, Time, Environment and Society," dated 11 November 1927, appears in Folder 6, together with three later drafts dated 11 November 1927, 19 November 1927, and 29 December 1927. Folder 7 contains five drafts of "The Data of Sociology Examined with Respect to Time and Space," 18 November 1927, 21 November 1927, 23 November 1927, 26 November 1927, and 28 November 1927.

29 See the 11 November 1927 draft of "Space, Time, Environment and Society," p. 7. Bentley's criticism of Locke's use of Newtonian categories in philosophy and so-

cial theory appears as well in "Sociology and Mathematics," *Sociological Review* 23 (1931): 85–107, 149–72.

30 I examine Bentley's criticism of Watson in chap. 7.

31 Carton 8 includes four folders containing notes and seven drafts for "Individual and Social—Terms and Facts." Bentley's manuscript was translated into French by Jeanne Duprat, with Bentley's assistance. It appeared as "L'individuel et le social: les termes et les faits," *Revue Internationale de Sociologie* 37 (1929): 243–70. Bentley had helped Duprat find an American publisher for her study of Proudhon's social theory. She deserves much of the credit for the essay's clarity.

32 Arthur F. Bentley, "New Ways and Old To Talk About Men," *Sociological Review* 21 (1929): 300–14. The essay is a plea for the "harmonization of speechways" among social scientists. The advantage of this consensus is assumed to lie in ontological neutrality.

33 David Lamb, "Hegel and Wittgenstein on Language and Sense-Certainty," *CLIO* 7 (1978): p. 285. Among the better interpretations of Wittgenstein's *Tractatus* are David Favrholdt, *An Interpretation and Critique of Wittgenstein's Tractatus* and Max Black, *A Companion to Wittgenstein's Tractatus*. Bentley's views are found in two drafts, dated 30 November 1927 and 14 January 1928, of "Words as Tools," in Carton 8, Folder 1. In addition, the 29 December 1927 draft of "Space, Time, Environment and Society" contains several references to the *Tractatus*, the most important being to 5.6.

34 Among the most lucid and comprehensive accounts of these connections is Allan Janik and Stephen Toulmin, *Wittgenstein's Vienna*, pp. 120–67.

35 Ibid., p. 166.

36 Ludwig Wittgenstein, *Tractatus Logico-Philosophicus*, 5.6, 5.61.

37 Ibid., 2.1–2.171.

38 Ludwig Wittgenstein, *Notebooks, 1914–1916*, p. 60.

39 Arthur F. Bentley to John Dewey, 12 December 1945.

40 See Arthur F. Bentley, "Words as Tools," 14 January 1928 draft. Wittgenstein's famous doctrine of the "mystical" begins with *Tractatus* 6.4 to the final proposition 7.

41 Wittgenstein, *Tractatus*, 1.2, 2.02, 2.027.

42 Ibid., 5.641.

43 P. W. Bridgman, *The Logic of Modern Physics*, p. 28.

44 See Carton 8, four folders, 1928–30 (MSS 1) containing notes and fourteen drafts of "The Postulates of Operational Physics." A short summary of Bentley's criticisms appears as a manuscript dated 4 January 1928.

6 The Logic of Scientific Inquiry

1 Arthur F. Bentley to John Dewey, 13 May 1945 in John Dewey and Arthur F. Bentley, *John Dewey and Arthur F. Bentley: A Philosophical Correspondence*, p. 412. Bentley criticized the view that the measurement of attitudes is a major contribution to social science in a folder labeled "1944–November 14, 1950."

2 Max Weber, *The Theory of Social and Economic Organizations*, pp. 99–100.

3 Ernst Nagel cited in Abraham Kaplan, *The Conduct of Inquiry: Methodology for Behavioral Science*, p. 176.

4 Stanley Rosen, *Nihilism: A Philosophical Essay*, p. 62.

5 Arthur F. Bentley, "Sociology and Mathematics," in *Inquiry into Inquiries: Essays in Social Theory*, p. 53.

6 Paul F. Lazarsfeld, "Notes on the History of Quantification in Sociology—Trends, Sources and Problems," pp. 147–203.

7 Martin Heidegger, *Being and Time*, p. 29.

8 A good history of these disputes is given in Morris Kline, *Mathematical Thought from Ancient to Modern Times*, chaps. 36–38. See also his *Mathematics: The Loss of Certainty*. For more technical studies of foundations of mathematics see Ernst Cassirer, *The Problem of Knowledge: Philosophy, Science, and History Since Hegel*, esp. chaps. 2–4; William S. Hatcher, *Foundations of Mathematics*; and Andrej Mostowski, *Thirty Years of Foundational Studies*.

9 Cassirer, *The Problem of Knowledge*, pp. 22–24.

10 Kline, *Mathematical Thought from Ancient to Modern Times*, p. 1036.

11 Felix Klein cited in Cassirer, *The Problem of Knowledge*, p. 30.

12 John Passmore, *A Hundred Years of Philosophy*, p. 148.

13 Felix Klein described arithmetic as having achieved "sovereign authority as the really fundamental discipline." See Klein cited in Cassirer, *The Problem of Knowledge*, p. 59. See also Hatcher, *Foundations of Mathematics*, p. 78.

14 Cassirer, *The Problem of Knowledge*, p. 61.

15 See Hilary Putnam, "The Thesis That Mathematics Is Logic," in *Mathematics, Matter and Method, Philosophical Papers*, 1:12–43.

16 For a useful discussion of Brouwer's teaching see William and Martha Kneale, *The Development of Logic*, pp. 672–81.

17 Max Black, *The Nature of Mathematics*, pp. 191–96.

18 Brouwer cited in ibid., p. 195.

19 Kneale and Kneale, *The Development of Logic*, p. 452.

20 I have used the following sources for my summary of Hilbert's views: Kline, *Mathematical Thought from Ancient to Modern Times*, pp. 1203–8; Kneale and Kneale, *The Development of Logic*, pp. 651–58; Hatcher, *Foundations of Mathematics*, chap. 6; and Constance Reid, *Hilbert*.

21 David Hilbert cited in Kline, *Mathematical Thought from Ancient to Modern Times*, p. 1027.

22 Mostowski, *Thirty Years of Foundational Studies*, p. 8.

23 David Hilbert cited in Kline, *Mathematical Thought from Ancient to Modern Times*, pp. 1027–28.

24. Arthur F. Bentley to Friedrich Waismann, 7 May 1929.

25 See the revised and augmented edition of Hermann Weyl, *Philosophy of Mathematics and Natural Science*, trans. Olaf Helmer (Princeton: Princeton University Press, 1949).

26 Bentley first explored these ideas in a number of unpublished manuscripts. These include: "Words as Tools" (1927–28), "Language, Knowledge, Experience, Fact" (1928), "The Background of Postulation" (1928–1930), "Semantic Analysis" (1928), "Betrachtungen vom soziologischen Standpunkte heraus uber die Neubegrundungsprobleme der Mathmatik" (1929), "Eine dreifache annäherung des Kontinuumproblemes: A. Die mathematische zweckmässigkeit. B. Die verschiebung des Kontinuumproblemes. C. Zur zerspaltung des Abzählbarkeitbegriffes" (1929). In 1929 Bentley experimented with writing his mathematical material in a mélange of German, English, and other European languages because

he doubted that translations were adequate to convey the linguistic contexts of mathematical concepts.

27 I have been unable to discover precisely when Bentley changed his mind about the title of his book.

28 Arthur F. Bentley to John Dewey, 29 May 1935.

29 For Bentley the notion of an uninterpreted term or formula resembled the empiricist notion of an incorrigible basis for knowledge in sense data.

30 Hermann Weyl in Reid, *Hilbert*, p. 270.

31 Bentley is concerned with what Stanley Rosen calls the "context of analysis" or, in the case of mathematical formalism, the context within which we construct formalism. He would disagree with Rosen's claim that "the problem of the context of analysis, or of the whole, is not one of the completability or incompletability of formalism" (Stanley Rosen, *The Limits of Analysis*, p. 151).

32 For an account of Hegel's position see Stanley Rosen, *G. W. F. Hegel: An Introduction to the Science of Wisdom*, pp. 266–80.

33 W. V. Quine, "Epistemology Naturalized," in *Ontological Relativity and Other Essays*, p. 71.

34 Arthur F. Bentley to Hermann Weyl, 20 January, 30 January 1929, MSS 2.

35 For a useful discussion of Mauthner see Allan Janik and Stephen Toulmin, *Wittgenstein's Vienna*, p. 130.

36 Gilbert Ryle cited in Arne Naess, *Four Modern Philosophers*, p. 151.

37 Imré Lakatos, "A Renaissance of Empiricism in the Recent Philosophy of Mathematics?" in *Mathematics, Science and Epistemology*, 2:40.

38 Sidney Ratner makes this claim in his introduction to *Dewey and Bentley: A Philosophical Correspondence*, p. 34. See Kurt Gödel, *On Formally Undecidable Propositions of Principia Mathematica and Related Systems*.

39 Arthur F. Bentley to John Dewey, 25 October 1946.

40 Barry Hindess, *Philosophy and Methodology in the Social Sciences*, pp. 148–49.

41 See Putnam, "Truth and Necessity in Mathematics"; "The Thesis That Mathematics is Logic," "Mathematics without Foundations," and "What Is Mathematical Truth?" in *Mathematics, Matter and Method*, pp. 1–79.

42 Putnam, "Mathematics without Foundations," ibid., p. 45.

43 Putnam, "What Is Mathematical Truth?" ibid., p. 73.

44 Ibid., pp. 61–69.

45 See Karl Popper, "The Demarcation between Science and Metaphysics," in *Conjectures and Refutations: The Growth of Scientific Knowledge*, pp. 253–92.

46 Frederick Suppe, "The Search for Philosophic Understanding of Scientific Theories," in *The Structure of Scientific Theories*, ed. Frederick Suppe, pp. 221–30.

47 Putnam, "The Logic of Quantum Mechanics," in *Mathematics, Matter and Method*, p. 179.

48 Rosen, *G. W. F. Hegel*, p. 89.

49 Arthur Pap, *Semantics and Necessary Truth*, p. 422.

7 Bentley's Behavioral Science

1 Bentley was concerned principally with American academic psychology, with the important exception of the Gestaltists who also engaged his interest.

2 For excerpts from reviews see Sidney Ratner, "Arthur F. Bentley's Inquiries into

the Behavioral Sciences and the Theory of Scientific Inquiry," *Life, Language, Law: Essays in Honor of Arthur F. Bentley*, ed. Richard W. Taylor, pp. 44, 56.

3 For good discussions of the state of psychology in the 1930s see Jean Matter Mandler and George Mandler, "The Diaspora of Experimental Psychology: The Gestaltists and Others" and Marie Jahoda, "The Migration of Psychoanalysis: Its Impact on American Psychology," in *The Intellectual Migration: Europe and America, 1930–1960*, ed. Donald Fleming and Bernard Bailyn, pp. 371–420, 420–46.

4 See John Passmore, *A Hundred Years of Philosophy*, chap. 17.

5 Paul F. Kress's account of this part of BKF is superb. See Paul F. Kress, *Social Science and the Idea of Process: The Ambiguous Legacy of Arthur F. Bentley*, pp. 146–52.

6 This is clearly the most important article Bentley published during the 1930s. "Sociology and Mathematics," in *Inquiry into Inquiries: Essays in Social Theory*, pp. 53–101.

7 William McDougall's "hormism" claimed to explain human behavior in terms of a hierarchy of instinct. His views were sufficiently influential to warrant a chapter in R. S. Woodworth's survey, *Contemporary Schools of Psychology* (1931).

8 Arthur F. Bentley, "A Sociological Critique of Behaviorism," in *Inquiry into Inquiries*, pp. 31–36.

9 Ibid., p. 35.

10 This "transcendental" argument, as we have seen, is present even in Bentley's earliest writings.

11 For a good summary of these views see Richard J. Bernstein, *Praxis and Action: Contemporary Philosophies of Human Activity*, esp. pp. 260–78.

12 Paul F. Lazarsfeld, "Historical Notes on the Empirical Study of Action: An Intellectual Odyssey," in *Qualitative Analysis: Historical and Critical Essays*, pp. 53–106.

13 John Dewey cited in BKF, 76. See John Dewey, *Experience and Nature*, pp. 8, 15, 19.

14 John Dewey, *The Quest for Certainty*, p. 165.

15 Dewey, *Experience and Nature*, pp. 351, 54, 351, 104–5.

16 John Dewey to Arthur F. Bentley, 14 November 1935, Arthur F. Bentley to John Dewey, 18 November 1935. See Dewey and Bentley, *John Dewey and Arthur F. Bentley: A Philosophical Correspondence*, pp. 57–58.

17 Noam Chomsky, *Reflections on Language*, pp. 28, 34.

18 J. R. Kantor to Arthur F. Bentley (undated), 1936.

19 See John Dewey and Arthur F. Bentley, *Knowing and the Known*, p. 126n. 3.

20 Bentley, "Sociology and Mathematics," in *Inquiry into Inquiries*, p. 90.

21 Dewey and Bentley, *Knowing and the Known*, pp. 208–12.

22 Hermann Weyl, cited in Gerald Holton, "Introduction," in *Thematic Origins of Scientific Thought*, p. 35.

23 Holton, *Thematic Origins*, p. 36.

24 Bentley, "Observable Behaviors," in *Inquiry into Inquiries*, p. 175. The article originally appeared in *Psychological Review* 47 (1940): 230–53.

25 Frederick Suppe, "The Search for Philosophic Understanding of Scientific Theories," in *The Structure of Scientific Theories*, ed. Frederick Suppe, pp. 14–15.

26 George A. Lundberg, "The Postulates of Science and Their Implications for Sociology," in *Philosophy of the Social Sciences*, ed. Maurice Natanson, p. 53.

27 Bentley, "New Ways and Old to Talk About Men," in *Inquiry into Inquiries,* pp. 42–43.

28 J. L. Austin, *Philosophical Papers,* p. 124.

29 Hilary Putnam, "What Theories Are Not," in *Mathematics, Matter and Method, Philosophical Papers,* 1 : 215–28.

30 These articles include: "The Positive and the Logical," *Philosophy of Science* 3 (1936): 472–85; "Physicists and Fairies," ibid. 5 (1938): 132–65; "Situational vs. Psychological Theories of Behavior" and "Postulation for Behavioral Inquiry," *Journal of Philosophy* 36(1939): 169–81, 405–13; "The Factual Time and Space of Behavior," ibid. 38 (1941): 477–85.

31 W. V. Quine, "Grades of Theoreticity," pp. 1–17.

32 With only a few exceptions, Bentley chose to reveal his interests in contemporary literature in his correspondence with Jules Altman more than with any other associate.

33 Dewey and Bentley, *Knowing and the Known,* p. 108.

34 Hans-Georg Gadamer, *Truth and Method,* pp. 460–91.

35 Bentley, "Situational vs. Psychological Theories of Behavior," in *Inquiry into Inquiries,* p. 151.

36 Bentley, "The Factual Space and Time of Behavior," in ibid., p. 217.

37 Bentley, "Observable Behaviors," in ibid., p. 175.

38 Charles Taylor, "Reply," in *Explanation in the Behavioural Sciences,* ed. Robert Borger and Frank Cioffi, p. 94.

39 Kress, *Social Science and the Idea of Process,* pp. 154–81, 233–39.

40 Ibid., pp. 178, 172–75.

41 I have in mind J. L. Austin's notion that it is possible to question "an age-old assumption in philosophy" that to say something is "always and simply to *state* something" (Austin, *How to Do Things with Words,* p. 12). Bentley's neologisms may be understood, I believe, as analogous in role to Austin's various classes of utterances, such as "constatives," "performatives," "verdictives," "exercitives," "commissives," "behabitatives," and "expositives."

42 Compare Bentley in "Kennetic Inquiry" with J. N. Findlay. Bentley: "I have never myself made observation of any such 'pure knowers' or 'pure reals'; I know no one who has" ("Kennetic Inquiry," in *Inquiry into Inquiries,* p. 338). J. N. Findlay: "I do not believe that there are such entities as particulars, and I am quite sure that I have never encountered any" ("Hegelianism and Platonism," in *Hegel and the History of Philosophy: Proceedings of the 1972 Hegel Society of America Conference,* ed. Joseph J. O'Malley, Keith W. Algozin, Frederick G. Weiss [The Hague: Martinus Nijhoff, 1974], p. 71).

43 Kress, *Social Science and the Idea of Process,* p. 168.

44 Ibid., pp. 248–53. I am not clear why Kress insists that Bentley's teaching should be judged in light of its supposed implications for "political theory." Kress seems to mean "political philosophy," but because he does not explain how political philosophy is or should be related to social science, he cannot show that Bentley's "failure" is of any importance for political philosophy.

45 Ibid., pp. 239, 243.

46 Peter F. Strawson, *Individuals: An Essay in Descriptive Metaphysics,* pp. 59–86, 10–14, 39.

47 Ibid., pp. 90–93, 104, 97, 100, 56, 113–14.

48 Ibid., pp. 103, 10.

49 Bentley, "The Human Skin: Philosophy's Last Line of Defense," in *Inquiry into Inquiries*, p. 211. Bentley adds that for the scientist the "person" resides not in the organism but "becomes a local description of an organic-environmental process from the behaviorally organic viewpoint." Earlier (p. 197 n. 4) Bentley argues more pointedly against the referential prior of mental states (and thus against Strawson before the fact): "The generalization of the 'inner' into a comprehensive or 'absolute' form is a more recent program of philosophical escape. Trailing its initial 'innerness' with it to the end, it remains a program rather than an achievement, critically of high importance, constructively of none. Its justification has rested in its importance as complement to the Newtonian absolutes, space and time. When these last disintegrated in modern physics this justification disappeared. When science ceases to have a base that is all 'outer,' then a complementary 'pure inner' is no longer needed; scientific techniques become available for direct application to cognitions, once we discover how to develop and use them."

50 See Bernstein, *Praxis and Action*, pp. 281–99 for a discussion of the displacement hypothesis.

51 Ibid., p. 297.

8 Pragmatism as Behavioral Naturalism

1 Sidney Ratner, "Introduction," in John Dewey and Arthur F. Bentley, *John Dewey and Arthur F. Bentley: A Philosophical Correspondence*, pp. 23–24.

2 Paul F. Kress believes that Bentley dominates the correspondence. Paul F. Kress, *Social Science and the Idea of Process*, p. 20. For a more balanced view see John J. McDermott, "Introduction," in *The Philosophy of John Dewey*, vol. 1, *The Structure of Experience*, p. xxii. Suggestive of the tone of the Bentley-Dewey relationship is the fact that, although their correspondence began in 1932, Dewey continued to use "Mr." in his letters to Bentley until 1939, while Bentley alternated between "Mr." and "Professor" in his letters to Dewey until 1942. They did not use first names until early in 1945. Although I have concentrated almost without exception upon the philosophical issues that dominate the correspondence, its wide-ranging character encompasses literature, politics, and contemporary events.

3 John Dewey to Arthur F. Bentley, 7 June 1944. Bentley benefited in turn from his association with Dewey, which gave him more opportunities to present his views in a wider philosophical forum. His correspondence with, among others, Otto Neurath, Ernst Nagel, John H. Randall, Jr., and Sidney Hook suggests that his views were given some attention. In 1941 he was invited by the philosophy department at Columbia University to participate in a seminar on philosophy and language with Nagel, Herbert Schneider, and others. While Bentley thought his own presentation of a paper on a "general theory of language" was a failure, Schneider later told Dewey that it had made a very favorable impression. See John Dewey to Arthur F. Bentley, 9 May 1942.

4 For a complete list of the Bentley-Dewey articles see the Appendix. The articles were collected and published as *Knowing and the Known* (Boston: Beacon Press, 1949). For all references to this work, however, I have used the complete reprint of the original text in Rollo Handy and E. C. Harwood, *Useful Procedures of In-*

quiry (Great Barrington, Mass.: Behavioral Research Council, 1973): 89–193.

5 Herbert Feigl, "The Wiener Kreis in America," in *The Intellectual Migration*, p. 645.

6 Three folders, January–June 1936. The material consists of 168 pages of notes and manuscript. See also "Conceptual Reliance in Logical Construction," an unpublished manuscript with notes dated May 1936.

7 Frederick Suppe, "The Search for Philosophic Understanding of Scientific Theories," in *The Structure of Scientific Theories*, ed. Frederick Suppe, p. 62.

8 See Peter Achinstein, *Concepts of Science*; Dudley Shapere, "Scientific Theories and Their Domains," in Suppe *The Structure of Scientific Theories*, pp. 518–66; Hilary Putnam, "What Theories are Not," in *Mathematics, Matter and Method, Philosophical Papers*, 1:215–27.

9 Arthur F. Bentley, "The Positive and the Logical," *Philosophy of Science* 3 (1936): 472–85.

10 John Dewey to Arthur F. Bentley, 21 November 1935. See *Dewey and Bentley: A Philosophical Correspondence*, p. 59. A sample of Bentley's invective can be found in a letter to Ernst Nagel on 11 December 1944, in which he says of the contributors to the *Encyclopedia of Unified Science* that they had found "it was not so easy to settle everything on earth in cheap schematisms in a year or so of scribbling." In October 1944 Bentley sent Nagel an abusive polemic titled "The Greased Pigs of Carnap, They are Damned Hard to Catch."

11 For a similar argument see Putnam, "What Theories Are Not" in *Mathematics, Matter and Method*.

12 See "The Positive and the Logical" in Arthur F. Bentley, *Inquiry into Inquiries*, p. 109n.

13 Arthur F. Bentley, "Comments on George Herbert Mead," 20 August 1937, MSS 1.

14 John Dewey to Arthur F. Bentley, 7 April 1939. See *Dewey and Bentley: A Philosophical Correspondence*, p. 69.

15 The Peirce materials are found in the 1939 carton although they span a period from April 1939–November 1946. Bentley's notes and manuscript fragments amount to 319 pages. In a fragment dated 15 April 1939, Bentley argues against the thesis that logical positivism is in any genuine sense a successor to pragmatism. It incorporates a confused psychology quite alien to Peirce, James, or Dewey. The outline sketch for "Peirce the Forerunner" appears in three forms in manuscripts dated 9 April 1939, 22 June 1939, and 4 July 1939. Bentley attempts to trace Peirce's unacknowledged or misunderstood influence on contemporary philosophy of logic in a manuscript dated 27 June 1939.

16 Bentley felt quite free to distinguish essential from nonessential elements in Peirce's teaching and he simply rejected Peirce's ethical and religious doctrines.

17 Arthur F. Bentley to John Dewey, 14 June 1939. See *Dewey and Bentley: A Philosophical Correspondence*, p. 73.

18 The memorandum in which Bentley expresses his belief that he is Peirce's successor, from which this chapter's headnote is taken, is dated 9 April 1939.

19 "The Human Skin: Philosophy's Last Line of Defense," *Philosophy of Science* 8 (1941): 1–19; "Decrassifying Dewey," ibid., pp. 147–56; "As Through a Glass Darkly," *Journal of Philosophy* 39 (1942): 432–39; "The Jamesian Datum," *Journal of Psychology* 16 (1943): 35–79. The first and last of these articles are reprinted in *Inquiry into Inquiries*, pp. 195–212 and pp. 230–68.

20 I have been unable to find any evidence that Bentley had studied James systematically before the late 1930s, although there are sporadic references to James's *Principles of Psychology* in some of his notes.

21 Bentley, "The Jamesian Datum," in *Inquiry into Inquiries*, p. 248.

22 Ibid., pp. 258–61.

23 This point is made clearly in BKF, 164, 225. See also Bentley, "Kennetic Inquiry," in *Inquiry into Inquiries*, p. 351.

24 Bentley, "The Jamesian Datum," in *Inquiry into Inquiries*, p. 259.

25 Ibid., pp. 260–61. Bentley's reference to James's "analysis of the 'selves'" is to *Principles of Psychology*, chap. 10.

26 John Dewey, *Logic: The Theory of Inquiry*, p. iv.

27 See *Dewey and Bentley: A Philosophical Correspondence*, pp. 293–96.

28 Arnold Brecht, *Political Theory*, p. 511. Brecht is one of the few political scientists to have given serious attention to *Knowing and the Known*.

29 Arthur F. Bentley to John Dewey, 30–31 August 1943. See *Dewey and Bentley: A Philosophical Correspondence*, p. 158. The expression "behavioral naturalism" appears in *Knowing and the Known*, p. 112.

30 W. V. Quine, "Ontological Relativity," in *Ontological Relativity and Other Essays*, p. 30.

31 For a clear discussion of some leading ideas of avowedly naturalistic philosophers of the period see Thelma Z. Lavine, "Note to Naturalists on the Human Spirit," in *Philosophy of the Social Sciences*, ed. Maurice Natanson, pp. 250–61.

32 Largely at Bentley's insistence, the ordinary philosophical meaning of "epistemology" had to be scrapped for it assumed, in his view, a subject/object dichotomy. See *Knowing and the Known*, p. 175.

33 Ibid., p. 179.

34 Ibid., p. 122.

35 Bentley praises Phillipp Frank, *Foundations of Physics* (Chicago: University of Chicago Press, 1946) for Frank's contextual position. In Bentley's view, Frank was especially aware that the physical reality of an elementary particle cannot be spoken of without an account of the theoretical/experimental situation in which the particle is implicated.

36 Niels Bohr cited in Gerald Holton, "The Roots of Complementarity," in *Thematic Origins of Scientific Thought*, pp. 149–50.

37 Dewey and Bentley, *Knowing and the Known*, pp. 91–103, 137, 138.

38 Quine, "Natural Kinds," in *Ontological Relativity and Other Essays*, pp. 130–38.

39 See, for example, Martin Heidegger, *Being and Time*, p. 67.

40 While Hilary Putnam believes that nonmaterial scientific objects such as structures and physical magnitudes can be incorporated into his own scientific realism, it is extremely doubtful if Bentley would have been willing to extend realism to include such objects. See Putnam, "Introduction," in *Mathematics, Method and Matter*, p. viii.

41 Dewey and Bentley, *Knowing and the Known*, p. 47.

42 Bentley's opinion is worth noting at some length. See his letter to Jules Altman, 17 August 1950, in which he calls Einstein a "crypto-realist." In "Kennetic Inquiry" he remarks: "Einstein, amidst the efflorescence of German philosophical terminology—the most resplendent in the world—maintains, largely in the Kant-

ian tradition, all the ancient self-actional treatments, inclusive of the wholly re-
dundant, entitatively personalized know*er*, at the very time that he has been the
greatest of all leaders in overcoming the rigidities of the old 'knowns' by expel-
ling that sort of reification from the physical range" (*Inquiry into Inquiries*,
p. 349). For confirmation of this reading see Holton, "Mach, Einstein, and the
Search for Reality," in *Thematic Origins*, p. 245: "In the end, Einstein came to
embrace the view that many, and perhaps he himself, thought earlier he had
eliminated from physics in his basic 1905 paper on relativity theory: that there
exists an external, objective, physical reality which we may hope to grasp—not
directly, empirically, or logically, or with fullest certainty, but at least by an intuitive leap, one that is only guided by experience of the totality of sensible 'facts.'
Events take place in a 'real world,' of which the space-time world of sensory experience, and even the world of multi-dimensional continua, are useful conceptions, but no more than that."

43 John H. Randall, Jr., to Arthur F. Bentley, 12 August 1943. Randall accused
Bentley of systematically apologizing for defects in the pragmatists he would not
tolerate in logical positivists.
44 For an argument that Tarski's semantic theory of truth is both metaphysically
neutral and can be employed to buttress realism, see Hilary Putnam, *Meaning
and the Moral Sciences*, pp. 9–34. For a criticism of Putnam, see Joseph Margolis, "Cognitive Issues in the Realist-Idealist Dispute," pp. 384–88.
45 See Karl R. Popper, "Truth, Rationality and the Growth of Knowledge," in *Conjectures and Refutations*, pp. 223–28.
46 Dewey and Bentley, *Knowing and the Known*, p. 179.
47 Ibid., pp. 150, 151 n.
48 Dewey, *Logic: The Theory of Inquiry*, pp. 22, 11.
49 Morris R. Cohen and Ernst Nagel, *An Introduction to Logic and Scientific
Method* (1937), cited in Dewey and Bentley, *Knowing and the Known*, p. 194.
50 Bertrand Russell, *An Inquiry into Meaning and Truth* (1940), cited in Dewey and
Bentley, *Knowing and the Known*, p. 154 n.
51 Dewey and Bentley, *Knowing and the Known*, p. 93 n.
52 Ibid., p. 151 n. See also Neurath's lengthy letter to Bentley dated 15 October 1945,
which shows his familiarity with Bentley's position (MSS 2).
53 Alonzo Church reviewed the first four Bentley-Dewey articles in *Journal of Symbolic Logic* 10 (1945): 132–33. Arthur F. Smullyan reviewed "Definition" in ibid.
12 (1947): 99.
54 Bentley's fullest response to Church and Smullyan was not published at the
time. It appears as "An Aid to Puzzled Critics" in *Inquiry into Inquiries*,
pp. 320–24.
55 Arthur F. Bentley to John Dewey, 6 December 1951. See *Dewey and Bentley: A
Philosophical Correspondence*, p. 646.
56 Bentley, "Logic and Logical Behavior," in *Inquiry into Inquiries*, pp. 286–319.
While I have devoted most of my attention to Bentley's understanding of "nature," this work is a wide-ranging restatement, often powerfully argued, of many
of Bentley's views.
57 Ibid., pp. 292–95, 302–14.
58 Arthur F. Bentley to John Dewey, 24 April 1945. See *Dewey and Bentley: A Philosophical Correspondence*, p. 403.

59 Dewey and Bentley, *Knowing and the Known*, p. 109.
60 Manuscript of "Human Living as Natural Transaction," dated 5 August 1951, p. 5 in MSS 1.
61 "Logic and Logical Behavior," in *Inquiry into Inquiries*, p. 312.
62 Arthur F. Bentley to Richard W. Taylor, 17 December 1953, MSS 2. See David Easton, *The Political System*, pp. 176–79, 189–90, 279–82.

9 Conclusion: Inquiry and the Limits of Form

1 For a comparison of Bentley's views with those of positive political theorists who base their teaching in microeconomics see James F. Ward, "Arthur F. Bentley's Philosophy of Social Science," *American Journal of Political Science* 22 (1978): 605–6.
2 Bentley's criticism parallels that of John C. Wahlke, "Pre-Behavioralism in Political Science," *American Political Science Review* 73 (1979): 9–31. Unlike Bentley, Wahlke assumes that there is a stable and unproblematic model of science to which political science should turn.
3 Richard J. Bernstein, *Praxis and Action: Contemporary Philosophies of Human Activity*, pp. 260–304.
4 This is the distinction between the "context of discovery" and the "context of justification" introduced by Hans Reichenbach, which calls for a clear demarcation between the study of the origins of scientific theories, which is the concern of psychology and history, and the philosophical analysis of scientific theories. See Hans Reichenbach, *Experience and Prediction* (Chicago: University of Chicago Press, 1938).
5 Stephen Toulmin, "Postscript: The Structure of Scientific Theories," in *The Structure of Scientific Theories*, ed. Frederick Suppe, p. 603.
6 David Bohm, "Science as Perception-Communication," in ibid., pp. 375–76.
7 Arthur F. Bentley, "Kennetic Inquiry," in *Inquiry into Inquiries*, pp. 338, 347.
8 The most important of recent works indebted to the pragmatic rejection of epistemology is Richard Rorty, *Philosophy and the Mirror of Nature*. For a statement of pragmatism somewhat closer to Bentley's own view of the pragmatic tradition in its emphasis on the role of science, see Nicholas Rescher, *Methodological Pragmatism: A Systems-Theoretic Approach to the Theory of Knowledge*.
9 John Dewey and Arthur F. Bentley, *John Dewey and Arthur F. Bentley: A Philosophical Correspondence, 1932–1951*, p. 637.
10 Leo Weinstein, "The Scientific Study of Groups," in *Essays on the Scientific Study of Politics*, ed. Herbert J. Storing, p. 179.
11 For an illuminating discussion of this view see Rorty, *Philosophy and the Mirror of Nature*, pp. 165–212.
12 The most important statement of this approach is Saul A. Kripke, *Naming and Necessity*. A useful collection is Stephen P. Schwartz, ed., *Naming, Necessity, and Natural Kinds*. See also Alvin Plantinga, *The Nature of Necessity*. For a comprehensive criticism of Kripke see Stanley Rosen, *The Limits of Analysis*, pp. 52–98.
13 Frederick Suppe, "Afterword—1977," in Suppe, *The Structure of Scientific Theories*, p. 716.
14 This opinion is given support by the logical empiricist thesis that a scientific theory is analogous to a logico-mathematical theory that is supposed to rest upon

undefined primitive terms. We have seen that Bentley rejects such an understanding of logico-mathematical theories as well.

15 See Róm Harré, *The Principles of Scientific Thinking*, pp. 295–315.

16 See Rorty, *Philosophy and the Mirror of Nature*, p. 300.

17 For a critical discussion of the notion of possible worlds as used in Kripkean essentialism see Rosen, *The Limits of Analysis*, pp. 73–80.

18 Nelson Goodman, *Ways of Worldmaking*, p. x.

19 G. W. F. Hegel, *Hegel's Science of Logic*, p. 236.

20 See Rosen, *The Limits of Analysis*, pp. 232–56.

21 Michel Foucault, *The Order of Things*, p. 318.

22 From a fragment written by Bentley sometime in 1951–52 in a folder labeled
"Phrasings," in MSS 1.

Bibliography

Achinstein, Peter. *Concepts of Science*. Baltimore: Johns Hopkins University Press, 1968.

Anscombe, G. E. M. *An Introduction to Wittgenstein's Tractatus*. London: Hutchinson University Library, 1959.

Antoni, Carlo. *From History to Sociology: The Transition in German Historical Thinking*. Translated with an introduction by Hayden V. White. Detroit: Wayne State University Press, 1959.

Austin, J. L. *How to Do Things with Words*. Edited by J. O. Urmson. Cambridge: Harvard University Press, 1962.

———. *Philosophical Papers*. Edited by J. O. Urmson and G. J. Warnock. Oxford: The Clarendon Press, 1961.

Ayala, Francisco Jose, and Dobzhansky, Theodosius, eds. *Studies in the Philosophy of Biology: Reduction and Related Problems*. Berkeley and Los Angeles: University of California Press, 1974.

Baker, Keith Michael. *Condorcet: From Natural Philosophy to Social Mathematics*. Chicago: University of Chicago Press, 1975.

Barnes, Harry Elmer, ed. *An Introduction to the History of Sociology*. Chicago: University of Chicago Press, Phoenix Books, 1967.

———. *Sociology and Political Theory*. New York: Alfred A. Knopf, 1924.

Bay, Christian. "Politics and Pseudopolitics: A Critical Evaluation of Some Behavioral Literature." *American Political Science Review* 59 (1965): 39–52.

Bendix, Reinhard. *Max Weber: An Intellectual Portrait*. Garden City, New York: Doubleday and Co., Anchor Books, 1962.

Bentley, Arthur F. *Behavior Knowledge Fact*. Bloomington, Indiana: Principia Press, 1935.

———. *The Condition of the Western Farmer as Illustrated by the Economic History of a Nebraska Township*. Johns Hopkins University Studies in Historical and Political Science, 11th series. nos. 7–8. Baltimore: Johns Hopkins University Press, 1893.

———. *Inquiry into Inquiries: Essays in Social Theory*. Edited by Sidney Ratner. Boston: Beacon Press, 1954.

———. *Linguistic Analysis of Mathematics*. Bloomington, Indiana: Principia Press, 1932.

———. *Makers, Users, and Masters*. Edited by Sidney Ratner. Syracuse: Syracuse University Press, 1969.

———. *The Process of Government: A Study of Social Pressures*. Edited with an introduction by Peter H. Odegard. Cambridge: Harvard University Press, John Harvard Library, 1967.

———. *Relativity in Man and Society*. New York: G. P. Putnam's Sons, 1926.

———. "The Units of Investigation in the Social Sciences." *Publications of the American Academy of Political and Social Science* 149 (1895): 87–113.

Bernard, L. L., and Bernard, Jessie. *Origins of American Sociology: The Social Science Movement in the United States*. New York: Russell and Russell, 1965.

Bernstein, Richard J. *Praxis and Action: Contemporary Philosophies of Human Activity*. Philadelphia: University of Pennsylvania Press, 1971.

———. *The Restructuring of Social and Political Theory*. Philadelphia: University of Pennsylvania Press, 1978.

Black, Max. *A Companion to Wittgenstein's Tractatus*. Cambridge: Cambridge University Press, 1964.

———. *The Nature of Mathematics*. London: Routledge and Kegan Paul, 1933.

Bohm, David. "On the Relationship between Methodology in Scientific Research and the Content of Scientific Knowledge," *British Journal for the Philosophy of Science* 13 (1961): 103–16.

———. *Problems in the Basic Concepts of Physics*. London: J. W. Ruddock and Sons, 1963.

———. *Wholeness and the Implicate Order*. London: Routledge and Kegan Paul, 1980.

Borger, Robert, and Cioffi, Frank, eds. *Explanation in the Behavioural Sciences*. Cambridge: Cambridge University Press, 1970.

Boyce, Neith, and Hapgood, Hutchins. *The Story of an American Family*. Chicopee, Massachusetts: Brown and Murphy, n.d.

Brecht, Arnold. *Political Theory: The Foundations of Twentieth-Century Political Thought*. Princeton: Princeton University Press, 1959.

Bridgman, P. W. *The Logic of Modern Physics*. New York: Macmillan, 1927.

Brodbeck, May, ed. *Readings in the Philosophy of Social Science*. New York: The Macmillan Company, 1968.

Burger, Thomas. *Max Weber's Theory of Concept Formation: History, Laws, and Ideal Types*. Durham, North Carolina: Duke University Press, 1976.

Campbell, Angus, and Cooper, Homer C. *Group Differences in Attitudes and Votes*. Center for Political Studies and Institute for Social Research, The University of Michigan. Ann Arbor: University of Michigan Press, 1956.

Cantril, Hadley, and Livingston, William K. "The Concept of Transaction in Psychology and Neurology." *Journal of Individual Psychology* 19 (1963): 3–36.

Cassirer, Ernst. *The Problem of Knowledge: Philosophy, Science, and History Since Hegel*. Translated by William H. Woglom and Charles W. Hendel. Preface by Charles W. Hendel. New Haven: Yale University Press, 1950.

———. *Substance and Function* and *Einstein's Theory of Relativity*. Translated by Curtis Swabey and Marie Collins Swabey. New York: Dover Publications, 1953.

Childs, Harwood L. *Labor and Capital in National Politics*. Columbus: Ohio State University Press, 1930.

Chomsky, Noam. *Reflections on Language*. New York: Pantheon Books, 1975.

Cohen, Robert S., and Wartofsky, Marx W., eds. *Methodological and Historical Es-*

says in the Natural and Social Sciences. Proceedings of the Boston Colloquium for the Philosophy of Science, 1969–1972. Dordrecht: D. Reidel, 1974.

Coleman, James S. *Community Conflict.* Glencoe, Illinois: The Free Press, 1957.

Cowley, Malcolm. *The Literary Situation.* New York: The Viking Press, 1958.

Crick, Bernard. *The American Science of Politics: Its Origins and Conditions.* Berkeley and Los Angeles: University of California Press, 1959.

Curti, Merle. *The Growth of American Thought.* New York: Harper and Brothers, 1942.

D'Abro, A. *The Evolution of Scientific Thought from Newton to Einstein.* New York: Dover, 1950.

Dewey, John. *Essays in Experimental Logic.* Chicago: University of Chicago Press, 1916.

———. *Experience and Nature.* Chicago: Open Court Publishing Company, 1925.

———. *Human Nature and Conduct.* New York: Henry Holt, 1922.

———. *Logic: The Theory of Inquiry.* New York: Henry Holt, 1938.

———. *The Philosophy of John Dewey.* Edited by John J. McDermott. New York: G. P. Putnam's Sons, Capricorn Books, 1973. Vol. 1. *The Structure of Experience.* Vol. 2. *The Lived Experience.*

———. *Philosophy, Psychology and Social Practice.* Edited by Joseph Ratner. New York: G. P. Putnam's Sons, 1963.

———. "The Present Position of Logical Theory." *Monist* 2 (1891): 1–17.

———. *The Quest for Certainty.* New York: Minton, Balch and Company, 1929.

———. *Reconstruction in Philosophy.* New York: New American Library, 1950.

Dewey, John, and Bentley, Arthur F. *John Dewey and Arthur F. Bentley: A Philosophical Correspondence.* Edited by Sidney Ratner, Jules Altman, and James E. Wheeler. Introduction by Sidney Ratner. New Brunswick, New Jersey: Rutgers University Press, 1964.

———. *Knowing and the Known.* Boston: Beacon Press, 1949.

Diesing, Paul. *Patterns of Discovery in the Social Sciences.* Chicago: Aldine-Atherton, 1971.

Dilthey, Wilhelm. *Der Aufbau der geschichtlichen Welt in den Geisteswissenschaften.* Edited by Manfred Riedel. Frankfurt am Main: Suhrkamp Verlag, 1970.

———. *Gesammelte Schriften.* 7 vols. Leipzig and Berlin: Teubner, 1922.

———. *Pattern and Meaning in History: Thoughts on History and Society.* Edited with an introduction by H. P. Rickman. New York: Harper and Row, 1962.

Dove, Kenley Royce. "Hegel and Creativity." *The Owl of Minerva* 9 (1978): 5–10.

Dowling, R. E. "Pressure Group Theory: Its Methodological Range." *American Political Science Review* 54 (1960): 944–55.

Easton, David. *The Political System.* Chicago: University of Chicago Press, 1953.

Eulau, Heinz. *The Behavioral Persuasion in Politics.* New York: Random House, 1963.

Eulau, Heinz; Eldersveld, Samuel; and Janowitz, Morris, eds. *Political Behavior: A Reader in Research and Theory.* Glencoe, Illinois: The Free Press, 1956.

Favrholdt, David. *An Interpretation and Critique of Wittgenstein's Tractatus.* Copenhagen: Munksgaard, 1964.

Federal Writers Project of the Works Progress Administration for the State of Nebraska. *Nebraska: A Guide to the Cornhusker State.* New York, 1939.

Fleming, Donald. "Attitude: The History of a Concept." In *Perspectives on American*

History. Vol. 1. Edited by Donald Fleming and Bernard Bailyn. Cambridge: Harvard University Press, 1967.

Fleming, Donald, and Bailyn, Bernard, eds. *The Intellectual Migration: Europe and America, 1930–1960.* Cambridge: Harvard University Press, Belknap Press, 1969.

Foucault, Michel. *The Order of Things: An Archaeology of the Human Sciences.* New York: Random House, Vintage Books, 1973.

Fox, Daniel M. *Simon N. Patten and the Transformation of Social Theory.* Ithaca: Cornell University Press, 1967.

Friedrich, Carl J. "The Political Thought of Neo-Liberalism." *American Political Science Review* 49 (1955): 509–25.

Gadamer, Hans-Georg. *Hegel's Dialectic: Five Hermeneutical Studies.* Translated with an introduction by P. Christopher Smith. New Haven: Yale University Press, 1976.

———. "The Problem of Historical Consciousness." Translated by Hans Fantel. *Graduate Faculty Philosophy Journal* 5 (1975): 2–52.

———. *Truth and Method.* New York: The Seabury Press, A Continuum Book, 1975.

Garson, G. David. *Group Theories of Politics.* Beverly Hills, California: Sage Publications, 1978.

———. "On the Origins of Interest-Group Theory: A Critique of a Process." *American Political Science Review* 68 (1974): 1505–20.

Giddings, Franklin H. *The Theory of Sociology.* Supplement to *Annals of the American Academy of Social and Political Science.* 1894.

Gödel, Kurt. *On Formally Undecidable Propositions of Principia Mathematica and Related Systems.* Edinburgh: Oliver and Boyd, 1962.

Golembiewski, Robert T. "'The Group Basis of Politics': Notes on Analysis and Development." *American Political Science Review* 54 (1960): 962–72.

———. "The Small Group and Public Administration." *Public Administration Review* 19 (1959): 149–56.

Golembiewski, Robert T.; Welsh, William A.; and Crotty, William J. *A Methodological Primer for Political Scientists.* Chicago: Rand McNally, 1969.

Goodman, Nelson. *Ways of Worldmaking.* Indianapolis: Hackett Publishing Company, 1978.

Gouldner, Alvin W. *The Two Marxisms: Contradictions and Anomalies in the Development of Theory.* New York: The Seabury Press, 1980.

Graham, George J., Jr., and Carey, George W., eds. *The Post-Behavioral Era: Perspectives on Political Science.* New York: David McKay Company, 1972.

Gross, Bertram M., ed. *A Great Society?* New York: Basic Books, 1966.

———. *The Legislative Struggle: A Study in Social Combat.* New York: McGraw-Hill, 1953.

Grünbaum, Adolf. *Philosophical Problems of Space and Time.* New York: Alfred A. Knopf, 1963.

Haldane, Richard Burton Viscount. *The Reign of Relativity.* New Haven: Yale University Press, 1921.

Hale, Myron O. "The Cosmology of Arthur F. Bentley." *American Political Science Review* 54 (1960): 955–61.

Handy, Rollo, and Harwood, E. C., eds. *Useful Procedures of Inquiry.* Great Barrington, Massachusetts: Behavioral Research Council, 1973.

Hanson, Norwood Russell. *Observation and Explanation: A Guide to Philosophy of Science.* New York: Harper and Row, 1971.

———. *Patterns of Discovery*. Cambridge: Cambridge University Press, 1958.

Hapgood, Hutchins. *A Victorian in the Modern World*. New York: Harcourt, Brace and Company, 1939.

Harré, Rom. *The Principles of Scientific Thinking*. Chicago: University of Chicago Press, 1970.

Hartz, Louis. *The Liberal Tradition in America: An Interpretation of American Political Thought Since the Revolution*. New York: Harcourt, Brace and World, 1955.

Hatcher, William S. *Foundations of Mathematics*. Philadelphia: W. B. Saunders Company, 1968.

Hegel, G. W. F. *Hegel's Science of Logic*. Translated by A. V. Miller. New York: Humanities Press, 1969.

———. *Phenomenology of Spirit*. Translated by A. V. Miller with analysis of the text and foreword by J. N. Findlay. Oxford: Clarendon Press, 1977.

———. *Philosophy of Right*. Translated by T. M. Knox. Oxford: Oxford University Press, 1942.

Heidegger, Martin. *Being and Time*. Translated by John Macquarrie and Edward Robinson. New York: Harper and Row, 1962.

Hempel, Carl G. *Aspects of Scientific Explanation*. New York: The Free Press, 1965.

Herring, Pendleton. *Group Representation Before Congress*. Baltimore: Johns Hopkins University Press, 1929.

Hindess, Barry. *Philosophy and Methodology in the Social Sciences*. Atlantic Highlands, New Jersey: Humanities Press, 1977.

Hofstadter, Richard. *The Age of Reform*. New York: Alfred A. Knopf, 1955.

———. *Social Darwinism in American Thought*. New York: George B. Braziller, 1959.

Holt, Robert T., and Turner, John E., eds. *The Methodology of Comparative Research*. New York: Macmillan Company, The Free Press, 1970.

Holton, Gerald. *Thematic Origins of Scientific Thought: Kepler to Einstein*. Cambridge: Harvard University Press, 1973.

Hughes, H. Stuart. *Consciousness and Society: The Reorientation of European Social Thought, 1890–1930*. New York: Alfred A. Knopf, 1961.

Hull, Clark L. *Principles of Behavior*. New York: Appleton-Century-Crofts, 1943.

Jacobson, Norman. "Causality and Time in Political Process." *American Political Science Review* 58 (1964): 15–22.

James, William. *Essays in Radical Empiricism* and *A Pluralistic Universe*. Edited by Ralph Barton Perry. New York: Longmans, Green and Company, 1958.

———. "On Some Omissions of Introspective Psychology." *Mind* 9 (1884): 1–26.

———. *The Principles of Psychology*. New York: Dover Publications, 1950.

Janik, Allan, and Toulmin, Stephen. *Wittgenstein's Vienna*. New York: Simon and Schuster, A Touchstone Book, 1973.

Jonas, Hans. "The Practical Uses of Theory." In *Philosophy of the Social Sciences: A Reader*, edited by Maurice Natanson. New York: Random House, 1963.

Kant, Immanuel. *The Critique of Pure Reason*. Translated by Norman Kemp Smith. New York: Basic Books, 1963.

———. *Prolegomena to any Future Metaphysics*. Translated by Paul Carus. Chicago: Open Court Publishing Company, 1909.

Kantor, Jacob R. *Psychology and Logic*. Bloomington, Indiana: Principia Press, 1945.

Kaplan, Abraham. *The Conduct of Inquiry: Methodology for Behavioral Science.* San Francisco: Chandler, 1964.

Kariel, Henry S. *Open Systems: Arenas for Political Action.* Itasca, Illinois: F. E. Peacock, Publishers, 1969.

Karl, Barry D. *Charles E. Merriam and the Study of Politics.* Chicago: University of Chicago Press, 1974.

Keat, Russell, and Urry, John. *Social Theory as Science.* London: Routledge and Kegan Paul, 1975.

Klein, Jacob. *Greek Mathematical Thought and the Origins of Algebra.* Translated by Eva Brann. Cambridge: The MIT Press, 1968.

Kline, Morris. *Mathematical Thought from Ancient to Modern Times.* New York: Oxford University Press, 1972.

———. *Mathematics: The Loss of Certainty.* New York: Oxford University Press, 1980.

Kneale, William, and Kneale, Martha. *The Development of Logic.* Oxford: The Clarendon Press, 1962.

Krausser, Peter. "Dilthey's Revolution in the Theory of the Structure of Scientific Inquiry and Rational Behavior." *Review of Metaphysics* 22 (1968): 262–80.

Kress, Paul F. *Social Science and the Idea of Process: The Ambiguous Legacy of Arthur F. Bentley.* Urbana: University of Illinois Press, 1970.

Kripke, Saul. *Naming and Necessity.* Cambridge: Harvard University Press, 1980.

Kuhn, Thomas S. *The Structure of Scientific Revolutions.* Chicago: University of Chicago Press, 1970.

Kuklick, Bruce. *The Rise of American Philosophy: Cambridge, Massachusetts, 1860–1930.* New Haven: Yale University Press, 1977.

Lakatos, Imré. *Mathematics, Science and Epistemology, Philosophical Papers.* Vol. 2. Edited by John Worrall and Gregory Currie. Cambridge: Cambridge University Press, 1978.

Lamb, David. "Hegel and Wittgenstein on Language and Sense-Certainty." *CLIO* 7 (1978): 285–303.

LaPalombara, Joseph. "The Utility and Limitations of Interest Group Theory in Non-American Field Situations." *Journal of Politics* 22 (1960): 29–49.

Latham, Earl. *The Group Basis of Politics: A Study of Basing Point Legislation.* Ithaca: Cornell University Press, 1952.

———. "The Group Basis of Politics: Notes for a Theory." *American Political Science Review* 46 (1952): 376–97.

Lazarsfeld, Paul F. "Notes on the History of Quantification in Sociology—Trends, Sources and Problems." In *Quantification,* edited by Harry Woolf, pp. 147–203. New York: Irvington, 1961.

———. *Qualitative Analysis: Historical and Critical Essays.* Boston: Allyn and Bacon, 1974.

Levison, Arnold B. *Knowledge and Society: An Introduction to the Philosophy of the Social Sciences.* Indianapolis: Bobbs-Merrill Educational Publishing, 1974.

Llewellyn, Karl N. "The Constitution as an Institution." *Columbia Law Review* 34 (1934): 1–40.

Lowell, A. Lawrence. "Oscillations in Politics." *Annals of the American Academy of Political and Social Science* 12 (1898): 69–97.

———. "The Physiology of Politics." *American Political Science Review* 4 (1910): 1–15.

Luebke, Frederick C. *Immigrants and Politics: The Germans of Nebraska, 1880–1900*. Lincoln: University of Nebraska Press, 1969.

MacIver, Robert M. *The Web of Government*. New York: Macmillan, 1947.

McWilliams, Wilson Carey. *The Idea of Fraternity in America*. Berkeley and Los Angeles: University of California Press, 1973.

Mannheim, Karl. *Ideology and Utopia: An Introduction to the Sociology of Knowledge*. Translated by Louis Wirth and Edward Shils. New York: Harcourt, Brace and World, 1936.

Margolis, Joseph. "Cognitive Issues in the Realist–Idealist Dispute." In *Midwest Studies in Philosophy V 1980: Studies in Epistemology*, edited by Peter A. French, Theodore E. Uehling, Jr., and Howard K. Wettstein, pp. 373–90. Minneapolis: University of Minnesota Press, 1980.

Marx, Karl, and Engels, Frederick. *Correspondence, 1846–1895*. Translated and edited by Dona Torr. New York: International Publishers, 1936.

Matson, Floyd W. *The Broken Image: Man, Science and Society*. Garden City, New York: Doubleday and Co., Anchor Books, 1964.

Merriam, Charles E. *New Aspects of Politics*. Third Edition. Enlarged with a foreword by Barry D. Karl. Chicago: University of Chicago Press, 1970.

Merton, Robert K. *On Theoretical Sociology*. New York: The Free Press, 1967.

Mises, Ludwig von. *Human Action*. New Haven: Yale University Press, 1963.

Montague, William Pepperell. "Professor Royce's Refutation of Realism." *Philosophical Review* 11 (1902): 43–55.

Mostowski, Andrej. *Thirty Years of Foundational Studies*. Oxford: Basil Blackwell, 1966.

Naess, Arne. *Four Modern Philosophers*. Translated by Alastair Hannay. Chicago: University of Chicago Press, Phoenix Books, 1965.

Nagel, Ernst. *The Structure of Science*. New York: Harcourt, Brace and World, 1961.

Natanson, Maurice, ed. *Philosophy of the Social Sciences: A Reader*. New York: Random House, 1963.

Oakeshott, Michael. *Experience and Its Modes*. Cambridge: Cambridge University Press, 1933.

———. *Rationalism in Politics and Other Essays*. New York: Basic Books, 1962.

Odegard, Peter H. "A Group Basis of Politics: A New Name for an Old Myth." *Western Political Quarterly* 11 (1958): 689–702.

Olson, James C. *History of Nebraska*. Lincoln: University of Nebraska Press, 1966.

Pap, Arthur. *Semantics and Necessary Truth*. New Haven: Yale University Press, 1966.

Parsons, Talcott. *The Structure of Social Action*. New York: The Free Press, 1968. Vol. 1, *Marshall, Pareto, Durkheim*. Vol. 2, *Weber*.

Passmore, John. *A Hundred Years of Philosophy*. New York: Basic Books, 1966.

Patten, Simon N. "The Failure of Biologic Sociology." *Annals of the American Academy of Political and Social Science* 4 (1894): 919–47.

Peirce, Charles Sanders. *Collected Papers of Charles Sanders Peirce*. Vols. 1–6. Edited by Charles Hartshorne and Paul Weiss. Cambridge: Harvard University Press, 1931–1935. Vols. 7–8. Edited by Arthur W. Burks. Cambridge: Harvard University Press, 1958.

Perry, Ralph Barton. "Professor Royce's Refutation of Realism and Pluralism." *Monist* 12 (1902): 446–58.

Plantinga, Alvin. *The Nature of Necessity*. Oxford: The Clarendon Press, 1974.

Popper, Karl R. *Conjectures and Refutations: The Growth of Scientific Knowledge*. New York: Harper and Row, Harper Torchbooks, 1968.

Putnam, Hilary. *Mathematics, Matter and Method*. Cambridge: Cambridge University Press, 1979.

———. *Meaning and the Moral Sciences*. London: Routledge and Kegan Paul, 1978.

———. *Mind, Language and Reality*. Cambridge: Cambridge University Press, 1979.

Quine, W. V. "Grades of Theoreticity." In *Experience and Theory*, edited by Lawrence Foster and J. W. Swanson, pp. 1–17. Amherst: University of Massachusetts Press, 1970.

———. *Ontological Relativity and Other Essays*. New York: Columbia University Press, 1969.

———. "Two Dogmas of Empiricism." *Philosophical Review* 60 (1951): 20–43.

Reichenbach, Hans. *Axiomatization of the Theory of Relativity*. Translated and edited by Maria Reichenbach. Foreword by Wesley Salmon. Berkeley and Los Angeles: University of California Press, 1969.

Reid, Constance. *Hilbert*. New York, Heidelberg, Berlin: Springer Verlag, 1970.

Rescher, Nicholas. *Methodological Pragmatism: A Systems-Theoretic Approach to the Theory of Knowledge*. New York: New York University Press, 1977.

Rice, Stuart A. *Quantitative Methods in Politics*. New York: Alfred A. Knopf, 1928.

Ringer, Fritz K. *The Decline of the German Mandarins: The German Academic Community, 1890–1933*. Cambridge: Harvard University Press, 1969.

Rorty, Richard. *Philosophy and the Mirror of Nature*. Princeton: Princeton University Press, 1979.

Rosen, Stanley. *G. W. F. Hegel: An Introduction to the Science of Wisdom*. New Haven: Yale University Press, 1974.

———. *The Limits of Analysis*. New York: Basic Books, 1980.

———. *Nihilism: A Philosophical Essay*. New Haven: Yale University Press, 1969.

Rothman, Stanley. "Systematic Political Theory: Observations on the Group Approach." *American Political Science Review* 54 (1960): 15–33.

Rucker, Darnell. *The Chicago Pragmatists*. Minneapolis: University of Minnesota Press, 1969.

Rudner, Richard S. *Philosophy of Social Science*. Englewood Cliffs, New Jersey: Prentice-Hall, 1966.

Schlesinger, Arthur M., Jr., and White, Morton, eds. *Paths of American Thought*. Boston: Houghton Mifflin, 1963.

Schumpeter, Joseph A. *History of Economic Analysis*. Edited by Elizabeth Boody Schumpeter. New York: Oxford University Press, 1954.

Schutz, Alfred. *Collected Papers*, edited by Maurice Natanson. The Hague: Martinus Nijhoff, 1973. Vol. 1. *The Problem of Social Reality*.

———. *The Phenomenology of the Social World*. Translated by George Walsh and Frederick Lehnert. Evanston, Illinois: Northwestern University Press, 1967.

Schwartz, Stephen P., ed. *Naming, Necessity, and Natural Kinds*. Ithaca: Cornell University Press, 1977.

Sellars, Wilfrid. *Science, Perception and Reality*. New York: The Humanities Press, 1963.

Shklar, Judith N. *After Utopia: The Decline of Political Faith*. Princeton: Princeton University Press, 1957.

Sklar, Lawrence. *Space, Time and Spacetime*. Berkeley and Los Angeles: University of California Press, 1974.

Simmel, Georg. *On Individuality and Social Forms*. Edited with an introduction by Donald N. Levine. Chicago: University of Chicago Press, 1971.

Small, Albion. *General Sociology*. Chicago: University of Chicago Press, 1905.

Somit, Albert, and Tannenhaus, Joseph. *American Political Science: From Burgess to Behavioralism*. Boston: Allyn and Bacon, 1967.

Stigler, George J. *Essays in the History of Economics*. Chicago: University of Chicago Press, 1967.

Storing, Herbert J., ed. *Essays on the Scientific Study of Politics*. New York: Holt, Rinehart and Winston, 1962.

Strauss, Leo. *Natural Right and History*. Chicago: University of Chicago Press, 1971.

———. *Thoughts on Machiavelli*. Seattle: University of Washington Press, 1958.

Strawson, Peter F. *Individuals: An Essay in Descriptive Metaphysics*. London: Methuen and Company, 1959.

Suppe, Frederick, ed. *The Structure of Scientific Theories*. Urbana: University of Illinois Press, 1977.

Tarski, Alfred. *Logic, Semantics, Metamathematics*. Edited and translated by J. H. Woodger. Oxford: Oxford University Press, 1956.

———. "The Semantic Conception of Truth and the Foundations of Semantics." *Philosophy and Phenomenological Research* 4 (1944): 341–76.

Taylor, Charles. *The Explanation of Behaviour*. London: Routledge and Kegan Paul, 1964.

———. *Hegel*. Cambridge: Cambridge University Press, 1975.

Taylor, Richard W. "Arthur Bentley's Political Science." *Western Political Quarterly* 5 (1952): 214–30.

———. "Groups and the Political Process: A Study of the Methodology of Arthur Fisher Bentley." Ph.D. diss., University of Illinois, 1950.

———, ed. *Life, Language, Law: Essays in Honor of Arthur F. Bentley*. Yellow Springs, Ohio: Antioch College Press, 1957.

Thayer, H. S. *Meaning and Action: A Critical History of Pragmatism*. New York: The Bobbs-Merrill Company, 1968.

Truman, David Bicknell. *The Governmental Process: Political Interests and Public Opinion*. New York: Alfred A. Knopf, 1951.

Von Wiese, Leopold, and Becker, Howard. *Systematic Sociology*. New York: John Wiley, 1932.

Wahlke, John C. "Pre-Behavioralism in Political Science." *American Political Science Review* 73 (1979): 9–31.

Wallas, Graham. *Human Nature in Politics*. London: Routledge and Kegan Paul, 1920.

Ward, James F. "Arthur F. Bentley and the Foundations of Behavioral Science." *Journal of the History of the Behavioral Sciences* 17 (1981): 222–31.

———. "Arthur F. Bentley's Philosophy of Social Science." *American Journal of Political Science* 22 (1978): 595–608.

———. "Consciousness and Community: American Idealist Social Thought from Puritanism to Social Science." Ph.D. diss., Harvard University, 1975.

Ward, Lester Frank. "The Political Ethics of Herbert Spencer." *Annals of the American Academy of Political and Social Science* 4 (1894): 582–619.

Weber, Max. *Basic Concepts in Sociology*. Translated by H. P. Secher. New York: Greenwood Press, 1962.

———. *Critique of Stammler*. Translated with an introductory essay by Guy Oakes. New York: The Free Press, 1977.

————. *From Max Weber: Essays in Sociology.* Edited and translated by Hans H. Gerth and C. Wright Mills. New York: Oxford University Press, 1946.

————. *Max Weber on the Methodology of the Social Sciences.* Translated by Edward Shils and Henry A. Finch. Glencoe, Illinois: The Free Press, 1949.

————. *Roscher and Knies: The Logical Problems of Historical Economics.* Translated with an introduction by Guy Oakes. New York: The Free Press, 1975.

————. *The Theory of Social and Economic Organizations.* Translated by A. M. Henderson and Talcott Parsons. Glencoe, Illinois: The Free Press, 1949.

Weingartner, Rudolph H. *Experience and Culture: The Philosophy of Georg Simmel.* Middletown, Connecticut: Wesleyan University Press, 1960.

Weyl, Hermann. *Philosophy of Mathematics and Natural Science.* Revised and augmented English based on a translation by Olaf Helmer. Princeton: Princeton University Press, 1949.

White, Morton G. *The Origin of Dewey's Instrumentalism.* New York: Octagon Books, 1964.

Whitrow, G. J. *The Natural Philosophy of Time.* London: Thomas Nelson and Sons, Ltd., 1963.

Wiebe, Robert H. *The Search for Order, 1877–1920.* New York: Hill and Wang, 1967.

Winch, Peter A. *The Idea of a Social Science and Its Relation to Philosophy.* London: Routledge and Kegan Paul, 1958.

————. "Understanding a Primitive Society." *American Philosophical Quarterly* 1 (1964): 307–24.

Wittgenstein, Ludwig. *Notebooks, 1914–1916.* Edited by G. H. von Wright and G. E. M. Anscombe. Translated by G. E. M. Anscombe. Oxford: Basil Blackwell, 1961.

————. *Philosophical Investigations.* Translated by G. E. M. Anscombe. New York: Macmillan, 1958.

————. *Tractatus Logico-Philosophicus.* Translated by D. F. Pears and B. F. McGuiness, with an introduction by Bertrand Russell. London: Routledge and Kegan Paul. New York: The Humanities Press, 1969.

Wolff, Kurt H., ed. *Georg Simmel, 1858–1918: A Collection of Essays, with Translations and a Bibliography.* Columbus: Ohio State University Press, 1959.

Index